T3-AJK-440

DATE DUE

MAR 2 3 1995	
DEC 2 3 1996	
DEC 1 6 1997	
APR 2 - 1998	
Nov. 14/04	

BRODART   Cat. No. 23-221

HAVEN'S GATE

HAVEN'S GATE

Canada's Immigration Fiasco

Victor Malarek

Macmillan of Canada
A Division of Canada Publishing Corporation
Toronto, Ontario, Canada

BRESCIA COLLEGE
LIBRARY
55139

Copyright © 1987 by Victor Malarek

All rights reserved. The use of any part of this publication, reproduced, transmitted in any form, or by any means, electronic, mechanical, photocopying, recording or otherwise, or stored in a retrieval system, without prior consent of the publisher is an infringement of copyright law.

Canadian Cataloguing in Publication Data

Malarek, Victor, date.
   Haven's gate : Canada's immigration fiasco

Bibliography: p.
ISBN 0-7715-9497-6

1. Canada — Emigration and immigration —
Government policy. I. Title.

JV7225.M34 1987   325.71   C87-094532-7

Editor: Anne Holloway
Design: Don Fernley

Macmillan of Canada
A Division of Canada Publishing Corporation
Toronto, Ontario, Canada

Printed in Canada

BRESCIA COLLEGE
LIBRARY

For Emilio and Ida Cipriani, my father-in-law and
mother-in-law, and to the memory of my grandparents,
Nicola and Maria Malarek and Nicola and Maria
Yashan. They left their homelands, their families and their
friends for a new life in Canada.

ACKNOWLEDGEMENTS

I would like to thank my wife, Anna, for her support and patience during the research and writing of this book, and my daughter Larissa for her hugs. I would also like to thank my editor Anne Holloway, Yury Boshyk, Thomas Szlukovenyi and the *Globe and Mail*.

CONTENTS

PREFACE

Canada's immigration program has had a major impact on the social and economic fabric of the country. Yet immigration policy has been, and remains, one of the least debated and least understood of the major public policy issues. It is responsible for bringing in tens of thousands of new people to Canada every year to build and strengthen the country both economically and culturally. It offers a safe haven to refugees fleeing persecution. It is also responsible for the control and security of our borders by ensuring that criminal elements and undesirables are kept out. In the past decade, Canada has settled nearly one million immigrants and processed almost 500 million visitors. This is truly a remarkable and laudable achievement, and the future will demand even more of Canadians as we attempt to settle large numbers of immigrants and refugees through to the end of the century. In 1987, we will accept 115,000 to 125,000 immigrants. To put that number and the magnitude of the work involved into perspective, Canada's gatekeepers are being asked to recruit and deploy almost a dozen army divisions. Yet today, it seems to have become more difficult to immigrate to Canada than at any time since the Second World War. The roadblocks, the paperwork, the delays, the complexity and the confusion that confront thousands of frustrated applicants each year make one wonder how anyone ever gets to Canada.

I began looking into immigration issues for the *Globe and*

Mail in the spring of 1984, mostly by happenstance. Until that time, it wasn't a subject to which I had given much thought. My grandparents on both my mother's side and my father's side of the family had immigrated to Canada from Ukraine in the early 1900s. They were the peasants in sheepskin coats. Treated with disdain for most of their time here, they scrounged a living for themselves and their children. It wasn't a happy or rewarding existence, but it was a far cry from the horrendous poverty they had endured in the Old Country. At least in Canada they had a chance to survive. My in-laws immigrated from Italy in the early 1950s, bringing with them three small children. They also had a very hard time in those early years, but they settled in and life has been good to them. The stories of the early years recounted by my late grandparents were both intriguing and upsetting. I often wondered how they managed to survive the struggles and the hardships. Today, my in-laws can look back at their early years and even laugh at some of the problems they overcame.

In early 1984, during research for news features on the legal-aid system in Ontario and the Law Society of Upper Canada, I met some lawyers who specialized in immigration matters, and it was their acerbic comments on various aspects of immigration that piqued my reporter's curiosity. My preoccupation with the issue began with a series of articles exposing the antics of certain immigration lawyers and consultants making a dirty living off the hopes and dreams of desperate people wanting to remain in Canada. The articles triggered the inevitable verbal sabre-rattling from Ottawa but no real concrete action to rid society of these unscrupulous leeches. From that time until June, 1987, I have written scores of newspaper articles describing the questionable and outright illegal activities of dozens of immigration consultants and lawyers operating in Toronto, Montreal, Vancouver, Calgary and Edmonton. Many of the schemes were international in scope, involving forgery rings, black-market racketeers and sleazy travel agents in such cities as Amsterdam, Hamburg, London, Lisbon, Istanbul, Karachi, New Delhi, Bangkok and Hong Kong. With each story, the Canadian government and various immigration ministers promised swift and firm action. It wasn't until June, 1987, that any charges were laid against lawyers or consultants involved in these blatant scams — scams in which almost 4,000 Portuguese citizens made bogus refugee claims from July, 1985, to June, 1986; in which more than 2,000 Turks filed phony refugee claims in a six-month period from June, 1986; and in which more than 800 Brazilians arrived in the first five months of 1987 claiming refugee status.

The unfortunate repercussion of these events is that genuine refugees — people fleeing war, vicious totalitarian regimes, civil disorder and calamities — were tarred with the same brush as the phony refugee claimants. Moreover, rather than dealing with the illegal flow, the government of Canada simply allowed this confusion to build in the minds of Canadians. Today, Canadians are demanding that the government crack down on people who use the refugee process as a means of jumping the immigration queues, and rightly so. However, the result has been a move by the Progressive Conservative government to implement a tougher and mean-spirited system that will in effect also keep out legitimate refugees.

In a public opinion poll published in the *Toronto Star* on June 3, 1987, 83 per cent of Canadians questioned said they supported a bill introduced in the House of Commons a month earlier that would make it far more difficult for people claiming refugee status to enter the country. The sad reality is that Canadians, for the most part, have been seriously misled by politicians and senior bureaucrats into thinking that the proposed law would curb the abusers while allowing genuine refugees access to the new process. The fact is that the legislation would slam the door in the face of most genuine refugees with the drive and tenacity to get here.

On various assignments, I have visited refugee camps in Thailand, Hong Kong, Iran, Pakistan, Austria, West Germany and Italy. They have had a marked effect on me. The conditions that these unfortunate people are forced to endure are, in a word, horrific. They are packed into tents or mud and bamboo huts, herded into aging, turn-of-the-century army barracks and literally banished to prison colonies on islands. Most of the time these people do nothing because there is nothing for them to do but wait — wait for some country to accept them for resettlement or wait for the hostilities in their homelands to end. These are the real refugees who desperately need our help and the help of the international community. Canada cannot resolve this incredible human drama alone. We simply cannot resettle all the refugees in the world. Yet while we have been applauded in the international forum for our humanitarian response to refugees, the fact is we certainly can do better than the meagre 12,000 places we have set aside in our 1987 immigration quota for refugees.

Being identified as a reporter on immigration issues inevitably attracts what often seems like every individual or family that has ever had a problem with the Immigration Department. The letters, phone calls and meetings I've had in the past three years on the subject with Canadians, landed immigrants, refugee claimants, lawyers, consultants and the many people who work with immigrants and refugees could fill volumes. They speak of a department ruled by a cold, unfeeling hand and riddled with confusion, incompetence and sometimes outright stupidity. I have been left with one inescapable conclusion: Canada's immigration system has become a fiasco. Much of the sharpest public criticism is aimed at the front-line officers when it should rightly be directed at the top echelons of power: the senior bureaucrats and their gutless political masters.

Criticism should also be directed at External Affairs and the foreign service officers who are responsible for the selection and processing of immigrants and refugees from abroad. It doesn't take long for even the most novice observer to discover that much of the delay and bungling is the direct result of activities in our embassies and consulates. There is a serious conflict in the relationship between the Immigration Department and External Affairs that must be resolved before the immigration system can have a chance of working efficiently and humanely.

Haven's Gate attempts to show Canadians the sorry state of the nation's immigration system. Immigration ministers often refer to the "integrity" of the system being challenged by bogus refugee claimants, illegal immigrants or unscrupulous lawyers and consultants. The fact is that Canada's immigration system has little integrity, and the blame lies squarely on the shoulders of a long line of weak immigration ministers who have failed repeatedly to put some order into the department. Since 1980, eight immigration ministers have tried to grapple with the department; more than 25 ministers have held the post since 1945. The blame also lies with senior bureaucrats both in the Immigration Department and in the Department of External Affairs. They are the gatekeepers who have allowed the system to deteriorate to the point where most Canadians have lost all faith in the ability of these civil servants to do the job.

It comes as no surprise that a public opinion poll carried out by Environics Research Group Ltd. for the *Globe and Mail* in early March, 1987, found that 65 per cent of Canadians questioned felt there was too much immigration into Canada. Much of the negative sentiment by Canadians toward immigrants can be directly traced to their lack of trust in the government's ability to handle immigration. While *Haven's Gate* is highly critical of the government's handling of immigration policy, there are a number of positive things I hope it will accomplish. For one, I have tried to give Canadians a look at the underbelly and insides of the system so they will understand what has been going on in recent years and not simply allow themselves to be duped into believing what the politicians and bureaucrats want them to believe. I also hope it will stimulate serious and open public debate on a variety of crucial issues such as increasing immigration to Canada; racism toward new immigrants; our humanitarian response to the worldwide refugee situation; our aging and declining population; the effects of immigration on our economy and more specifically on employment; and the politics behind immigration.

Canada is on the threshold of making some very dramatic changes to its immigration policy. Before this is done, public confidence must be restored in the process. Our future depends on it.

1 IMMIGRATION: THE BEGINNINGS

THE HISTORY OF CANADIAN IMMIGRATION IS far from idyllic. Contrary to the myth cherished by most Canadians that this country was built on rich libertarian traditions, immigrants were not always welcomed with an outpouring of compassion for the world's downtrodden, oppressed and displaced. They were brought here to work and Canada was not about to coddle them. They toiled at back-breaking jobs plowing farmland, laying railroad track, mining and cutting timber. They were sometimes shunned, patronized and exploited.

In the very early years, there was no legislation of any kind to govern the entrance of people into what is now Canada. On the eve of the American Revolution in 1776, the population of Canada was about 110,000, of whom about 65,000 were French. The American Revolution soon added 40,000 people — disbanded British troops, refugees and United Empire Loyalists — to Canada's tiny population. The general philosophy during the first period of major immigration during the nineteenth century was essentially one of *laissez-faire*. During this era, the British government viewed emigration to the colonies as a release valve for chronic unemployment, misery and poverty at home rather than as a means of advancing the interest of the colonies. The colonies, on the other hand, welcomed the able-bodied, for whom there was no lack of employment, but increasingly protested against the unloading of paupers and the physically and mentally unfit who had been assisted to leave Britain for Canada and the United States because they were a burden at home. The early adoption of strict immigration control measures by several American states resulted in shipload after shipload of unwanted human cargo being diverted to Canada. In 1831 and 1832 at least 20,000 of these wretched souls, denied entry into the U.S., arrived in Halifax and Saint John.

The ocean voyage to the New Land was arduous and dangerous. By the mid-1800s the average trip took about a month and a half. Ships, often referred to as "floating coffins," were few, small, crowded and lacking sanitary facilities. Deaths at sea were commonplace. Because of the horrific conditions aboard the ships, most immigrants arrived in a frightful state. Preparations for their arrival were grossly inadequate. The port cities were often overcrowded and their resources taxed to the limit in caring for and protecting themselves from the newcomers. During the height of the immigration season, the threat of contagious disease — smallpox, typhus, cholera — hung continually over the port cities.

The first measures to control immigration to Canada resulted from the appalling state of ocean transportation. The failure of shipping companies to act responsibly toward their human cargos gave rise to quarantine areas at the receiving ports of Halifax, Saint John, Quebec and Montreal. Canadians demanded that the British government enact tough regulations to police the shipping industry, for it had become brutally clear that the ship owners were unable and unwilling to police themselves. In 1802, a British Parliamentary committee was set up to look into the industry. Its findings showed an urgent need for immediate legislation, but the Passenger Vessels Act of 1803 triggered violent protest from ship owners and left conditions little better than they had been for another half-century. In the summer of 1827, shiploads of new settlers arrived in Halifax, Quebec and Montreal starving, diseased and dying. In Halifax alone, disease killed more than 800 of a population of 11,000. A year later, a new imperial statute was passed to control the shipping industry, but the problems continued unabated. Out of

90,000 Irish immigrants embarking for Canada in British ships in 1847, 15,000 died on the way. Continued public protests eventually forced Nova Scotia, New Brunswick and Lower Canada to pass legislation imposing a head tax on every immigrant entering the country. The money was to be used for the care of the sick and destitute coming off ships and for forwarding immigrants to their final destinations inland.

The abuses which inquiry after inquiry revealed and successive laws attempted to control became the focus of a Royal Commission in Britain in 1851. It found that, along with the overcrowding of ships, immigrants destined for Canada had become the victims of vicious exploitation. At the point of departure, immigrants were set upon by latter-day versions of today's unscrupulous immigration consultants — "crimps," fast-talking con men who specialized in fleecing the unsuspecting and naive. The crimps sold tickets at inflated prices, often for non-existent ships. They dispensed bad advice and bogus information and enticed their trusting quarry to boarding houses where they would be robbed at knifepoint or gunpoint. At sea, the exploitation continued. The food was poor, thinly rationed and supplied uncooked so that more money could be exacted for the use of stoves. Passengers also had to endure constant bullying and physical abuse from the ship's crew. Few dared to complain on the high seas, and the law on land was too slow to act forcefully. Often ship captains dumped their passengers at the wrong ports, hundreds of miles from their original destination, or on deserted beaches. Upon arrival, the newcomers would be set upon by the Canadian version of crimps, and the process of exploitation would start all over again.

At Confederation in 1867, the population of Canada was some 3.5 million. The French were the single largest group with slightly more than one million. The Irish were the second largest with about 846,000. The English numbered some 706,000 and the Scots 549,946, while those of German origin numbered about 202,000. There were, of course, other ethnic groups such as the Dutch with 29,000, "Africans" with

21,000, as well as Spanish, Portuguese, Italian, Swiss, Welsh and Chinese.

Two years after Confederation, the federal government placed immigration under the Department of Agriculture and adopted its first legislation governing the arrival of immigrants. The bill covered federal-provincial responsibilities, the establishment of immigration agents in Britain and elsewhere, and quarantine stations. It also stated that no immigrants were to leave a ship until the passenger list had been checked and the ship inspected by quarantine officers. The passenger list was to include the names of single persons as well as of the heads of families and the number of persons accompanying them, occupation, country of origin and destination. The legislation also required that the passenger list show whether the ship carried any person who was insane, idiot, deaf-mute, blind or infirm and whether such persons were accompanied by parents or a relative able to support them. If any such individual was likely to become a public charge, the Collector of Customs could exact a bond of $300 from the ship's captain to reimburse the government for any expenses incurred by the immigrant during the first three years in the country. In addition, a ship's captain was required to give a detailed report of any immigrant who died en route to Canada and to account for the personal effects of the deceased.

For the protection of immigrants, penalties were set out for the captain and crew found guilty of a breach of contract with their passengers. Perhaps the most significant innovation was to prohibit the landing of indigents unless the ship's captain deposited sufficient funds to cover the costs of temporarily sheltering, feeding and moving these immigrants to other parts of the country. This provision, however, did not come into force until 1879. Although shipping conditions improved as steamships superseded sailing vessels, there was a constant drive to make the maximum use of ship space at the expense of passenger welfare. The legislation established the number of passengers a ship might carry as one adult per 12 square feet of clear superficial deck available for passenger use and not occupied by stores or other goods, or one person per two tons of capacity. An adult was defined as a person over 14 years of age, or two persons over one year but under 14. The new law said nothing about what categories or classes of persons should be admitted or excluded as immigrants. This silence on admissible classes continued until 1872 when the Act was amended to prohibit the landing of criminal and "other vicious classes," and seven years later an order-in-council was passed excluding paupers and destitute immigrants.

From 1867 to 1895, nearly 1.5 million immigrants came to Canada, the great majority of them from Britain and the United States. But many thousands of Italians and a considerable number of Finns came after 1880 to do railway construction.

In general, the easygoing attitude toward immigration policy remained basically intact during these early years, with one important exception. The province of British Columbia had become very concerned about the number of single male Chinese who had entered when the American gold fields had run out in the 1860s. Agitation against the Chinese began in 1864. Ten years later, the B.C. legislature passed a law excluding them from the franchise. But since the Chinese made good manual labourers on the railroad and in the mines, much of the criticism was ignored. When in 1881 construction of the Canadian Pacific Railway through the Rocky Mountains began in earnest, contractors brought in 17,000 "coolies" from the province of Kwangtung in south China. The work was brutally hard but the Chinese saw in it the possibility of quick riches and a life of luxury back home when they returned. Later, as mining and railroad construction declined, many of these Chinese workers decided to remain, becoming farmers, gardeners, restaurant keepers, laundrymen and domestic servants. Their hard work and acceptance of a low standard of living enabled them to compete successfully against European settlers. In 1884, a Royal Commission investigating the question of Chinese immigration exonerated "the Orientals" of the allegations of bad morals and criminal tendencies frequently levelled against them. Nevertheless, the commission recommended restricting their immigration and a year later Parliament passed a law aimed at doing just that. The law did not ban Chinese immigration outright but imposed a stiff "head tax" of $50 on every Chinese entering the country. Despite this measure Chinese immigration, although very limited, continued.

The appointment in 1896 of Clifford Sifton as minister of the interior, whose department was responsible from 1892 for lands administration and immigration, marked a major shift in immigration policy that was to change the face of the nation. Canada was just recovering from the depression of the early 1890s, and the completion of the Canadian Pacific in 1885 had opened vast new regions of the West to settlement. Sifton, a struggling young lawyer from Winnipeg and the youngest member of the Cabinet of Sir Wilfrid Laurier, was obsessed by a dream of promoting Canada's prosperity by developing the prairies with pioneer farmers. Tradition and sentiment favoured immigration from Britain, the United States and France, but when the lure of "free land" failed to produce enough immigrants from the traditional sources, Sifton focussed his attention on new sources of supply. Sifton's policy was radical for its time but he convinced Prime Minister Laurier that the path he had chosen was the right one. Cabinet colleagues, who were committed to an aggressive policy of opening up the Canadian West, were baffled as to where Canada would get the immigrants to make the conquest of the prairies. Sifton said he knew of people who would do the work and he knew where to get them. His plans, when revealed, were daring, unorthodox and in some ways ruthless.

"I think that a stalwart peasant in a sheepskin coat, born on the soil, whose forebears have been farmers for ten generations, with a stout wife and a half dozen children, is good quality," Sifton revealed. And his "sheepskins" arrived by the thousands — poor Ukrainian peasants, Poles, Doukhobors, Hutterites, all willing to work the land. The immigration of Ukrainians began in 1891 with the arrival of two adventurous peasants from western Ukraine. They were followed three years later by nine families who settled near Star, Alberta, and by 1901 the number of Ukrainian immigrants exceeded 5,000. Ten years later, it reached 75,000. But these new settlers were not welcomed warmly by established Canadians, who derisively referred to the Ukrainians as "Sifton's Sheepskins" and "Scum of the Empire."

Sifton remained constant in his defence of this new breed of immigrants. "The cry against the Galicians is the most absolutely ignorant and absurd thing that I have ever known in my life. There is simply no question in regard to the advantage of these people," he commented. In her book *Men in Sheepskin Coats* (1947), Vera Lysenko poignantly described the plight of these newcomers, "systematically underpaid . . . tortured by physical labor, torn by nostalgia for the old country, crushed by loneliness in a strange land, and by the fear of death which [they] often looked in the face. . . ."

The arrival of these exotic newcomers united the most disparate elements in Canadian society at the time, from the Anglican Church to the Trades and Labor Congress. Preachers and politicians assailed the Sheepskins at every turn, and journalists went so far as to describe the Ukrainian immigrants as "ignorant . . . creatures of the mud who must be made over in the superior British pattern." In 1899, Toronto's *Mail and Empire* branded Sifton's immigration policy as an attempt to turn the prairies into "a sort of anthropological garden" colonized by "the waifs and strays of Europe, the lost tribes of mankind, and freaks of creation." In 1919, John W. Dafoe, the influential Liberal editor of the *Winnipeg Free Press*, captured mainstream opinion in the West when he suggested shipping the immigrants back to their happy homes in Europe "which vomited them forth a decade ago."

The most virulent criticism of this new wave of immigration came from Quebec. Laurier's energetic immigration policy was denounced from every pulpit—in the province which had given the Liberals 49 of its 65 seats. The man who spearheaded the French-Canadian attack was Henri Bourassa, a nationalist Member of Parliament. He charged that the aim of the government's immigration program was to swamp the French minority in a sea of "drunkards, paupers, loafers and jailbirds." His vicious attack was aimed particularly at eastern Europeans and especially Jews, yet it seemed at the time that no new group was free from hostility.

During the 1920s, the racist Ku Klux Klan made its way north from the United States and established itself in Saskatchewan. Some Canadians joined because of what one Klansman described as disgust and hatred for "men who tighten their bellyband for breakfast, eat spaghetti and hot dog and rye bread for lunch and suck in limburger cheese for supper." The Klan, a secret brotherhood of white supremacists and anti-Semites given to wearing bedsheets and burning wooden crosses as they terrorized minorities, quickly spread across Canada. In 1932, it was even granted a charter from the Alberta government which it held until 1952.

However miserable the lives of the men in sheepskin coats, they were privileged when compared with the "Orientals," blacks and Jews. In the early 1900s, fear of the "Yellow Peril" was deep and desperate. British Columbia was still concerned about the number of Chinese entering the province and the result was a doubling of the head tax to $100 in 1900, and a further increase to $500 three years later.

The federal government would have liked to have imposed the same head tax on the Japanese but was prevented from doing so for diplomatic reasons. Although the head tax on Chinese had largely achieved its purpose, British Columbia's concerns about immigration from the Orient continued to mount. Substantial numbers of immigrants were arriving from Japan and India, and among the rumours being spread throughout B.C. was the bizarre notion that Japan was attempting to found a colony on the Pacific coast. In the years 1906 to 1908, a total of 11,565 Japanese immigrants entered Canada. In September, 1907, a protest demonstration in Vancouver against Japanese immigration ended in a riot in which several lives were lost. The federal government expressed its regrets to the Japanese government and compensated the victims for their losses.

The more important outcome of this unfortunate incident was a settlement of the Japanese immigration question that would remain in force for almost two decades. The Japanese government was persuaded into a "gentlemen's agreement" restricting the number of its countrymen immigrating to Canada to not more than 400 per year. However, by 1921 the number of Japanese began to increase beyond those numbers and a demand arose for further restrictions. In 1923, after prolonged negotiations between Canada and Japan, the Japanese government agreed to limit the number of passports to 150 domestic servants and farm labourers annually. On June 8, 1928, Prime Minister William Lyon Mackenzie King told the House of Commons that the Japanese consul general in Ottawa had informed the Canadian government that Japan "does not contemplate that the total number of emigrants to Canada . . . will exceed a total of one hundred and fifty annually." In the six years from 1929 to 1934 inclusive the average yearly number of Japanese immigrants was 154. In 1923, the federal government also passed the Chinese Immigration Act, which severely restricted the "entry to or landing in Canada of persons of Chinese origin or descent, irrespective of allegiance or citizenship. . . ." There was no Chinese immigration recorded in 1925, 1926 and 1927. Three immigrants came in 1928; one the following year; and none for the years 1930, 1931 and 1932. One Chinese immigrant came in 1933; two in the following year; and none in 1935.

During 1907 and 1908, more than 4,700 East Indians, mainly from British India, entered Canada. There was bitter opposition to their immigration but the task of blocking their arrival was more complex because they could, at least in theory, claim special rights as citizens of the British Empire. However, in 1908 the federal government devised and passed immigration regulations to keep them out. The regulations required that each immigrant have at least $200 in his own name and that he should come to Canada with a through ticket on a ship that had made a non-stop journey from the land of his birth. An unfortunate incident occurred in 1914 when a shipload of 400 would-be immigrants from India arrived in Vancouver harbour aboard a Japanese freighter, the *Komagata Maru*. They were denied entry and held aboard the ship for nearly three months before one-half of Canada's two-ship navy forced the vessel to turn around and sail back home.

In 1918, Canada's decision to exclude immigrants from India was debated at the Imperial War Conference in London, England. Canada's efforts to keep out East Indians had sparked some controversy over the concept of free movement between members of the Empire. Nonetheless, the conference declared that "it is the inherent function of the governments of the several communities of the British Commonwealth that each should enjoy complete control of the composition of its population by means of restriction by immigration from any of the other communities." It was a decision that would influence immigration policy toward non-white British subjects for many years to come. (In 1919 and 1920, no immigrants from India were recorded, and from 1921 through 1930, only 418 East Indians, mostly wives and children of those already in Canada, were admitted as immigrants.)

The period from 1896 to 1914, during which the prairie wheatfields were settled, is considered the most spectacular era in Canadian immigration history. Nearly three million immigrants came to Canada during this time, of which almost half arrived in the years 1910 through 1913. It was during this period that six of the eight largest annual immigration movements were recorded. The all-time high ever recorded for any single year was 1913 with 400,870 arrivals. This period also marked the beginning of selective immigration to Canada. More importantly, it was during this time, with the arrival of European immigrants, that the cultural diversity of Canada became clearly defined. Nevertheless, the bulk of immigration continued to come from Britain and the United States. Between 1910 and 1914, these two sources provided 1.2 million new immigrants, compared with 440,000 from all other countries.

The outbreak of the First World War in 1914 may have saved the government of the day from having to come to some very tough decisions about immigration. Pressures to change the immigration policy were mounting, but during the war, Canadian immigration entered a period of uncertainty. It was during this period that more than 8,000 Ukrainians, many of them Canadian citizens, were rounded up as enemy aliens and interned in two dozen camps across Canada. Some lost property and many lost their right to vote. Six were killed trying to escape from forced labour camps, and another hundred died of illnesses related to the squalid living conditions imposed on them.

When the war ended in 1918, there was expectation in some quarters that there would be a resumption of large-scale immigration, but the demobilization of army units threw thousands of workers into the labour market at a time when the economy was suffering. High unemployment, labour unrest and a general recession ensued and continued until 1922, and until 1923 immigrants other than those going to assured farm work or domestic service were required to possess stated sums of money in order to enter the country.

In 1919, the government passed an order-in-council under the Immigration Act of 1910 enshrining its discriminatory policies in law by creating a general excluded class of immigrants deemed undesirable because of climatic, industrial, social, educational, labour or other conditions or requirements of Canada, or because their customs, habits, modes of life and methods of holding property were deemed to result in a probable inability to become readily assimilated. Selection would also be carried out on the basis of whether applicants belonged to "preferred" countries or "non-preferred" countries. Traditional affinities to the United Kingdom and the United States naturally favoured immigrants from those countries. Next in order of preference came immigrants from northern and western Europe, followed by those from central and eastern Europe and by those from southern Europe including Greece, Italy, Syria and Turkey. Jews, regardless of citizenship, were treated separately.

In 1923, with the return to prosperity, the Canadian government moved to adopt a more aggressive approach to finding immigrants to settle the land. There was a substantial movement of Ukrainians, Poles, Finns, Hungarians, Slovaks, Lithuanians, Yugoslavs and Scandinavians. The economic boom also brought considerable numbers of Italian labourers who found ready employment in construction and heavy industry. One significant development in that year was the government's decision to accept several thousand Jewish refugees from Romania on compassionate grounds. These people, notwithstanding the fact that they were inadmissible under the existing regulations, were allowed to come to Canada if they had relatives here and were endorsed by the Jewish Immigrant Aid Society.

Under a series of agreements from 1925 onward, the recruitment and forwarding of immigrants from the "non-preferred" European countries was given to the Canadian railway companies. Their role in the promotion of immigration and in the settlement of the West was far-reaching and outstanding. Steadily improving social and economic conditions brought further amendments to the Immigration Act. The prohibition of Doukhobor immigration was revoked in 1926 and, in the same year, the admissible classes were extended to non-British immigrants with occupations in demand in Canada, and to parents, unmarried children and unmarried brothers and sisters of Canadian residents. These adjustments, however, did not apply to Orientals. The preferential category was extended to include citizens of Belgium, Denmark, France, Sweden, Norway, Switzerland and the Netherlands.

A consolidation of the Immigration Act of 1927 produced nothing new, but a year later, the labour movement finally succeeded in its decades-long effort to overcome Senate opposition to the repeal of a provision under which strike leaders could be deported. The stock market crash of 1929 and the depression beginning in 1930 cut deeply into immigration policy. The number of immigrants admitted into Canada dropped in spectacular fashion. By 1935, the figure reached a low of 11,277 from all countries, due to the effects of an order-in-council passed by Parliament in August, 1930, that restricted immigrants entering the country to wives and children of heads of families already established in Canada, and farmers with sufficient capital to establish and maintain themselves on farms.

The outbreak of the Second World War in 1939 brought what little immigration activity there had been during the decade to a virtual halt. During the war Canada earned its blackest mark in immigration history. Amid heightened suspicion and fear, there occurred some of the most flagrant manifestations of racism ever witnessed in this country. Parliament passed a regulation barring enemy aliens. Several hundred Germans and Italians suspected of being supporters of the Nazis and more than 22,000 Canadians of Japanese descent were rounded up and interned in prison camps.

In 1942, after Japan's attack on Pearl Harbor, the Liberal government of Mackenzie King cited national security reasons and invoked the War Measures Act against Canadian residents of Japanese heritage living in British Columbia. Racial intolerance on the west coast had blocked many Japanese Canadians, the majority of them Canadian-born, from holding Canadian citizenship. Under the War Measures Act, their homes, farms, fishing boats, cars, businesses and other assets were confiscated and later sold at far below market value. The money was used to pay for the lodging and feeding of the Japanese, who were forcibly moved to camps in the B.C. interior and farther east because of fears that they still had allegiances to the Emperor of Japan.

In an article in the *Globe and Mail* on July 20, 1984, Toronto lawyer Maryka Omatsu noted that while national security interests were cited as the reason behind the mass expulsions, Prime Minister Mackenzie King disclosed in the House of Commons in August, 1944, that "no person of Japanese race born in Canada has been charged with any act of sabotage or disloyalty during the years of the war." The U.S. government released its Japanese-American internees months before the end of the war in 1945. In Canada, it was not until 1947 that the camps were emptied, and it was 1949 before Canadian Japanese were allowed to resettle on the west coast.

As news reports of the rounding up, imprisonment and slaughter of millions of European Jews at the hands of the Nazis reached North America, the federal government remained unmoved and adamantly opposed accepting Jewish refugees from Nazi Germany. Anti-Semitism, most notably in Quebec, had rendered Canada deaf to humanitarian pleas that Jewish refugees from Hitler's reign of terror be granted haven in Canada. In 1939 a passenger liner, the *St. Louis*, steamed into the port of Halifax carrying more than 900 Jews who had fled Nazi Europe. Prime Minister Mackenzie King refused to allow the Jews to land and the ship steamed back to France. As a result of that decision many of its passengers perished in Nazi concentration camps.

In their book *None Is Too Many*, historians Irving Abella and Harold Troper identified the three individuals who had a strong influence on Canada's immigration policy toward the Jews: Frederick Charles Blair, director of immigration, and a well-known anti-Semite in Ottawa; Thomas Crerar, the minister responsible, who was described as weak and naive and who deferred to Blair; and Ernest Lapointe, Prime Minister Mackenzie King's Quebec lieutenant, who was able to impose his narrow views on Jewish immigration whenever the prime minister's humanitarian tendencies threatened to change the closed-door policy. Abella and Troper pointed out that during the 12 years of Nazi terror, the United States accepted more than 200,000 Jewish refugees; embattled Britain, 70,000; Argentina, 50,000; penurious Brazil, 27,000; distant China, 25,000; tiny Bolivia and Chile, 14,000 each. Canada found room for fewer than 5,000. "What Canadian history books do not mention and what few Canadians talk about — because they don't know, or worse, don't care — is that, of all the nations of the Western world, of all the states that could have received refugees, theirs has, arguably, the worst record for providing sanctuary to European Jewry,"

Abella and Troper wrote. It was only after the war, when the full horror of what the Nazis had done to the Jews was exposed to the world, that Canada began to dismantle its racist barriers to immigration.

As soon as the war ended, there was a strong movement for a liberalization of immigration, and it has been since 1945 that Canadian immigration policy has evolved most rapidly and most profoundly. New challenges and shifting priorities provided the framework for substantial development of Canadian immigration policy. The thrust of the government's policy, pockmarked with polite racism, was enunciated by Prime Minister Mackenzie King in a House of Commons debate on May 1, 1947. Mr. King affirmed Canada's need for a larger population. "This it will seek to attain through the development and energetic application of productive immigration measures." Regarding long-term objectives, Mr. King said that "apart from all else, in a world of shrinking distance and international insecurity, we cannot ignore the danger that lies in a small population holding so great a heritage as ours." Mr. King also said that it was of the utmost importance to relate immigration to absorptive capacity, a factor that would vary from year to year in response to economic conditions.

With regard to the selection of immigrants, the prime minister stressed that "much has been said about discrimination. I wish to make it quite clear that Canada is perfectly within her rights in selecting the persons whom we regard as desirable future citizens. It is not a fundamental right of any alien to enter Canada. It is a privilege." He added: "There will, I am sure, be general agreement with the view that the people of Canada do not wish, as a result of mass immigration, to make any fundamental alteration in the character of our population. Large-scale immigration from the Orient would change the fundamental composition of the Canadian population. Any considerable Oriental immigration would, moreover, be certain to give rise to social and economic problems of a character that might lead to serious difficulties in the field of international relations. The government, therefore, has no thought of making any change in immigration regulations which would have consequences of the kind."

Immigration in the years immediately after 1945 was characterized by the arrival of thousands of persons who had been uprooted by the war and scattered throughout Europe, and who were unable or unwilling to return to their former homelands. The first movement of the post-war period took place during the winter of 1946-47 when some 7,000 Polish war veterans, most of whom had served with the Polish division of the First Canadian Army, arrived in Canada. They were followed by a veritable flood of displaced persons, derisively referred to as "DPs." Prominent among these groups were refugees from Ukraine, Lithuania, Latvia and Estonia. Meanwhile, the mainstream of immigration from Britain and continental Europe began to build up again. There was also an upsurge in the number of Italian, Dutch and German immigrants. From 1946 to 1973, immigrants from Italy totalled 463,970; the Netherlands, 177,612; and Germany, 315,161. Immigrants also began to arrive from Greece and Portugal, mainly from the Azores. From 1946 to 1973, immigrants from Greece totalled 115,836 and from Portugal, 111,626. In 1947, the Chinese Immigration Act was repealed and in 1951 special agreements were reached with the Commonwealth countries of India, Pakistan and Ceylon (Sri Lanka) respecting the entry of their nationals.

In 1952, a new Immigration Act was passed. The accumulated amendments of the old law had made it too unwieldy. However, the new Act was merely a consolidation of all the earlier changes. It reeked of prejudice outmoded even at the time it was passed, and contributed little to immigration policy. Its focus was one of sharper control and enforcement. Section 5 of the Act, for example, provided an update on the prohibited classes, which included mental defectives and the mentally ill or those with a history of such illness, epileptics, persons afflicted with tuberculosis, trachoma, or any contagious disease and immigrants who were dumb, blind or otherwise physically impaired. Entry by some in these categories was permitted if they had sufficient means of support or were taken care of by family members so as not to become public charges. Also excluded were persons who had been convicted of any crime involving "moral turpitude." Barred were prostitutes, homosexuals, pimps, persons seeking entry for immoral purposes, professional beggars and vagrants, persons who were public charges or judged likely to become such, alcoholics, drug addicts and persons who had trafficked in drugs. In addition, persons deemed likely to advocate the overthrow of the system of government by force or subversion, persons who were or had been associated with any subversive organization, spies and saboteurs were denied admission.

The most controversial aspect of the Act was Section 61, which gave the government the power to limit or prohibit the entry of immigrants for reasons of nationality, citizenship, ethnic group, class or geographical area of origin, peculiar customs, habits, modes of life or methods of holding property, unsuitability having regard to climatic, economic, social, industrial, educational, labour or health factors or probable inability to become readily assimilated. Over all, the Act maintained the preference for British, American and French immigrants, but otherwise left the determination of admissibility to the judgement of the immigration minister, who could use Section 61 to exclude Chinese, East Indian or black immigrants.

Throughout the 1950s legislative changes to the Immigration Act were relatively few compared with the years immediately after the Second World War and there was little development of immigration policy. It was a period of uncertainty as to the future course of immigration policy. There were strong concerns expressed over maintaining high immigration levels as an economic recession took hold in the mid-1950s. There was also constant pressure to preserve the system of preferred nationalities. Sponsored immigration by relatives in Canada, which before 1947 was virtually non-existent, had become a major force. During this period the problem of increasing numbers of visitors applying for landed-immigrant status from within Canada also began to emerge, partly because of restrictions on non-European immigration and partly because of controls on sponsorship.

The 1950s marked a greater public awareness of immigration issues and a push for social and humanitarian considerations in immigration policy. The decade saw the increasing involvement of non-governmental groups in the formulation of that policy, and growing objections to restrictions on non-white immigration, particularly from Canada's sister Commonwealth nations. About 2.5 million immigrants came to Canada in the 22 years after the war, only a third of them from Britain. A notable characteristic of the immigration flow in those years was the sharp decline in the number of people from countries lying within the Soviet sphere of influence. For many years, such countries as Poland and Ukraine had provided substantial numbers of immigrants. For example, in 1912, 19,222 Ukrainian immigrants were admitted to Canada. Fifty years later, the number had dwindled to 128.

By 1960, policy-makers had begun to think seriously about ways to end the discriminatory features of Canada's immigration policy. However, slack economic conditions at that time militated against immediate change. Canada's "whites-only-need-apply" policy would remain in effect for some years to come, although the racial barriers gradually began to fall. In 1962, the government agreed to take in one hundred Chinese refugee families from Hong Kong; a year later, Canadians were allowed for the first time to adopt non-white children from abroad.

During the early years of the decade, manpower measures became increasingly linked with the development of Canada's economic policy. Rapid changes in the workplace had resulted in shortages of certain skills and the obsolescence of others. Yet even though times were prosperous, unemployment levels still remained unacceptably high. Meanwhile, the arrival of large numbers of visitors, especially from Greece, Italy and Portugal, who sought to become landed immigrants after their arrival, triggered widespread public criticism of immigration policy. In response, in June, 1964, the government commissioned an independent inquiry headed by Joseph Sedgwick, a lawyer, to look into the issue of visitors seeking immigrant status from within the country.

In December, 1964, the Department of Citizenship and Immigration undertook the preparation of a White Paper on immigration to provide a statement of the government's views on immigration policies and procedures in relation to national problems and interests. Emphasis on employment policies had led the government to conclude that existing systems were inadequate. More attention had to be devoted to the integration of Canada's working population with the labour market and this could be done only with the closest possible coordination between employment and immigration policies. The outcome was the creation of the Department of Manpower and Immigration in January, 1966.

In the meantime, the visitor-immigrant problem had grown out of control, but the government was unwilling to deport all the offenders. It was also not willing to grant an amnesty. Instead it steered a middle course, announcing that it would grant landed status to applicants who met normal immigration requirements, were successfully established in employment or business, had ten years of education or had married Canadian residents. All others would be refused landing and would be deported. This policy was expected to clear the backlog without causing serious hardship, while discouraging future flows of unskilled, under-educated workers. Recommendations from Mr. Sedgwick's inquiry were tabled and led to the creation of the Immigration Appeal Board (IAB) in 1967. The IAB was designed to relieve the minister and his officials of pressures to make exceptions to immigration law by transferring the matter to an impartial, non-political arbitrator.

In 1966, the White Paper on immigration was finally released. It was expansionist in philosophy, stressing traditional reasons to encourage immigration: population growth, enhancement of domestic markets, lower per capita costs of government and services, and cultural enrichment. But the White Paper also reflected reservations about unselective immigration, emphasizing the upgrading of the employability and productivity of the labour force and the vulnerability of the unskilled and semi-skilled to rapid technological change. The document unambiguously heralded the end to official racial discrimination in immigration policy. It was referred to a special Parliamentary committee, and the outcome was the introduction of the 1967 regulations which introduced four new elements into immigration law:

- the elimination of discrimination on the basis of race or nationality for all classes of immigrants;
- the presentation in detail, for the first time, of the selection criteria for independent immigrants;
- the narrowing of the sponsored class to dependent relatives, and the creation of a totally new class, nominated relatives, which included sons and daughters of any age or marital status, brothers and sisters, parents and grandparents, uncles, aunts, nieces, nephews and grandchildren likely to enter the workforce; and
- the establishment of a specific provision for visitors to apply for immigrant status while in Canada.

Even with these changes, the 1952 Immigration Act was a thorn in the side of successive immigration ministers. It was a political minefield of outdated thinking and it desperately needed to be redrafted. On September 17, 1973, Robert Andras, minister of manpower and immigration, announced plans for a comprehensive review of Canada's immigration policy as a first step toward a new national policy. Briefs, letters and papers were submitted by national organizations, provincial authorities and the public, and the results were released on December 1, 1974, in a series of thought-provoking discussion documents collectively known as the Green Paper.

 The Green Paper discussed the domestic and international challenges facing future immigration programs. "The development of Canada's future immigration legislation must be inspired by a sense of purpose about Canada's immigration goals and the place of the immigrant in Canadian life," it said, adding that responsibility for articulating those goals belongs to the Canadian people. Following its release, a special joint committee of the Senate and House of Commons was established to conduct a nationwide series of hearings, conferences and seminars, leading toward the formulation of a new Immigration Act.

The current Immigration Act was tabled in Parliament on November 24, 1976, and, was subsequently passed by the House of Commons. On August 5, 1977, it received royal assent, and it became law upon proclamation in early April, 1978. The 1976 Immigration Act and Regulations brought Canada's immigration policy and practices into much sharper focus than ever before. At a glance, the Act states, for the first time in Canadian law, the basic principles underlying immigration policy: non-discrimination, family reunification, humanitarian concern for refugees, and the promotion of national goals. It contains provisions that link the immigration movement to Canada's population and labour-market needs, and it provides for an annual forecast of the number of immigrants Canada can comfortably absorb, a figure arrived at after consultation with the provinces and other groups.

The Act establishes the "family class," allowing Canadian citizens to sponsor close relatives to come to Canada as long as they meet basic standards of good health and character, and it confirms Canada's commitment and responsibilities under the United Nations Convention Relating to the Status of Refugees. It also requires immigrants and visitors to obtain visas or authorizations abroad before coming to Canada, and it prohibits visitors from changing their status from within Canada. Security measures to protect Canada from international terrorism and organized crime are outlined, as are safeguards of the rights of immigrants and visitors through an improved inquiry and appeal system. Less drastic alternatives than deportation are provided for cases involving minor violations of immigration law, and the powers granted to the government and its officials are stated in specific terms. Central to the Act is an increased role for provincial governments, which get a say in setting annual immigration levels and are permitted the option of entering into separate agreements with the federal government that give them a greater hand in setting priorities and more consultation on policy. In the case of Quebec, the provincial government was granted the right to select immigrants planning to settle within its borders.

The development of Canada's immigration policy since Confederation has been marked by constant change. Rarely have more than a few years gone by without some amendment to the Act or adjustment of the regulations and procedures to meet the events of the day. The development of that policy has also been marked by an ongoing battle of opposing interest groups. The present situation is no different. Each of the various groups involved in immigration has its own vision of Canada. Some demand that the door to immigration be shut. Others want it opened wider. Some want more restrictive measures imposed on people arriving in Canada claiming to be refugees. Others want the government to allow refugees to enter unhampered so they can state their case. Some want more wealthy immigrants who can invest in Canada and create jobs for unemployed Canadians. Others want only educated immigrants. Caught in the middle of this constant struggle are Canada's gatekeepers, the immigration officials who must ultimately decide who gets into the country.

2 HOW TO IMMIGRATE TO CANADA

THE GOVERNMENT BROCHURES ARE COLOUR-
ful and full of information about immigrating to Canada.
They make the entire matter sound simple, routine and free
from aggravation. All you have to do is paint by the numbers
and you're in. Like those of all other countries, Canada's
immigration laws are based on the premise that admission to
the country is a privilege, earned only after certain conditions are met. These conditions are spelled out in the Immigration Act and Regulations and apply to all persons seeking
to enter and remain in the country. The only exemptions are
Canadian citizens and persons registered under Canada's
Indian Act who, whether or not they are Canadian citizens,
have an absolute right to come into or remain in the country.
"The Canadian government has offices in many parts of the
world where visa officers help people who wish to make
Canada their new home," begins one glossy brochure.
"These officers can tell you about the country's immigration
law, its climate, geography, living and working standards,
and other aspects of Canadian life. If you apply to immigrate
to Canada, they will process your application." The brochure
notes that there is a fee for processing applications ($125 for
an application for permanent residence) and points out in
bold black type: "There are no refunds for unsuccessful
applicants." Then it adds that all the information and help
given by visa officers "is free of charge."

According to the Immigration Act, virtually anyone can

23

apply to immigrate to Canada, as long as he is of sound body, mind and character. But he must apply to immigrate from outside the country at a Canadian embassy, High Commission or consulate. Persons visiting Canada and deciding they would like to live here cannot remain and apply for landed-immigrant status from within the country. This *must* be done while living abroad. Prospective immigrants can apply on their own or with the financial assistance of a close relative living in Canada; if the application indicates that an individual will probably settle successfully in the country, he will be called to a personal interview for a full assessment of his chances.

Section 3 of the Immigration Act states that the principles concerning admission of immigrants to Canada are to be applied without discrimination on grounds of race, national or ethnic origin, colour, religion or sex. Immigrants are to be selected according to universal standards designed to assess their ability to adapt to Canadian life and to settle successfully. Because of the tens of thousands of applications received each year, a broad processing-priority system has been established under which immediate family members of Canadian residents and refugees receive the highest priority.

Section 6 of the Act sets out the three basic categories of immigrants, categories which reflect the economic, social and humanitarian objectives of Canada's immigration policy. Those categories are family class, Convention refugees, and independent and other immigrants who apply on their own initiative.

Under the family class, any Canadian or permanent resident who is at least 18 years of age has the right to sponsor certain close relatives. Eligible relatives include the spouse; unmarried children under the age of 21; parents or grandparents who are 60 years of age or older, plus any accompanying dependents; parents or grandparents under the age of 60 who are widowed or incapable of working; unmarried, orphaned siblings, nephews, nieces or grandchildren under the age of 18; and a fiancé(e). Family-class members must only meet the basic standards of good health and character.

However, before an immigrant visa can be issued, the sponsoring relative in Canada is required to sign an undertaking of financial support. In this undertaking, the sponsor promises to provide for lodging, care and maintenance of his family members for a period of up to ten years. If an application is refused, both the sponsor and the applicant have the right to know why. Family-class members have been the major source of immigration in recent years, accounting for more than 54 per cent of the total movement of approximately 89,000 immigrants in 1983.

The humanitarian objective of immigration policy is evident in the admission of Convention refugees, as defined by the United Nations Convention and Protocol on refugees. Refugees seeking resettlement in Canada are assessed according to the same criteria used to select independent applicants. However, they do not receive a point rating. Instead, the assessment is used to evaluate their general ability to adapt successfully to Canadian life. This, and the amount of settlement assistance the federal government or private groups provide, determines whether they will be admitted to Canada under the refugee class. Local groups of at least five Canadian citizens or permanent residents 18 years or older, or legally incorporated organizations, have the right to sponsor refugees and their families. Groups offering to help refugees resettle here must promise to provide them with food and shelter for a period of one year. There are also thousands of people who do not technically qualify as refugees under the United Nations refugee definition but who, in times of crisis, may be admitted into Canada as members of a "designated class" under relaxed selection criteria on humanitarian grounds. In recent years, the federal government has placed people fleeing from Vietnam, Poland and certain Latin American countries in the designated class. Refugees accounted for almost 16 per cent of all landings in 1983, although their numbers have varied considerably from year to year.

The independent class includes a wide range of immigrants: selected workers, the self-employed, entrepreneurs, investors, retirees and assisted relatives. To be eligible to immigrate as an entrepreneur, a person must intend to establish a business in Canada that will employ one or more Canadians. An investor is required to have a net worth of $500,000 or more and must make a minimum investment of $250,000 for at least three years in a business venture which will contribute to the creation or continuation of employment opportunities for Canadians. A self-employed person, on the other hand, is someone who intends to establish a business that will create employment for that person, or who will contribute to the cultural and artistic life of Canada, for example farmers, athletes, artists and operators of small businesses needed in certain communities. To qualify as a retiree, a person must be at least 55 years old and have enough money to retire in Canada. He will not be allowed to work.

As of January 1, 1986, a revised immigrant selection system was introduced for independent immigrants coming into the Canadian labour force, both with and without relatives already in Canada. Emphasis is placed on the applicant's education, vocational training, experience, chances of finding a job, having pre-arranged employment, age, knowledge of the English or French language, personal suitability and having relatives in Canada. Points are awarded for each category to a maximum of 100. The pass mark is 70, and there is a bonus of ten points awarded to all applicants with relatives in Canada who are willing and have the ability to become guarantors by submitting an undertaking of assistance. The independent class constituted approximately 30 per cent of all immigrants in 1983.

Applications are processed as quickly as possible but there is a priority rating with the highest priority supposedly going to family class and refugees. Entrepreneurs and investors are next and then other independent immigrants, who may find themselves waiting some time before their application is approved and a visa is issued. The government brochures note that unnecessary inquiries about the status of an application may slow the process, so they advise that applicants call only when asked to do so, or if it is a matter of giving new information, such as a change of marital status, the birth of a child or change of address. "You should wait until you have been *told officially* that you can go to Canada before quitting your job and selling or giving away your possessions," one government brochure warns.

3 DOES CANADA NEED MORE PEOPLE?

CANADA IS ON THE THRESHOLD OF A POPULA-
tion crisis, but not a population crisis in the usual sense. We
are certainly not experiencing the explosive birthrates of
many Third World nations. In fact, Canadians are having too
few children. Our fertility rate of 1.66 births per woman is
below the population replacement rate of 2.1, and immigration over the past few years has not been sufficient to com-
pensate for the significant drop in the national birthrate and
the number of people leaving the country each year.

Canada's population is also aging, and that factor will
have a major effect on our society in years to come. On April
14, 1987, Statistics Canada released its final figures from
the June, 1986, census. They put Canada's population at
25,354,064, up from 24,343,181 in 1981. The growth rate —
only 4.2 per cent since 1981 — is the lowest in a quarter-
century and Statistics Canada attributed the decline directly
to lower immigration levels and a falling birthrate.

Some observers have sounded the warning knell. They are
telling Canadians that the country is in desperate need of
people, and that unless Canadians start having a lot more
babies, the only way to get those people is through a robust
immigration policy that will serve the nation's needs well into
the next century. In the 1984 *Annual Report to Parliament on
Future Immigration Levels,* concern about population decline
was raised for the first time. "The continuing decline in the
Canadian fertility rate and the recent sharp downward trend

28

in net immigration (gross immigration minus emigration) has given rise to concern among academics and others about the longer-term demographic future of Canada. Should fertility continue at below-replacement levels, and gross immigration continue at considerably less than 100,000 per year, population decline would begin shortly after the turn of the century. The federal government will be giving serious early consideration to the relationship between immigration levels and Canada's demographic future," the report said.

A 1984 federal government background paper on future immigration levels suggested that if current trends continue, the remaining years of the 20th century will be the last period of any significant demographic growth in Canada. "The following twenty-year period will be greatly influenced by the demographic events of 1980-2000. Were fertility to stay at or below current levels and annual net immigration be held to a minimum of 50,000, growth would diminish and decline would begin by about 2020." Lower net immigration would advance the timetable and move the onset of decline closer to the year 2001.

While a net immigration of 50,000 may not seem much, considering Canada has always selected considerably higher numbers of immigrants annually, it must be kept foremost in mind that the operative word here is "net." Government studies show that tens of thousands of people leave Canada each year; they either return to their homelands or emigrate to warmer and greener pastures to the south. Although there are no firm studies to show just how many people emigrate, because Canada does not have exit visas or other forms of exit controls, a Statistics Canada study estimates that with gross immigration at 118,000 in 1971-72, emigration was 66,000. Therefore, *net* immigration was 52,000. The analysis, which looked at actual and projected immigration and emigration from 1971 to 2006, estimates net immigration to be roughly half the gross figure. The actual projections on emigration were gleaned from census data and family-allowance and income-tax files.

A population and fertility survey of 18 developed countries

compiled for a working group on migration for the Organization for Economic Co-operation and Development (OECD) in 1984 revealed that none of these countries used immigration as a demographic tool to offset declining fertility. The U.S.S.R., Poland and Yugoslavia have no immigration programs, while Yugoslavia and, to a lesser extent, Poland, have been eager to increase their levels of emigration. In the European Community, virtually no country was considering the use of immigration to meet demographic considerations. Moreover, restrictions have been introduced to curtail non-European immigration and to encourage the emigration of foreign resident workers. By and large, the survey found that Western European countries have adopted restrictive immigration policies, apparently prompted by changing economic conditions, labour surpluses and an increasingly negative attitude toward certain culturally distinct groups.

According to the study, Canada, the United States and Australia were the only major immigrant-receiving countries, and while all three shared similar immigration policies aimed at social, economic and humanitarian concerns, none had specific population policies to support its immigration activities. In contrast, France has introduced a variety of measures aimed at encouraging increased fertility through social services, tax benefits and allowances to assist families with children. In May, 1985, the French government launched a year-long campaign dubbed *Ouvrons la France aux enfants* (Let us open France to children). Politicians and business and labour leaders were urged to construct playgrounds and to do everything they could to make parents feel that children were welcome. Other countries in Western and Northern Europe have also initiated programs to make their societies more *kinderfreundlich* (child-friendly) and many have established national agencies to explore the question of population decline.

Public participation in the population debate has been steadily growing throughout Europe since the mid-1970s. Former right-wing French prime minister Michel Debré wrote in *Le Monde* on December 14, 1978, that policy-makers,

politicians, priests, teachers and journalists have a responsibility to "make it understood that in France everything is at
stake with this catastrophe of the decline in births — pension
plans, social legislation, economic prosperity, freedom. . . .
And you, gentlemen, are doing nothing!" At the other end of
the spectrum, feminist Vera Slupik fiercely attacked what she
called "brainwashing with population policy" in West Germany. In a 1981 issue of the feminist journal *Emma*, Ms Slupik warned that women should keep a watchful eye on these
"childbirth technocrats." She argued that it was not women
who were expressing concern over the birthrate in West Germany. The debate, she said, is controlled by men and is a
male ploy to send women back to the kitchen. She asked
why women should be concerned about the decline in the
birthrates of Germany and Europe when the planet is
already over-populated, women from Third World nations
are being forced to undergo sterilization, and the West German government is steadfastly refusing to let in thousands of
refugees and economic migrants from Afghanistan, Iran, Sri
Lanka and Turkey?

Most Eastern European nations have adopted pro-natalist
measures in an attempt to stem declining birthrates. The
U.S.S.R., in particular, has initiated a policy aimed at increasing the proportion of the ethnic Russian population. Soviet
authorities are very worried about the declining birthrate of
ethnic Russians and the high birthrate of Moslems, who
dominate the Soviet Asian republics. There were an estimated 50 million Moslems among the Soviet population of
280 million in 1986, and with a birthrate in Moslem areas
almost three times that of the rest of the country, these peoples could increase to one-quarter of the Soviet Union's population by the end of the century while ethnic Russians drop
to less than one-half.

In a paper called *Europe's Second Demographic Transition*,
published in March, 1987, Dirk J. van de Kaa, director of the
Netherlands Institute for Advanced Study in the Humanities
and Social Sciences, suggested that there are really only two
scenarios that would ward off any long-term population

decline in Europe: increased fertility or increased immigration. "The second scenario would be much simpler. It assumes that immigration becomes a major component of population growth," Mr. van de Kaa wrote. However, he pointed to the growing anti-immigrant trend throughout Europe and concluded that large-scale immigration in this atmosphere "is likely to be unacceptable."

While a number of Western European and Scandinavian countries have initiated studies on the issue of declining fertility, most governments are reluctant to introduce pro-natalist programs. The Netherlands and Belgium actually seem to welcome a moderate decline in their populations, arguing that a smaller, more stationary population than at present would be good. Mr. van de Kaa noted that opponents of the pro-natalist position vehemently dismiss "as exaggerated the spectre of Europe as a decrepit society of ruminating octogenarians." He pointed out that opponents attach no special value to their own cultures, welcome a pluralistic society "and fiercely oppose racial discrimination. More generally, they consider it Europe's duty to let others share in its resources and not to stimulate population growth when this is a serious problem at the global level."

The population debate in Canada is still in its infancy and appears to be taking its cues from events in Western Europe. Canada is in an enviable position, having plenty of space, abundant resources, and a high standard of living, yet the spectre of a declining and aging population hovers on the horizon. Throughout much of this country's history, arguments supporting rapid and large population increases were compelling. In 1966 the federal government's expansionist White Paper on immigration policy emphasized the need for a larger population. "The Government's view is that it is in Canada's interests to accept, and if need be encourage, the entry into this country each year of as many immigrants as can be readily absorbed. There is little dissent from the proposition that Canada still needs immigrants. Canada is an underpopulated country by most standards of measurement," the White Paper said.

"A bigger population means increased domestic markets for our industries. A larger home market permits manufacturing firms to undertake longer, lower-cost production runs, and it broadens the range of industry we can undertake economically; for both these reasons, population increase in turn improves our competitive position in the world markets. A bigger population also yields lower per-capita costs of government, transportation, and communications, and stimulates the development of more specialized services."

Forceful as these arguments were in bygone years, and although they still have some support today, their validity in current circumstances needs to be scrutinized more closely than ever. In 1974, the government's comprehensive Green Paper on immigration policy challenged the assumptions made by the advocates of high immigration and substantial population expansion. The Green Paper noted that to many Canadians, "living in a modern industrialized and increasingly urbanized society, the benefits of high rates of population growth appear dubious on several grounds. Canada, like most advanced nations, counts the costs of more people in terms of congested metropolitan areas, housing shortages, pressures on arable land, damage to the environment — in short, the familiar catalogue of problems with which most prosperous and sophisticated societies are currently endeavouring to cope."

The Green Paper stressed that when all the arguments were sifted, "it would probably be a not unfair assessment of our understanding of the economic consequences of higher against lower population growth rates for a country in Canada's present position to conclude that the evidence in favour of higher rates is uncertain. Furthermore, the hidden costs that they entail in terms of social strains and the impairment of the quality of life, admittedly extremely difficult to quantify, have thus far tended to be neglected in expert appraisals."

Advocates of increased immigration still feel strongly that Canadian industry would derive significant benefits from the larger domestic market generated by a larger population, which in turn would create more jobs and prosperity for all. In a newspaper column in the *Toronto Star* on January 11, 1987, Hugh Segal, political aide to former Ontario premier William Davis, spoke for the pro-immigration lobby when he said that the real challenge for the Canadian government is not how to keep immigrants out "but how to massively increase the numbers of people coming into Canada. If one believes in this country's future, one knows that future is not shaped by geography, natural resources and a new constitution alone. People — human beings who want to build their own lives and find opportunities for themselves and their families — that is what shapes the future. And that is what built this country in all its present dimensions."

Mr. Segal argued that on almost every front — from trade relationships with other countries to the need to generate domestic growth and prosperity — "our one problem is people, or lack of people, to form the critical mass and market size essential to sustain this country's ambitions." He also maintained that nationalists who do not favour a massive increase in immigration champion a diminished view of Canada, "not one that sees this nation increasing in economic might, technological capacity and international stature in the decades ahead. No country has shown greater success at integrating different racial, ethnic and cultural backgrounds into a broad framework. No nation would benefit more from a population of 50 million by the year 2050."

Progressive Conservative MP Jim Hawkes, chairman of the Parliamentary Standing Committee on Labour, Employment and Immigration, is another forceful advocate of increasing immigration. In an interview in November, 1986, Mr. Hawkes argued that Canada needs at least 175,000 new immigrants a year just to maintain a static population. "Canada needs far greater immigration if it wants to keep the population increasing at an annual rate of one per cent," he said. The Alberta MP stressed that Canada simply has to start admitting more immigrants, and that "now is the time to take a long, hard look at exactly how we are going to do that." His concerns, he said, began with "a sense of the size of Canada and how few people we have for a country so vast. Then there is the pressing question of demographics. If you were to stop immigration, we'd have a declining population fifteen years down the road, and an aging population. We would reach the point where you'd get about 1.5 people in the workforce for every retired person," Mr. Hawkes warned.

Mr. Hawkes also suggested that policy-makers will have to consider the role of immigration in changing the structure of the population — particularly the age make-up. Without new and younger blood, the problems Canada faces in coming years could be critical. The present Canadian population is characterized by an aging trend. With the maturation of the baby-boom generation, and a much lower birthrate in the 1970s and 1980s, the smallest-ever proportion of the population is now under age fourteen. The largest share is held by the baby-boomers who are now creeping into the midriff-bulge years. Who is going to care for all those wizened baby boomers in the first half of the 21st century? Several studies indicate that the greying baby-boomers will increase the burden on a diminishing productive labour force striving to provide social and health services to an expanding number of non-working elderly citizens. These studies contend that immigration can alleviate problems associated with an aging population by bringing in younger immigrants to augment the size of the labour force and reduce the relative proportion of the population over 65.

Proponents of slower population growth have their own arguments. Many wonder where increased numbers of immigrants will find work, especially when the so-called developed nations are moving more and more into the "information age." The information society, already benefiting from high technology and soon to profit from robotic technology, will be knowledge-intensive rather than labour-intensive. In a paper entitled *Technological Advance, Economic Growth and Income Distribution*, published in September, 1983, U.S. economist Wassily Leontief suggested that the ability of the service sector to absorb displaced workers will decline. "As soon as not only the physical but also the controlling 'mental' functions involved in the production of goods and services can be performed without the participation of human labour, labour's role as an indispensable factor of production will progressively diminish," Mr. Leontief wrote.

Ken MacKay, chairman of the Population Committee for the Conservation Council of Ontario, wrote in a letter to the *Toronto Star* on February 7, 1987, that the slow rate of population growth in Canada "is a very minor crisis. In contrast, the population problem of the Third World is a major crisis not only for those countries but for Western countries as well. It is unlikely that international aid will ever become truly effective as long as population growth in the Third World continues at its present rate." Mr. MacKay also warned that Canada has long since passed the time when it could ignore the limitations imposed by fragile environmental systems. Canada "must not ignore the impact of population change on environmental problems and natural resource supplies. . . . Many in Canada see rapid growth in population as a positive step in our growth-oriented economy. We think it is essential to examine that growth, not only from the viewpoint of economic and social issues but also from the viewpoint of environmental issues. Rapid population growth without regard to the environmental consquences is short-sighted and unwise," Mr. MacKay wrote.

In November, 1984, Employment and Immigration Minister Flora MacDonald said she wanted to rethink immigration policy. She expressed concern about the continual decline in immigration levels brought on by the severe economic slump and high unemployment at the start of the decade. (Immigration dropped from a high of 143,117 in 1980 to a low of 84,273 in 1985.) Given current population projections, Ms MacDonald also said she wanted her officials to look into the long-term relationship between immigration and Canada's demographic future. Late that year, and in early 1985, the first phase of a major consultation process was undertaken. A series of seminars with academics and other experts was held on population issues.

In June, 1985, Ms MacDonald tabled a special report to Parliament, *Review of Future Directions for Immigration Levels.* Demographic trends indicated that the Canadian population would begin to decline shortly after the turn of the century, if fertility continued at its current below-replacement rate and if net immigration continued at the low levels experienced over the past few years. With this in mind, the report stressed that there "is a need to consider the broader economic and social implications" of this trend. It also suggested that immigration is the readily available mechanism for shaping the future population of Canada. While advocating the need for a change in policy, the document went only as far as calling for a moderate, controlled increase in future immigration levels. It concluded that Canada needs, and will continue to need, a vigorous, balanced immigration movement both to maintain national social and humanitarian ideals and to complement strategies for economic growth. In presenting its case for increased immigration, the report stated: "Contrary to myth, immigrants do not take jobs away from Canadians." It noted that immigrants contribute to economic growth and job creation by augmenting the pool of capital, expanding consumer demand for Canadian goods and services, and bringing needed skills and energies to the labour market.

In August, 1985, the second volume of the report of the Royal Commission on the Economic Union and Development Prospects for Canada was released. Commission chairman Donald S. Macdonald devoted an entire chapter to immigration policy, and the most significant point that emerged was the conviction that Canada should set its immigration levels on the basis of long-term objectives, rather than short-term labour force considerations. "Given the uncertainties involved in deciding both on an appropriate population size and on its age composition, Canada should follow that course which, in the past, has served our country well: that is, a less restrictive policy than that currently in place," Mr. Macdonald recommended. Canada, he also suggested, should increase its immigration flow to one closer to the historical average of the post-war years.

In late autumn of 1985, the federal government announced it would admit 105,000 to 115,000 immigrants to Canada in 1986, an increase of 30,000 over the previous year's level. It also said that it would plan for the admission of 115,000 to 125,000 immigrants in 1987. In announcing these increased levels for 1986 and 1987, which the immigration minister noted were aimed in part at helping forestall the projected decline in the Canadian population, Flora MacDonald stressed the need for a comprehensive review of the link between immigration levels and future demographic needs, and of the economic and social implications of the future size, rate of growth, and structure of the Canadian population. Any further increases in immigration levels for demographic reasons would have to await the outcome of such a review, she said.

The details of a three-year review of demography and its implications for economic and social policy, to be carried out by Health and Welfare Canada, were announced in May, 1986, by Health and Welfare Minister Jake Epp. The review team, headed by Dr. E. M. Murphy, an assistant deputy minister with the department who holds a PhD in demography, will report its conclusions to Cabinet by March, 1989. They will look into and assess population projections for Canada to the year 2025 and examine the impact Canada's changing age structure will have on federal policies and programs during the next four decades. The team will also assess the relationship between Canada's population growth and economic growth; examine the impact of immigration on such factors as urban, suburban and rural growth and the labour market; and investigate the policies and programs of other countries in regard to changes in size, structure and distribution of their populations. Whether the demographic review will in fact become a new blueprint for Canadian immigration policy or yet another tome in the weighty pile of glossy government reports gathering dust on some forgotten shelf won't be known until 1989.

The population question demands a serious study and a major public debate on the implications of future government policies relating to immigration, covering all aspects of this important public policy issue. The purpose of such a debate would be, of course, to help determine what policy options can be addressed on the basis of the findings. The government's comprehensive review of population issues is an excellent starting point, but it must be kept in mind that it is only one aspect of the issue.

A broad range of questions will require careful study. Discussions of population size and composition are political minefields; arguments on all sides are frequently charged with emotion and tainted by prejudice, and the government will require courage and commitment to undertake such a debate. The following are some of the possible questions and issues that merit public discussion:

- *What is the ideal population for Canada?* Twenty-five million, thirty million, fifty million? The question of population growth may not even be the issue in this debate. The fact is that Canada will need substantially increased immigration just to hold the population at its present level. Without immigration, Canada's current population of 25 million would begin to drop by the year 2001, and it would fall to about 11.6 million by the year 2051! Even if it was found desirable from an economic and social perspective that our population remain at its current level, immigration would have to be increased significantly or programs would have to be established to encourage Canadians to have larger families.
- *Should the government consider a pro-natalist policy as a method of arresting population decline?* What kinds of moral and social questions would such a policy raise? What experience or knowledge can be learned from European countries such as France in implementing pro-natalist policies? What are the advantages and disadvantages of population decline for overall economic development?

What lessons can we learn from industrialized European countries, some of which have been experiencing population decline for a number of years?

- *How can immigration influence the size, rate of growth, and structure of the Canadian population at the national, provincial and regional levels?* This leads to the question, how successful have immigration policies in the recent past been in attracting immigrants to sparsely populated or less economically developed regions of the country? Many proponents of increased immigration point to the vastness and emptiness of Canada. Yet the overwhelming majority of Canadians are concentrated on a relatively narrow band along the U.S.-Canada border. Immigrants, for the most part, head for the big cities and do not want to settle in remote, undeveloped parts of the country.

- *What are the social and economic implications of an aging Canadian population?* Specifically, how will the overall costs of government social programs be affected, taking into consideration the higher-cost programs such as health care for an increasing elderly population? Furthermore, what impact will a declining and aging labour force have on productivity? Will mandatory retirement become an outdated concept to be replaced by a policy of flexible retirement? What impact will this have on the workforce? Can older workers adapt to the workforce demands of a rapidly changing technological society? Are they willing and able to be retrained? Will advanced technology and computerization make obsolete the routine, low-skill jobs in the economic structure that many immigrants are called upon to fill? Should we seek to select immigrants who are relatively young, well-educated and skilled? After all, they will be more likely to adjust to technological change. More importantly, they will increase the proportion of the overall population in the workforce and decrease the relative proportion of the group over age 65.

- *What are the costs and benefits of increased immigration?* Do immigrants augment the pool of capital and skills? Does the importation of skills reduce Canada's commitment to develop its own training and apprenticeship programs? And is there not a moral issue here, in that Canada would be benefiting from the investments made in education by other countries, especially Third World nations? The flow of young, professionally and technically qualified people from developing to developed countries, often referred to as the "brain drain," has been the subject of intense debate. The majority of Third World countries are on record in the United Nations and elsewhere as stating unequivocally that they view the outward flow of highly skilled persons as harmful. The Canadian government must remain keenly aware of the anxieties of these countries about the loss of people whose talents they desperately require. This particular issue also puts Canada in a dilemma because it cannot unilaterally refuse to process immigration applications from any specific source. Not only would such a step be inconsistent with our non-discriminatory immigration policy, it would also be incompatible with the principle of freedom of movement for all people enshrined in the Universal Declaration of Human Rights.

- *Do immigrants create employment or do they take jobs away from Canadians?* The studies on this question are inconclusive, despite recent pronouncements by various politicians that immigrants actually create jobs for Canadians and generate economic activity. A report called *The Employment Effects of Immigration: A Balance Sheet Approach*, presented in Winnipeg at a meeting of the Canadian Population Society in June, 1986, concluded that "on balance, immigrants may create more employment than they take in Canada. The report was prepared by T. John Samuel, chief of the immigration and demographic analysis division of Employment and Immigration Canada. Mr. Samuel analyzed five major studies which used "macroeconomic models" to measure the impact of immigration on the Canadian economy and, more specifically, on the unemployment rate. All concluded that increased immigration tended to yield higher unemployment rates.

Mr. Samuel suggested that the effect on the unemployment rate "depends heavily on the underlying assumptions of the model in question. The lack of empirical data on the economic behaviour of immigrants has made the macroeconomic modelling of the impact of immigration a difficult task." Instead, Mr. Samuel made a detailed analysis of the "supply and demand side effects" on the labour market using 1983-84 immigration data, hoping that his conclusions would provide a reference for future modelling. His results indicated that immigrants do in fact create more jobs than they take. "There is no suggestion, however, that the best possible solution to Canada's unemployment problem is to drastically increase the number of immigrants allowed into Canada each year," Mr. Samuel said. "Nevertheless, it does raise the perplexing question of how to determine the optimal immigrant inflow which maximizes the economic, demographic, and multicultural aspects of immigration."

In the meantime, Mr. Samuel pointed out that his analysis has led him to conclude that "immigration should be seen in a more positive light in regard to its employment effects." While his study is convincing, the footnote on the cover page sounds a note of caution: "The views in this paper are those of the author only and do not necessarily represent those of Employment and Immigration Canada." But whether they do or not, Mr. Samuel's study must have had a convincing effect on the current minister of state for immigration, Gerry Weiner. In virtually every speech he has given since he was appointed minister on June 30, 1986, Mr. Weiner has stressed that "immigrants do not take jobs from Canadians. As often as not they end up creating them for others."

- *What problems have been associated with past large influxes of immigrants and refugees?* Will the immigrants and refugees of the 1980s and 1990s be willing to wait a generation, as their predecessors did, to integrate into Canadian society, or will they come with a set of demands and expectations? Will this new wave of immigrants experience more difficulty in adjusting? What types of settlement and integration programs will be needed — in particular, orientation classes and English or French language training? And if immigration is to be expanded significantly, can it be handled by the current organizational structure?

- *How can different interest groups and sectors of Canadian society be encouraged to become actively involved in the debate and management of immigration policies?* This last question is of paramount importance. Many Canadians are expressing concern that the federal government has lost control of immigration policy. They do not feel that the government can manage the size of immigration movements being projected, or the proper settlement of newcomers, preferably away from already congested cities and into underpopulated regions of the country. They have also been traumatized by the recession, and to a large extent that experience has altered their behaviour and the way they now see things. It has made the population somewhat more skeptical and less generous, and, like many Europeans who have turned against the large immigrant communities in their midst, some Canadians are leaning toward more restrictive measures against anything they perceive as a threat to their battered social order. They hear the calls for a massive infusion of new immigrants, and they are frightened that Canada will change in ways they do not favour. For many, the argument that what has worked well in the past will work in the future is not reassuring. The questions they are asking demand answers, not political pipe dreams wrapped in bureaucratic bafflegab.

4 A RUDDERLESS SHIP

IN NOVEMBER, 1983, GAÉTAN LUSSIER, THE deputy minister and chairman of Employment and Immigration Canada, circulated a document within the department outlining the "functional authority" or chain of command of the Immigration Department. The document, which was formally approved in June, 1984, stressed that the growing complexity of an organization as large as and as decentralized as the Department of Employment and Immigration, "coupled with the constraints and guidelines applicable to the management of government programs, makes it essential to adopt and circulate a coherent and balanced policy which defines and regulates the concepts of line and functional authority. . . . The purpose of this circular is to introduce a policy on line and functional authority which is to be used to link the planning and accountability process to the executive managerial contract, and the corporate goals and objectives contained therein. The policy is based on the premise that service to the public is the primary objective of the department."

After this somewhat verbose but nonetheless comprehensible introduction, the memo went on for several pages to explain the framework for the chain of command and define the "authority relationships" within the department in indecipherable bureaucratic jargon. At the end, the author provided a final section entitled "Interpretation." It reads:

Functional authority, applied within the [department],

is based on the principle that the level of authority must be consistent with the office of accountability. Correspondence originated by a region or NHQ [national headquarters] at the level of chief would be considered as requesting or extending advice; under normal circumstances, and with prior consultation, regions would be expected to follow that advice. If the advice offered adversely affects regional operations, yet is required in the interests of standardization, or as a result of central agency requirements, the matter is to be referred to the next higher NHQ and regional level for resolution. Guidance requested by a regional director or extended by a NHQ functional director general/director should be viewed as expert, and prudence suggests that it should be followed; however, in the judgement of regional management, when such guidance does not act in the best interests of the public, or if it contravenes instructions previously received, it must be referred to the next higher NHQ and regional level for resolution. Direction requested by a regional executive head, or extended by a NHQ functional executive head, should, under normal circumstances, be accommodated quickly and in an appropriate manner. However, executive heads may refer any matter to the deputy minister/chairman for consideration or decision.

In March, 1986, an internal audit by senior departmental staff of the quality of service provided to the public by the Immigration Department concluded that the above policy on functional authority had — not surprisingly — caused uncertainty throughout the entire department, from headquarters to the regional and local offices across the country. The confusion, the report added, "has had an unfavourable impact on resolving the issue of responsibility/accountability for the achievement of the program's stated mission." The mission, as set out in the department's 1985/1986 Main Estimates, is: "To administer the admission of immigrants and visitors to Canada in accordance with the economic, social and cultural interests of Canada."

In their searing report, the audit team concluded that senior immigration officials at national headquarters were failing to ensure that policies, procedures and guidelines were being followed in regional and local immigration offices right across Canada. The report added that the entire immigration system lacks firm direction and control from senior officials in Ottawa. The quality of service to the public is unsatisfactory, the audit team noted: "The present immigration system . . . causes long delays for clients, involves excessive paperwork, is bound by outdated procedures and makes little use of modern technology." As a result, immigration policy is not being applied consistently across the country; front-line staff are inadequately trained; and morale problems are severe. "Over all, service to the public has suffered, the image of immigration has been tarnished, and management has not been very innovative in improving and streamlining service to the public at the point of contact."

At various immigration offices around the country, the audit team found that clients were not always served in a courteous, timely and professional manner. "Basic conditions required to provide high quality of client service were deficient." At these offices, the audit team found:

- a reluctance of immigration counsellors to identify themselves, and an indifferent and hostile attitude toward clients;
- inadequate initial, refresher, developmental and management training for staff, which has contributed to low morale and a recognition by many employees that they were not properly trained for their jobs;
- overcrowded waiting rooms with little or no immigration information material, such as brochures or pamphlets, on display;
- a cumbersome appointment system with waiting times of up to three or four months; and
- reception areas staffed by personnel who were not always knowledgeable about immigration matters.

Armed with these findings, it wasn't difficult for the audit team to determine where to lay the blame: at the top echelons of power in the Immigration Department executive offices in Hull, Quebec, across the river from the Parliament buildings. "At the present time, senior immigration management is unable to protect the integrity of program effectiveness" because priorities are not clearly stated to guide management at lower levels in dealing with immigration activities, the report said. In the absence of strong direction from national headquarters, regional operations had assumed the responsibility of implementing immigration policy. "Some instructions are altered at the regional level and, therefore, not implemented according to their national intent," the report commented. It also pointed out that participation by national headquarters "in a coordinated effort to manage and allocate resources was not evident." Moreover, there was no national plan by which senior management could even justify and allocate resources throughout the department, and there was "almost a complete absence of national standards by which management could effectively measure quality of service."

In keeping with the essence of bureaucratic tradition, the audit team unearthed a plethora of statistics on how much business was done by the department. The report pointed out somewhat sardonically that while the department was heavy on figures, charts, graphs and percentages, there was very little in the way of statistics on just how *well* the work was being carried out. National headquarters placed strong emphasis on monitoring, the report said, but the question of just what was monitored arose, since current methods were directed mainly at measuring quantity of activities rather than the quality of the results. Unless headquarters were to institute a formal and effective monitoring system to inform itself about service quality, the current system would continue to yield "vast amounts of data and very little useful information," the audit team noted. In the absence of a meaningful nationwide monitoring system and the failure to apply national standards uniformly across the country, the auditors stressed that there was simply no way the department could say with any assurance that the Immigration Act and Regulations were being applied with any degree of quality and consistency.

The auditors then tackled the question of procedures used by the department and concluded that they were overly complex, required excessive documentation and delayed service to clients. These procedures and a proliferation of special programs had mushroomed over the years without any regular review mechanism to eliminate the unnecessary or the inefficient. When outside groups that dealt on an almost daily basis with the department were questioned by the audit team, their strongest criticism centred on the deteriorating attitudes of immigration staff. Again, the auditors wagged the finger of blame in the direction of Ottawa, saying senior immigration bureaucrats had failed to address these problems, and as a result, many front-line immigration officers and their clients "are frustrated."

A key factor in many of the day-to-day problems was that the department has fallen far behind the times in terms of modern technology. "There is a lack of knowledge and appreciation of current technology that could enhance immigration services and make more efficient use of resources," the report said. In this area, the audit team found:

- insufficient use of word processing equipment at a time when word processors are being used increasingly by people in their homes. "It is surprising to find offices with high volumes of reports and repetitive letters not using such equipment." The secretaries simply retype form letters;
- inadequate telephone systems for handling large volumes of calls;
- the potential application of computers had not been fully explored, especially in areas such as monitoring, budgeting and scheduling, where manual tasks are cumbersome and repetitive.

The reasons for the department's technological rut were

traced to a reluctance by management to allocate funds to buy new equipment, which, in turn, was blamed on current financial restraints imposed by the federal government and a concern by union representatives that efficient equipment might endanger job security.

Soon after receiving the audit team's findings, senior bureaucrats at national headquarters responded to the complaints and recommendations in the audit report. The following is a sample of those responses. On the recommendation that the department clarify the responsibilities and accountabilities of "functional authority," the management response was: "The document on functional authority is being reviewed currently at this headquarters. . . ." On the question of simplification of procedures, management said that a "special projects unit" was reviewing all immigration procedures with a view to reducing or eliminating those aspects of immigration work which are unnecessary and unproductive. The waters became murkier with management's response to the recommendation to improve the department's quality of service and its performance measures and standards. "The development and promulgation of quality of service measures and standards is an urgent requirement. It will follow and then be part of greater emphasis in immigration toward the client. Once the process of thinking in terms of the client is underway, we can develop measures and standards which the immigration officers both understand and support."

The bureaucratic bafflegab grew even more confusing in management's responses to staff problems, particularly its failure to communicate effectively the intent of immigration program objectives when issuing policies and procedures to front-line staff. Although management agreed unequivocally that there was a need to improve communication with front-line and field staff, the convoluted language they used to express their commitment to this goal was scarcely encouraging: "Communication will be enhanced by a headquarters structure with a built-in focus on headquarters-field liaison. Field involvement in program and procedural change will help as will placing a greater focus on program rationale in operational memoranda." The response to a number of other major recommendations dealing with staff training, organizational and operational issues, and intelligence and investigation units was that they were being reviewed as part of a study of headquarters organization currently under way, adding, of course, that observations concerning these areas "have merit and warrant implementation."

In March, 1987, a full year after the report was officially presented to department officials, the front-line and middle-management staff at headquarters and at regional and local offices throughout the country were still waiting for concrete action. The situation hadn't improved; in fact, some senior managers in the Quebec and Ontario regions complained that in some instances matters had deteriorated. Backlogs and delays were getting worse, directives and memos from headquarters were pouring in, staff morale was at an all-time low, and the ultimate victim in this descending spiral of pathetic confusion, the would-be immigrant or refugee, was expected to grin and bear it.

My first face-to-face interview with the newly appointed minister of state for immigration, Gerry Weiner, took place over tandoori chicken in an Indian restaurant in Ottawa. On several occasions we had spoken over the phone, but we hadn't had the opportunity to meet and talk in more depth about the department and the minister's thoughts on immigration. Mr. Weiner had been in the portfolio for almost ten weeks, and less than six weeks into his reign he had already undergone baptism by fire over the 155 Tamils found bobbing in lifeboats off the coast of Newfoundland in August, 1986. Those were tense moments, calling for tough decisions, Mr. Weiner recounted. But sitting back and looking at the episode in retrospect, he said that he felt he had handled the Tamil affair with political aplomb and flair — an opinion not shared by political analysts from coast to coast who agreed that the new minister had bungled the entire affair.

This particular evening Mr. Weiner didn't want to discuss his handling of past events. He wanted to talk about the day-to-day operations of the Immigration Department. To set the scene, Mr. Weiner had ordered his officials earlier in the day to release the audit report dealing with quality of service. Not unexpectedly, the bureaucrats had objected before complying. They felt it was an internal document, and hotly maintained it was not for public consumption. But they had already inserted a vague reference to it in a speech delivered by the minister to the Ontario Bar Association, Immigration Section, in August.

Mr. Weiner had vowed, after he was sworn into Cabinet, that during his tenure as minister there would be no secrets: everything was on the record. It became evident early in our interview that discussing the audit report in any serious detail would be an exercise in futility; either the minister hadn't read it or the seriousness of its import had escaped him. The report itself was nothing short of an indictment of the entire management of his department, vindicating the critics, but Mr. Weiner responded to questions in a manner that suggested he felt the problems uncovered were minor mechanical ones that could be fixed with a little oil here and some fine tuning there.

When I suggested that the report's negative findings might lead to a clean-up at senior levels in the department, Mr. Weiner said that he didn't see why heads should roll. He didn't think it was necessary to be punitive, and steadfastly avoided entering any discussion that could be perceived as criticism of senior officials for the current state of the department. "I don't want to blame anybody. I think we have a unique opportunity to do something about it. I think what we see is an analysis of a situation, fairly and openly done with nothing hidden under the carpet." He said he felt his senior people now had a firm grasp of the problems plaguing the department, but he added, curiously, that "you might say we had a grasp of it three years ago, five years ago and before. I'm not saying there is something wrong with management. You could say that if you want. There are eleven levels of reporting between the minister and the desk officer. There's a lot of bureaucracy involved . . . I'm saying that the buck stops here because it is my responsibility to do something about it now." The audit report, he continued, gave the department the blueprint to put the ship back into shape. He reported that he and his senior officials had taken immediate action by establishing a special unit within the department to improve the quality of services to the public. To his credit, the minister went to bat for the little guy in the department, stressing that he firmly believed "there are many dedicated, well-meaning immigration officers who want to do a good job, but they've been hamstrung by a department which put them under a very severe hardship and handicap."

Mr. Weiner then reflected nostalgically on bygone days when he was a pharmacist and owner of a drugstore on the West Island of Montreal. "If I learned one thing, it was to answer the phone and say: 'Pharmacist speaking. How may I help you?'" Leaning intently across the table, Mr. Weiner put down his knife and fork. His eyes were flooded with sincerity, and, as if swearing a solemn oath, he said that his legacy in the immigration portfolio, should he leave one behind, was to have every immigration officer in every office and cubicle across Canada and in foreign posts abroad answer their phones: "Immigration officer speaking. How may I help you?" (In the fall of 1986, a departmental memorandum was sent to all regional immigration offices in Canada from national headquarters urging officers to comply with the following edict: "When answering the telephone, would you please say, 'Immigration officer speaking. How may I help you?'" The memo, however, was not Telexed to posts abroad.)

Mr. Weiner's intentions might have been honourable, but the serious shortcomings uncovered by the audit report amounted to no less than the ingredients of a full-scale government inquiry into a department that was and is rudderless. The audit was a damning indictment of an inept senior management, of bureaucrats who didn't care about the troops below and who were seriously out of touch with the realities facing immigrants. "It's all very fine to tell us to be friendly over the phones, but have you ever tried to call the main immigration phone number for information?" an immigration manager in Toronto responded when asked about Mr. Weiner's memo. "It's easier to get in on a radio game show for a free trip to Barbados than to get through on our numbers." He swung around in his swivel chair and slammed his hand on the top of a metre-long stack of binders jammed into a book rack along a wall in his cramped office. "Those things are filled with regulations, procedures, programs and directives on immigration. They all filter down from headquarters attached to official memos that tell us in vague, confusing and annoyingly mindboggling bureaucratic prose how to implement them. It's no wonder there's a very real problem in immigration today. What pisses me off most is that me and my staff have to suffer the brunt of the criticism, attacks, barbs and cheap shots from lawyers, consultants, the public, clients and you hound-dog reporters. We don't deserve it."

The bottom line, a manager at a Montreal immigration centre said, is that the quality of services being provided by the Immigration Department is still in woeful disarray. "Anyone needing these services has a right to expect that Canada's immigration centres be accessible, that information is available and that decisions be rendered in a reasonable period of time. For them, the most pressing problem is the delay in processing applications. It takes far too long to get an appointment. It takes far too long for a decision. It takes far too long to reunite families, and it takes far too long to process refugee claimants," he admitted. "Hours and hours are wasted in stuffy waiting rooms to get an appointment with an immigration counsellor. The telephone is an unrealistic alternative. The lines are always busy, and if you get through, you'll be put on hold. It is no wonder that after so many hours of waiting, that scarcely anyone could be in a calm, rational mood, regardless of how courteous we try to be."

During research for this book, another confidential audit report was uncovered. Completed early in 1986, it revealed an ongoing feud between Employment and Immigration Canada (EIC) and the Department of External Affairs (DEA). The report gave a detailed and unsettling description of just how deep is the rift between the departments and how it affects the selection of new immigrants from overseas. "Currently, most relationships [between EIC and DEA] are characterized by some suspicion and antagonism," the report began. "Problems with regard to resource use, which seem to be a major irritant between EIC and DEA, should clear up when each organization has a clear understanding of its own and the other's role."

The mission of the immigration program, as set out in Part III of the 1985-86 Main Estimates submitted to Parliament, is "to administer the admission of immigrants and visitors to Canada in accordance with the economic, social and cultural interests of Canada." Within the country, the administration of admission to Canada is done primarily by field offices reporting to Department of Immigration regional headquarters, while outside the country it falls under the control of External Affairs. The key to the strained relationship between EIC and DEA is that no umbrella organization exists to coordinate the immigration program. "What is absent is a headquarters operation that sits atop all program activities orchestrating their interaction." There are strategic planning and delivery units but no person or group charged with managing the various parts to produce a specific result.

The crux of the dispute dates back to 1981, when responsibility for the overseas immigration staff of the Immigration Department was transferred to External Affairs. A 1981 memorandum of understanding (MOU) signed by the two departments stated that Immigration would retain the responsibility for setting policy, while External Affairs would take on the responsibility for the day-to-day operation of the programs overseas. The audit report noted that Immigration did not want its foreign component taken over by External Affairs. "EIC was a reluctant participant at best, transferring resources and signing the MOU because the Prime Minister ordered that this be done and not because they felt it was in their own best interest to do so. Subsequent events can be viewed as an interaction of skepticism and resentment that led to the realization of self-fulfilling prophecies," the report said.

The intervening years, the report added, have been marked by "a series of disagreements, acrimony, bitterness and mutual recrimination. Both departments have established bargaining positions and little or no progress has been made in establishing a cooperative long-term relationship." Immigration officials have approached the problem as a structural one that requires a hierarchy of interlocking committees and formal agreements, while the approch of External Affairs remains unknown "although the tone of deputy ministerial correspondence is that relations are fine and require no alteration." After consolidation the status of the DEA group gradually rose until now the head of that unit is a *de facto* equal to the executive director of immigration as a program head. "Rising status implies broader responsibilities, yet consolidation was only supposed to organizationally shift the foreign delivery arm. Again, without a clear agreement as to the basic roles of the two departments, organizational drift and normal departmental territoriality have contributed to a poor working relationship," the report commented.

In their more candid remarks to the audit team, some Immigration staff members said they felt the only solution would be to take back immigration resources from External Affairs. In all the various exchanges between the feuding factions, the report notes, no attempt appears to have been made to build a cooperative relationship. What is urgently needed, the report recommended, is a clarification of roles on both sides.

Another serious problem lies in ministerial accountability. The minister of immigration designates numerous foreign service officers who are employed by External Affairs as "immigration counsellors" for the purposes of the Immigration Act, yet he does not have the authority or capability to choose who those officers will be or the standards to which they will be trained. Moreover, the immigration minister can use only "moral suasion" if DEA fails to meet the immigration level targets — and shortfalls have occurred in four of the last five years. One aspect of authority is the ability of the person in charge to take legal or personnel actions if an order is not followed. Yet it is clear from the report that while the immigration minister exercises this authority within his department, the current perception is that within DEA he does not. "This weakness in the accountability system gives employees of DEA the potential opportunity to ignore direction from the Minister of Immigration."

All of those interviewed saw the issue of resources and their method of allocation as critical to the EIC-DEA relationship. Central to that issue is the role of External Affairs: whether it is responsible for delivery of services as a partner to the immigration program, or as a contractor working on behalf of Immigration. Difficulties constantly arise between the two departments in all aspects of the resource question. "EIC headquarters staff are of the virtually unanimous opinion that DEA has diverted immigration resources to consular and other duties. . . . This causes frustration when DEA claims that it requires more resources to maintain its program." Quality of service is "a topic that has fallen through the cracks" throughout the entire immigration network, including the component handled by External Affairs. "Part of the reason for the lack of attention to quality of service is the lack of clarity over mission. In the absence of a uniform idea of what is to be done, different groups are at odds over what is to be done well. The immigration process can deal with an immigrant in a day, a month, a year or years. As long as the process is followed correctly, headquarters is currently neutral as to how long it takes," the report said. The study found that the absence of quality-of-service standards has been at the root of many EIC-DEA disagreements.

The operations of Canada's immigration program are subject to constant — and mostly negative — attention from the news media. Staff at immigration headquarters have become hardened to this phenomenon, accepting it as a natural consequence of running the program. "Their perception is that the public is against immigration, seeing it as a threat to both their physical and job security." The study suggests that a communications strategy would identify the key issues in immigration, allow for their monitoring, and dictate appropriate methods for disseminating information. "In the absence of this, support for a very valuable program will probably continue to deteriorate." Internal communications are in no better condition, the report noted. Headquarters personnel are isolated from the field, EIC has had an ongoing dispute with DEA, headquarters staff disagree or are unclear about the purpose of the organization, and program information flowing to the executive director "is sporadic at best."

On April 10, 1987, a beaming Gerry Weiner faced a throng of immigration officers, lawyers, consultants and political well-wishers at the opening of a new Canada Immigration Centre in downtown Toronto. He boasted that the new centre symbolized one of his top priorities: "to improve the quality of service we offer the public." He reminisced about visiting a Canada Immigration Centre in Toronto soon after he became minister on June 30, 1986: "I saw for myself the problems that clients and staff face. Long line-ups, no counters, frequent slow service, confusion, overloaded telephone lines. . . . Something had to be done. We had to improve. For our clients, we wanted faster, streamlined and simplified procedures. For our staff, we needed to improve working conditions, expand technology and increase training facilities. We had to remind ourselves that our goal is to give service."

Mr. Weiner noted that concrete measures taken over the past year were beginning to have a marked effect. The minister said the department was streamlining procedures and improving facilities in an all-out effort to improve service. He added that immigration offices abroad "are a reflection of Canada" and with that in mind, "External Affairs is improving the training of foreign service staff in immigration law, interviewing skills, and languages." Delays, he announced with an air of exuberance, had gone "from years and months to weeks and days." Ironically, in a letter to Tory MP Bill Attewell on January 22, 1987, regarding an immigration matter, Mr. Weiner wrote: "I must reiterate . . . that while we acknowledge that the quality of service to our clients is less than we would like, we are hampered in our efforts to improve. As you know there is only so much money in the public purse . . . and we have not been able to obtain approval from Treasury Board to increase staff. In fact, we are compelled to cut staff to meet the Prime Minister's promise to reduce the size of the public service."

During a brief "scrum" with reporters after the ribbon-cutting ceremony, a young Sri Lankan man confronted Mr. Weiner to ask why the Canadian High Commission in London had not acted for almost a year on his sister's immigration application. "We have not even had the decency of a reply," the man said. An aide to Mr. Weiner promised he would investigate personally. A full month later, the man still hadn't received even a response from the minister's office or the department despite 34 long distance phone calls.

Shortly after Mr. Weiner's speech, 24 lawyers and consultants both at the Canada Immigration Centre and around the country were canvassed about his claim of improved quality of service. A handful said they had noticed *some* improvement, but the majority wondered what the minister was crowing about. Sukhram Ramkissoon, a Toronto paralegal specializing in immigration, said that he continues to be dissatisfied with the quality of service "being meted out" to most of his clients. "I think Gerry Weiner is trying to convince the public that all is well and there is no need to panic because order has been restored to the department and we now have the best service in the world. That sounds very nice in a speech but when it comes to reality it is a horse of a different colour."

Denis McCrea, a Vancouver lawyer and chairman of the immigration branch of the British Columbia Bar Association, said he hadn't seen any improvements in the last year that "I would write home to Mom about. I think things are still very slow. Generally, it is very difficult to get anything done quickly. It's the same problem that has always existed in bureaucracy. Nobody wants to be criticized and the way to avoid criticism is avoid making decisions. Always leave it for somebody else." Mr. McCrea complained that there are just too many needless steps for the average, run-of-the-mill case "that everyone knows is going to be accepted. We're being put through hoops that really aren't necessary. The bureaucrats are not willing to take those necessary shortcuts."

Ottawa immigration lawyer Hugh Fraser noted that after eight years of immigration work, he felt the system was moving more slowly now than ever before. "The system is really clogged up right down the line." He also said he found morale to be at an all-time low among immigration officers. "Some of the things they tell us off the record make you wonder what is going on at the top. They feel the pressure when the system gets knocked by the media. They feel the pressure from the top when memos are fired off chastizing them when the fault is not theirs. I wonder how some of them could even interpret some of the conflicting messages they are getting in terms of policy. One day it's this and the next day it's something else, and they have to administer it."

Gerry Van Kessel, director of special projects for the Immigration Department and the man charged with improving the quality of service in Canada, recently responded to the criticisms. "First of all, it is a question of how quickly one wants to see results, and how quickly we can achieve them. Quality of service in our opinion really means meeting reasonable expectations of people in a timely, courteous and appropriate manner. That's an easy statement to make, but it encompasses a lot of things." Mr. Van Kessel said projects were in the works to answer many of the problems raised by the various audit reports. However, he stressed, "it is going to be around the end of 1987 before we can make any solid determinations. So much is riding on this that we've got to be careful that it's heading in the right direction. It has to be the result of good planning." He also emphasized that it would be 1988 before Canadians would see firm programs being established as a result of the pilot projects.

Mr. Van Kessel said the key concern for the department was improving family-class processing. "It has simply been taking far too long and that more than anything else must be reduced." On the question of improving line authority, he said he didn't know what was happening. However, on the issue of the relationship between the Department of External Affairs and the Immigration Department, he insisted that the situation "is now historical in that the kind of things the audit report revealed about the relationship are not the case right now." That opinion was not shared by several immigration officials who were later asked about the current relationship. They maintained that the two sides were still at odds over the numerous issues raised by the audit report. Mr. Van Kessel conceded that there are inevitable problems whenever one program has to be delivered by two departments. "Whenever one program marches to two drummers you have to make sure they're in step and the question is how to make sure they stay in step."

Mr. Van Kessel also said that while he understood the frustrations and anger of the lawyers and consultants, he wasn't quite sure what their expectations were "and how legitimate their expectations are. I don't have a good handle on it. Part of our business is saying no and if you don't like it, I can understand that, and lawyers don't always like that." With a seemingly monumental challenge ahead of him, Mr. Van Kessel revealed that he had been given "no additional resources" to achieve his objective. Nonetheless, he said he was absolutely convinced he could do the job "within the context of existing resource levels. I am absolutely convinced that you will see quite some improvements in 1988, but that doesn't mean you're not going to hear of delays in the isolated cases."

Readers of the audit reports can come to only one conclusion: the Immigration Department is in desperate need of reorganization and a thorough house-cleaning, and the Department of External Affairs must be part of that process. The issues of mission, roles, direction, management, accountability, quality of service, resource allocation and communications must be tackled immediately and with commitment. The public has a right to know that a critical public policy issue like immigration is being handled professionally and responsibly. Services offered to immigrants and refugees must be improved dramatically before confidence in the system is restored.

5 CONFRONTING CANADIAN RACISM

MOST CANADIANS DON'T WANT TO THINK about racism. They believe it is something that exists elsewhere — in the United States, Britain, France or West Germany. They prefer to think that incidents of racism in this country are isolated and do not reflect the thinking of the mainstream. Many will vehemently defend this position, arguing that most blacks or East Indians use their "visibility" as an excuse whenever they don't get their own way. They insist that immigrants, if they keep their noses to the grindstone and don't make any trouble, will have prosperous, happy and fruitful lives here.

But just how good is that life? Does Canada offer its immigrants a fair shot at the greener pastures? Do newcomers have the same equal opportunities as other Canadians? On March 28, 1984, the all-party Parliamentary Special Committee on Visible Minorities tabled its unanimous report *Equality Now!* in the House of Commons. While it praised some specific actions by governments to help non-white minorities in Canada, it pointed out that as many as 15 per cent of the Canadian people "exhibit blatantly racist attitudes, while another 20 to 25 per cent have some racist tendencies." Moreover, it added, even those individuals who are very tolerant can, with the best intentions, engage in racism without knowing it or meaning to do so. "Similarly, institutions can unintentionally restrict the life chances of non-white individuals through a variety of seemingly neutral rules, regulations

62

and procedures." The report concluded that a tension exists in Canadian society between the original European partners in Confederation, who dominate Canadian institutions, and the other peoples who wish to share fully in the institutional life of the country. "Inherent in the notion of the diversity of Canadian society as a mosaic is the equal participation of the pieces making it up, yet Canadian society is in reality a vertical mosaic with some pieces raised above others; the surface is uneven."

Trapped on the bottom rung of this vertical mosaic are the newcomers to Canada, especially visible minorities from Third World countries. Most come to this country with their hopes and dreams stuffed in a suitcase, only to have them threatened by a sometimes unfeeling and intolerant Canadian society. Like the hundreds of thousands of immigrants who came before them with strange habits, cultures, languages and religions, they find it difficult to adjust and, no matter how good life is here, they nurse a nagging nostalgia for their real home. It is cold comfort to them to know that the backlash against virtually all newcomers has historical precedents that go back even before the birth of Canada as a nation.

The first outright expression of racism in Canada toward immigrants was the concern voiced over "the assimilability" of black settlers arriving from Bermuda. In 1815, the Nova Scotia Assembly protested to the British Government against bringing in more "negroes" from Bermuda. It was stated that "the proportion of Africans already in this country is productive of many inconveniences; and [that] the introduction of more must tend to the discouragement of white labourers and servants, as well as the establishment of a separate and marked class of people, unfitted by nature to this climate, or to an association with the rest of His Majesty's Colonists."

In 1869, two years after Canada entered nationhood, the federal government passed the country's first Immigration Act. It would foreshadow those restrictions on entry which later developed into blatantly racist policies aimed at keeping out various nationalities, especially visible groups such as

Chinese, Japanese and East Indians. Donald Avery, in his book *Dangerous Foreigners*, documented the condemnation heaped on each new wave of immigrants between 1896 and 1932 — Ukrainians, Poles, Hutterites, Doukhobors, and the others. Every decade since has brought out some form of anti-immigrant sentiment in Canadians. Over the years, Jews, Italians, East Indians, Pakistanis and others have complained bitterly of racism and the refusal of established Canadians to welcome them.

While the Immigration Act of 1976 completely eliminated all the discriminatory references that for so long had barred admission to certain nationalities, it could not erase the racism inherent in Canadian society. Unlike the vast majority of those who came before them in the early years of Canada's immigration booms, these more recent arrivals, for the most part, are different in a most visible and significant way: the majority are not white.

On January 21, 1985, the Urban Alliance on Race Relations and the Social Planning Council of Metro Toronto released a disturbing report called *Who Gets the Work: A Test of Racial Discrimination in Employment*. The findings clearly indicate that there is a considerable amount of racial discrimination in Toronto and probably elsewhere in Canada. Co-authored by Frances Henry and Effie Ginzberg, the study was exceptional because it demonstrated for the first time in quantifiable terms that discrimination exists in employment.

During the study, professional actors who assumed various roles were sent out to apply for jobs listed in the classified sections of a major Toronto newspaper. The job applicants were matched with respect to age, sex, educational and job histories, and each carried a résumé carefully constructed to meet the requirements of the jobs being advertised. The only major difference between the applicants was race. In one case, Mary, a young black woman, applied for a job in a downtown coffee shop. "I went inside and there were two men at the counter. I asked about the job and one pointed to the other. I went over and spoke to him about the job, but he said he had already filled it." Sylvia, the white applicant, walked in five minutes later and was offered the job. In another case, Paul, one of the white male testers, walked into a gas station and approached the owner and asked if he needed any help. He said he didn't have a vacancy right then but asked Paul if he had any experience. Paul showed him his résumé and the station owner kept it, saying that Paul would be the first one he called if something came up. A half-hour later, Larry, a black tester, approached the same man and asked if he needed any help. The owner said no. "When I asked if I could leave him my résumé," Larry recounted, the man said: "Shit, I said no, didn't I?"

On another day, Mary, the black woman, followed up on an ad for counter help in an ice-cream parlour. "The lady said that the owner does the hiring and since he wasn't in, she would call me." Mary noted that three or four other black applicants were in the store. Outside she asked if any of them had got the job. None had been hired. Sylvia entered the shop ten minutes later. The same woman asked her a few questions about her past experience and she was hired on the spot. At a car leasing firm Andy, a white male, applied as a salesman. He was asked about his experience in sales, and his résumé was taken to another man in one of the inner offices. A short time later, a man, probably the manager, came out, introduced himself and took Andy into the inner office where he was given an extensive interview. After a while, the manager said, "I think you've got the right atti-tude, you can start immediately." An hour earlier, Robert, a black man, had gone to the same company to apply for the sales job. "I approached a salesman who told me the job was filled. I asked to speak to the manager. I was referred to someone else in the showroom. The man was one of three people standing around carrying on a conversation about a cookbook. Without looking up from the book, he informed me that the job was taken. The entire process took less than two minutes. It hurt quite a bit too," Robert recounted.

In total, 201 jobs were applied for in person, and 237 were queried over the phone. The results for the in-person method revealed that of 36 job offers received, the white applicant was hired 27 times and the black applicant received only 9 offers. In another 38 cases, blacks were treated discourteously and even with hostility. White applicants were never subjected to rude treatment but were, in all cases, dealt with as potential employees. In the most extreme cases, differential treatment took the form of black applicants being told that the job had been filled or was no longer available, whereas the white applicants received application forms or were even interviewed by the same employer for the same job on the same day. "The result of the in-person method reveals that some form of preference for whites took place in nearly one-quarter of all job contact which could not have occurred by chance alone. This is clear evidence of significant levels of racial discrimination in employment," the study said.

In an interview, Frances Henry, a professor of anthropology at York University and co-author of the study, said Canada has no claim to special status. "A lot of people in Canada work under the myth that 'sure these things happen in Britain and the United States but they don't happen here, because we're not a racist society, and we don't practise discrimination and we've got laws against discrimination' and so on," Ms Henry said. "The facts of the matter in day-to-day life are that there is as much racism and as much racial discrimination in employment [in Canada] as there is in every major industrial country in the world." She noted that when job applicants who are qualified and well trained for the positions they seek are denied access to employment because of the colour of their skins or their foreign accents, society loses the productive value of many of its members, "and it creates in them deep-seated frustration, bitterness and alienation. The long-term effects of these conditions create social unrest, disorder and rebellion."

Another striking implication of the study, the researchers pointed out, was that it roundly debunks the so-called "lunatic fringe theory," that acts of racism including the barring of non-whites or members of other minority groups from access to employment are simply the isolated actions of a few pathological people. It is overly simplistic and erroneous to suggest that employers, with the exception of a handful of bigots, apply fair-minded criteria to the process of employee selection, the researchers said. "The employment arena, as any system in modern society, is riddled with barriers created to deny access to certain categories of people to the full benefits of that system."

In May, 1985, the Urban Alliance on Race Relations and the Social Planning Council of Metropolitan Toronto released another unsettling report, called *No Discrimination Here?* Co-authors Brenda Billingsley and Leon Muszynski surveyed 199 large employers in the city, all with more than 50 employees, and found that only 9 per cent stated a firm belief in racial equality. "In their unsolicited remarks, approximately half of employers expressed a negative view of racial minorities, either assuming the inferiority of non-whites, indicating a willingness to exploit non-white immigrant labour, conveying fears about loss of white dominance in the labour force, or revealing outright bigotry," the study concluded.

A study of attitudes done by Policy Concepts Inc. for Employment and Immigration Canada and released in November, 1985, uncovered a disturbing level of racism among Canadians — primarily in Montreal, Edmonton and Vancouver — based on fear that Canada's predominantly Anglo-Saxon and European culture could be swallowed up by increased immigration from Third World countries. Over all, people surveyed believed that immigrants add to unemployment, compete with Canadians for educational and employment opportunities, and add to their tax burden if they are unable to find work. The study also found that there was a general feeling among the respondents that new Canadians do not make sufficient efforts to assimilate. Visible groups such as Chinese, Indo-Pakistanis and blacks were singled out repeatedly. The respondents said they would like future immigrants to Canada to be "monied, well-trained, well-educated and ready to assimilate." They saw present immigrants as poor, mostly from Third World countries, uneducated, untrained, reluctant to assimilate, prone to congregate in urban ghettos and a potential tax burden. "This immigrant is seen as posing a threat to our economy and our social fabric and a quality of life Canadians are reluctant to relinquish," the study stated, adding that there was serious apprehension among respondents of Anglo-Saxon and northern European background "about becoming a minority group in one's own country." Most respondents also favoured strict immigration controls. Some said they would like to see immigration stopped completely "until we get our house in order" and take care of those already here.

Subhas Ramcharan, author of *Racism: Nonwhites in Canada*, published in 1982, warned in his book that Canada's predilection for a self-image of equality of opportunity for all racial and ethnic groups, and its refusal to accept the evidence of racism in its midst, "bodes ill for the successful resolution of inter-racial conflict." He noted that when black immigrants were asked to describe their experience of prejudice and discrimination in Canada as compared to that in the United States, they noted one subtle difference: Canadians were the epitome of "polite racists." Mr. Ramcharan found that all the evidence suggested that prejudicial negative stereotyping and discriminatory behaviour against non-white groups "is as deeply rooted in the Canadian as it is in the American system. In fact, one could suggest that the American society, in accepting the reality of its racism, is a step ahead of Canada in the struggle to eradicate individual, institutional, and structural inequalities in the social order."

Mr. Ramcharan, a sociologist, pointed out that while all immigrants are expected to start at the bottom rung of the ladder when they come to Canada, the non-white immigrant soon perceives that he cannot expect to follow the pattern of the white immigrant. "Not only is he initially ascribed to an inferior socio-economic status and role, but in the second generation his children find that there is no way out for them. While they may or may not be ghettoized, it is a fact that while they physically live within the society, for most practical purposes they remain outside it." The author stressed that in terms of racial conflict this attitude has grave consequences for the non-white immigrant. "The catastrophes are evident in the chaotic and violent race relations scene in Great Britain today, and the key to the problem lies in the value system of a society which includes the notion of the inferiority of nonwhite people."

Think-tanks across Canada are currently studying the immigration question with a deep sense of concern and urgency. They are looking at the perceptions held by many Canadians that immigrants steal jobs. They are studying cultural and societal misconceptions about immigrants. They are looking at language training and resettlement programs. And they are trying to make sense of an immigration process that is cumbersome, confusing and inflexible. Yet in this entire debate, the issue of just *who* will be allowed to immigrate to Canada is being side-stepped by politicians and bureaucrats alike, who are afraid of what they will hear. They are afraid of a racist backlash. But the question of racism — distasteful and repugnant as it may be — must be dealt with, openly and publicly.

Traditional sources of immigrants to Canada are drying up. Virtually every country in continental Europe is facing a population decline and most will certainly not be encouraging their countrymen to emigrate. In the past two decades there has been a dramatic shift in immigration to Canada from primarily European to primarily non-European. Statistics indicate that immigration from Europe dropped from almost 65 per cent of Canada's total intake in 1968-69 to 24 per cent in 1984. The share of immigration from Asia, primarily from Indo-China, rose from 12 per cent to almost 50 per cent in the same period. Prior to 1967 less than 3 per cent of all immigrants to Canada were black or Asian. For example, in 1961, the top ten major source countries of immigration to Canada were all European. In 1978, three out of ten were Asian and in 1984, that number jumped to five, with the largest suppliers of immigrants being Vietnam and Hong Kong.

Immigrants are coming to Canada from around the world, but in particular from all over the Third World. Public opinion polls indicate that most Canadians are reluctant to put out the welcome mat for increased immigration; yet, the federal government resolutely ignores their feelings by announcing higher and higher levels of immigration. The gap between public opinion and government policy is a dangerous one that could lead to serious problems unless the reasons behind negative public sentiment are fully and properly explored, discussed and resolved.

Howard Adelman, a founder of the Operation Lifeline movement to help Indo Chinese refugees during the late 1970s, said in his book *Canada and the Indochinese Refugees* that the federal government's dramatic offer in 1979 to accept 50,000 Vietnamese boat people was made not in response to public opinion, but in spite of it. "The Canadian public as a whole was opposed to the Government's actions," the York University professor wrote. He went on to cite three public opinion polls that showed anywhere from 50 to 63 per cent of Canadians were "clearly opposed" to the humanitarian gesture which won the country international praise and respect. "Government policy was far ahead of public sentiment on this matter. . . . Because of this lack of [public] support, many argued that the Canadian government policy on Indochinese refugees was undemocratic," Mr. Adelman wrote.

In December, 1982, a particularly sordid but not atypical incident involving a recent immigrant group to Canada came under the public spotlight in Montreal. The Quebec Human Rights Commission was compelled to launch a public inquiry into a Montreal taxi company that had fired 24 black Haitian drivers earlier in the year. The company owner claimed he had lost a 14-year contract to a competing firm that employed solely white drivers. In the highly publicized inquiry, the commission found that two taxi companies systematically refused to hire black drivers and had even gone so far as to use the whiteness of their fleet as a marketing tool. The commission learned that problems of blatant racism had festered in the city's taxi industry for years. It was common practice, for example, for Haitians to be "bumped" or skipped over at taxi stands when they were next in line for a call. The policy was referred to in the industry as *au suivant* (on to the next). That radio message meant dispatchers were passing over black drivers waiting in a taxi line in favour of white drivers *at the request of customers*. Montrealers requesting white drivers threatened cab company owners with switching to other companies if they sent a Haitian. Moreover, several cab companies routinely marked PN — *pas de noirs*, or no blacks — on their order books when callers asked for white drivers.

When questioned mid-way through the ten months of hearings, Beaubien St-Michel Radio Taxi inspector Adrien Galarneau told Quebec human rights commissioner Nicole Trudeau-Bérard that managers knew about the policy and did nothing to stop it. Mr. Galarneau noted that the company he worked for modified the practice in 1981. "Drivers were then given the choice of answering a white-only request. If a black driver went and the client didn't want him, we'd send another car." Dispatchers honoured the requests for white-only drivers, Mr. Galarneau added, because "the customer is always right." He then declared that the practice of bumping was stopped altogether in 1982 because "it was illegal." When Ms Trudeau-Bérard held up a March, 1983, telephone log pockmarked with the letters PN, Mr. Galarneau sheepishly responded that it must have been a mistake. The commissioner then noted that the "mistake" occurred 357 times in that month.

The inquiry by the commission may have stopped the overt anti-Haitian practices, but it hasn't stopped the racism, especially within the taxi industry. The battle pits about 1,500 black drivers against 14,500 white drivers in a city oversupplied with taxis. (In Montreal, with a population of about 2.9 million, 16,000 drivers share 5,218 cabs, while Toronto with a population of 3.4 million has close to 8,000 drivers sharing 2,519 cabs.) Forced to work up to 80 hours a week to make a decent living, the white Montreal drivers blame the Haitians for their miserable incomes. The white cab drivers accuse the blacks of having dirty cars, not knowing the city and being rude to customers. Driver Roger Saint-Laurent said: "I've got to defend my livelihood when the government comes shoving its fingers into my pockets. I would like to see those [human rights] commissioners come down and work the taxis. Then they'd see what racism is and who is doing it. It is in every company."

In its report made public in the spring of 1984, the Quebec Human Rights Commission confirmed the allegations of widespread discrimination in the taxi industry. But the first two judgements from the courts, handed down in the early summer months, shook the faith of Quebec's black community and civil-liberties groups in the power of the province's lauded Charter of Rights and Freedoms. A judge found one company which used the *au suivant* policy guilty of discrimination and fined the manager a mere $150. A demonstration by several hundred people organized by the Quebec Civil Liberties Union and the Haitian community described the low fine as a slap in the face. In a second case, brought by a Haitian driver who said he lost as many as five fares a day because of the *au suivant* policy, the judge found the company guilty of discrimination but upheld the company manager's contention that his business would have suffered and the jobs of the majority of white drivers would have been in danger had the policy not been pursued.

The ruling stunned the black community and civil-rights groups who were still steaming over the first decision. "I simply do not understand it," an embittered Paul Dejean, president of the Christian Haitian Community, told the *Globe and Mail* in an interview in mid-July, 1984. "I understand that owners have the rights and blacks have rights. But does the majority have more rights than the minority?" (Montreal's Haitian population climbed to roughly 34,000 in the mid-1980s from 2,000 in 1965, largely because of a special immigration program sponsored by the Quebec Immigration Department in 1980.)

For a while, racism in Montreal's taxi industry simmered down, but in the summer of 1986 a spate of attacks on Montreal bus drivers provoked concerns in certain quarters that they were racially motivated because a couple of the incidents involved black youths. Some community leaders described the assaults as outbursts of frustration by minorities who remain on the margins of life in Quebec. "Montreal is the only city in North America where you can get on a bus and 95 per cent of the bus drivers are white," Arthur Heiss, Quebec executive director of the B'nai B'rith League of Human Rights, said in an interview with the *Globe and Mail*. "It's just not acceptable."

While some Montrealers refuse to accept that the attacks were racially motivated, there is almost total agreement that Montreal and the province as a whole have abysmal records in drawing ethnic and racial minorities into the social mainstream. At every level of public-sector employment, racial and ethnic minorities are woefully under-represented. Although such minorities (including English-speaking whites) represent 40 per cent of the population on the island of Montreal, they fill fewer than 12 per cent of the jobs in the municipal civil service of the Montreal Urban Community. In the province, minorities constitute 17 per cent of the population, yet almost 98 per cent of the jobs in the Quebec public service are held by white, Quebec-born francophones. The problem is especially pitiful on the 4,400-member Montreal Urban Community police force. About 12 per cent of Montreal's population is made up of visible minorities, yet in 1986 the police force had a grand total of five blacks and one Oriental on its staff.

In December, 1986, and the first two months of 1987, more than 10,000 people arrived in Canada claiming to be refugees. They came from such far-flung places as Turkey, Iran, Afghanistan and Sri Lanka and such not-so-far-off places as El Salvador, Guatemala and Chile. Their arrival, accompanied by the comments of certain Members of Parliament and immigration officials that most of the claimants were simply jumping the immigration queue, sparked an unsettling anti-immigrant backlash throughout the country. In opinion polls, open-line radio talk shows and furious letters to MPs and newspapers, a rising chorus of so-called ordinary Canadians began to drown out the entreaties of immigrant-aid and refugee-aid advocates for compassion and understanding. The hosts and producers of the open-line shows reported that 80 to 90 per cent of their callers were adamant against accepting more immigrants and refugees, said a banner front-page story in the *Globe and Mail* on March 6, 1987.

In Winnipeg, radio host and newspaper columnist Peter Warren told *Globe* reporter Susan Delacourt that he was disturbed by the tone of some of his callers. "Amongst us, I fear, there are many Archie Bunkers and Ku Klux Klanners. I'm hearing people say they want to keep Canada white." The calls to radio shows in the Maritimes were no different. "There is a racist sentiment that is creeping into this. Obviously, that's when the debate begins to be reduced," said Steve Murphy, host for six years of the open-line show at CJCH-AM in Halifax. In Vancouver, callers to the highly rated Jack Webster television show were quite bitter concerning the refugee claims of people arriving in Canada. "The feeling here is quite staunch — let these people wait their turn like everybody else who immigrated to this country," said Anne Davidson, a researcher for the BCTV show. "Everybody gets his back up over this issue."

The sentiments expressed in B.C. were virtually identical to those expressed on a CKAC-AM radio talk show in Montreal. Host Pierre Pascau said: "There's a mistaken assumption in the media that most people feel compassion for these refugees. Well, I can tell you that's not the way people feel." The reasons for the backlash against immigrants and refugees were varied. High unemployment was cited most often. However, pollster Peter Regenstreif of Policy Concepts Inc., in Toronto, sees a more fundamental attitude as the source of the backlash. A major part of the problem is that many Canadians see the country changing right before their eyes and they don't like it, Mr. Regenstreif said. Some people "just don't like the idea that when you get on the subway at working time, drive time, morning or night, it looks like the UN. They don't like it, they really don't. They thought they lived in a white middle-class society and they want to recapture it."

In the midst of the uproar, Gerry Weiner, minister of state for immigration, stumbled into the debate with a feeble and ill-advised attempt at putting a silver lining around a threatening black cloud. "What I am hearing very clearly is that [Canadians] do understand the contributions immigrants have made. They realize how good they've been for the country." A senior immigration official acknowledged that the minister was certainly rowing against the current and that his comment was contrary to what he was being told by his own advisors. "I guess he really wants to believe that Canadians are good, compassionate people. The reality is, they're not," the official said. Mr. Weiner's comment was also in conflict with the musings of Employment and Immigration Minister Benoît Bouchard who, in an interview in January, 1987, voiced concern that Canadians were "expressing a sort of fear" about the recent influx of refugees because the new arrivals "are from such places like Asia, whereas in the old days they came from Europe." Mr. Bouchard said this recent phenomenon of Third World asylum-seekers was worrying Canadians, "and they are demanding that the Government treat this question with great care."

Meanwhile, refugee- and immigrant-aid groups tried to put on a brave front, countering stories of negative attitudes with reports that their phone lines were humming with overwhelming support for the newcomers. But one worried person working the telephone lines for a beleaguered refugee-aid group in Montreal admitted to a reporter, without any prodding, that the majority of calls were of the "send them back where they came from" variety.

On March 10, 1987, Gerry Weiner addressed the Toronto Mayor's Committee on Community and Race Relations. In a sophomoric speech, Mr. Weiner drew attention to the *Globe and Mail* article of March 6. "There is not a politician in Canada, federal, provincial or municipal, who does not know that people are concerned about unemployment," he began. "They are worried about greater competition for few jobs. They are worried about higher taxes for welfare and social assistance. They are worried about a world of often bewildering complexity and change which seems to threaten the orderly routine of years. And when people are worried, are afraid, they look for a cause for their fear. If the news stories are correct, a good many Canadians have found the cause, and it is immigration." The minister said that he hoped the news stories were not correct. "I hope the information upon which they are based is erroneous or that those polled or giving their opinions are not representative of the great majority of Canadians."

Although seemingly possessed of a Pollyanna view of Canadians' racial attitudes, Mr. Weiner finally did admit somewhat begrudgingly that not all Canadians are well intentioned, generous or simply frightened by the unknown. "Discrimination is a fact of life which far too many of us have faced some time or other, be the reason race, religion, colour or physical handicap. I like to think Canada has less discrimination than other countries, but we are not free of it."

In an interview with the *Globe and Mail* on May 24, 1980, Lloyd Axworthy, then employment and immigration minister, pointed out that the federal government had done no studies on the racial impact of immigration, but it was an issue, he stressed, "that has to be addressed. We can't ignore it. There are people in this country who take exception to the changing composition of communities, and evidence probably points out, here and in other countries, that it can be the cause of friction." Mr. Axworthy noted that concerns about Canada's changing composition was not something new, and reminisced about growing up in the north end of Winnipeg. "I remember the enormous strains when immigrants from the Ukraine and Poland and Germany were shunned and discriminated against. If you didn't have the right surname, you didn't go to the right schools or work for the right department stores. That doesn't happen any more. Large numbers of new members of a community have always been seen with a certain degree of apprehension," he said. "Now, maybe, we are viewing those coming from the Caribbean or East Asia with the same apprehension. But in some ways our society has become a little bit more liberal. We don't accept some of the practices that were commonplace a couple of generations back. And that's progress." Mr. Axworthy stressed that what the country needed was better and faster methods of settling immigrants: better social services aimed at integrating immigrants smoothly into the community; more courses on Canada's racial and cultural diversity in our school system; better surveys of the job market.

Neither the Liberal government that Mr. Axworthy served nor the succeeding Progressive Conservative government has seen fit to act on the call for an assessment of the racial impact of immigration. In a brief telephone conversation in January, 1987, Kirk Bell, the Immigration Department's director general of policy and planning, said flatly: "It isn't our responsibility." The department uses only two criteria in determining who comes to Canada: economic and humanitarian. In other words, Canada only accepts the number of immigrants it thinks the economy can absorb in a given year on a first-come, first-serve basis, provided that the applicant either has close family ties in Canada, has been selected on humanitarian grounds as a refugee or meets the standards of an independent immigrant. Race, colour, religion and politics supposedly do not enter into the equation, the Immigration Department claims.

In August, 1985, volume 2 of the report of the Royal Commission on the Economic Union and Development Prospects for Canada raised the question of potential racial and ethnic tensions which may be created by the government's future direction in immigration policy. "It seems likely that in future years, a substantial proportion of newcomers will be attracted from non-European nations and these new Canadians will continue to expand the diversification of our cultural and ethnic mix," commission chairman Donald S. Macdonald wrote in the report, noting that these important changes in Canada's racial and ethnic composition will continue to transform the nation's economic and political life in the coming decades. "They are also likely to generate a certain amount of social conflict, and future generations of Canadians will need to invent new policies and techniques for coping with the stresses of a vibrant and dynamic multi-cultural society."

Mr. Macdonald also stressed that while many Canadians are understandably reluctant to encourage public debate on policies framed to deal with racial and ethnic conflicts, "it is essential that we recognize and come to terms with one of the most potentially explosive sources of political conflict in our increasingly multi-racial community." He noted that while the large influx of Canadian immigrants of non-European origin has not led to anything like the racial strife that the United States experienced in the late 1960s, or that Britain suffered just a few years ago, "it would be imprudent to ignore early signals indicating the possibilities of racial strife in the years ahead. Problems experienced by Haitian taxi drivers in Montreal, by Sikhs and Hindus in Vancouver, and by West Indians in Toronto indicate a need for all Canadians not only to help 'settle' our new immigrants, but also to promote their full integration and participation in all occupations and walks of life." Mr. Macdonald concluded that the political viability of a less restrictive immigration policy will depend on our capacity to deal with the domestic challenges likely to flow from it, and he strongly recommended that immigration policy be debated more openly among Canadians, and that governments in Canada actively consider the "management" implications of a return to the large-scale immigration of the 1960s.

Mr. Macdonald's comments open the door for a wide-ranging public debate on the immigration question, but so far, predictably, no public forum has been provided by the federal government. The government prefers to have private consultations with the provinces, which it is required to do under the Immigration Act, before announcing future annual immigration levels to Parliament. Government officials also invite opinions from scores of non-governmental organizations, representing business, labour, ethnocultural and humanitarian interests, along with qualified academics. For the most part, these consultations deal with labour-market needs and demographic issues. Advocacy groups have an opportunity to express their views on immigration levels with respect to certain aspects of the immigration program such as humanitarian concern for refugees and increases in family class immigrants. But the wide-ranging open public debate so urgently needed is missing.

Gerry Weiner announced in mid-March, 1987, that the federal government was working on a major program to educate Canadians about immigrants and refugees. He said the Immigration Department was consulting with advertising agencies to map out an awareness campaign that he hoped would be launched before the end of the year. The major focus of the campaign would be the economic and cultural benefits that immigrants and refugees bring to Canada. The junior immigration minister said he believed that if Canadians understood that newcomers are creating rather than stealing jobs, and that they enhance rather than detract from the economic and cultural life of the country, they would be as welcoming as the immigrant- and refugee-aid groups. But until Mr. Weiner and his department abandon their wilful disregard of the scope of racism among Canadians, it is unlikely that their advertising program will have a discernible impact on public attitudes toward immigration.

The Canadian public wants to know, and has a right to know, where the government is going with immigration policy. Canadians are worried about the immigration process, and the government hasn't adequately explained it to them. The government must put recent events and Canada's immigration policy in context. The immigration minister must tell Canadians what the policy is, and why.

Some Canadians are asking: will large-scale immigration significantly alter the character of Canada? This is an extremely delicate issue which, if ignored by wavering politicians fearful of offending certain elements of the electorate, could place control of immigration in the hands of bigots who argue that increased immigration threatens our way of life. The same complaint was voiced when thousands of eastern Europeans — Ukrainians, Poles and Jews — and southern Europeans — Italians and Greeks — poured into Canada during various immigration waves. If the racial question is not dealt with openly and honestly, public anxiety may finally provoke in Canada the deplorable interracial confrontations that have struck the United States and Europe.

6 THE GLOBAL REFUGEE CRISIS

I swore never to be silent whenever and wherever human
beings endure suffering and humiliation. We must always
take sides. Neutrality helps the oppressor, never the victim.
Silence encourages the tormentor, never the tormented.
Sometimes we must interfere. When human lives are
endangered, when human dignity is in jeopardy, national
borders and sensitivities become irrelevant. Whenever men
or women are persecuted because of their race, religion or
political views, that place must — at that moment — become
the centre of the universe.
— *Elie Wiesel, accepting the 1986 Nobel Peace Prize.*

PEOPLE HAVE ALWAYS BEEN UPROOTED BY
wars, natural disasters and persecution. Throughout history,
refugees have existed, but never until now have they existed
in such appalling numbers. Since the Second World War, the
world's refugees have numbered in the millions.

Statistics can only reveal the outline of the problem. They
cannot speak of the cruelty, indignities, violence and torture
these victims of displacement have suffered. There are now
an estimated 15 million refugees and they are to be found on
every continent and in virtually every country of the world.
They include not only intellectuals, university students, professionals and exiled politicians, but farmers, fishermen,
labourers, widows and their children. Many have fled perse-

cution for reasons of race, religion, nationality or politics. Most have been uprooted by war, revolution, civil strife and famine. Others are the victims of forcible relocation programs and internal exile within their own countries. As the years go by their numbers continue remorselessly to rise.

The U.S. Committee for Refugees graphically detailed the magnitude of the refugee problem in a survey published in early 1987. The statistical breakdown overwhelms the reader. The country-by-country reports are numbing.

The largest single refugee population is the estimated 5 million Afghans who have fled the war in their homeland since 1979. The next largest concentration is in the Horn of Africa, with more than 900,000 refugees in Sudan, more than half a million in Somalia, and smaller but significant numbers in Ethiopia and Djibouti. Throughout Africa, the refugee population is estimated at more than 3.1 million people. Thailand remains the dramatic focal point of the continuing Indo-Chinese refugee saga. At least 800,000 Kampucheans, Laotians and Vietnamese have fled to that country since 1975. Of these, about 370,000 have been resettled in other countries, but more than 115,000 still remain in refugee camps and an additional 260,000 Kampucheans live in displaced-persons camps along the Thai-Kampuchean border.

Countries throughout Latin America harbour more than 323,000 refugees, the largest groups having fled from El Salvador and Guatemala to Mexico, Honduras and Costa Rica. Not included in these figures are the estimated 500,000 Salvadoreans and 100,000 Guatemalans who live without documentation in the United States. More than 2 million Palestinian refugees are housed in over-crowded camps strewn across the Middle East. An estimated 300,000 live in camps in Lebanon, where almost daily throughout 1986 they were subject to attack from competing Lebanese militias, infighting among Palestinian factions, and Israeli military strikes.

A visit to a refugee camp anywhere in the world is a sobering experience. Ethiopian mothers worry desperately about where their children's next meal will come from. Afghan women and children in Pakistan and Iran live under the constant threat of bombardment by Afghan government jets. Kampucheans slog through ankle-deep mud during the rainy season. Vietnamese "boat children" inhabit a prison compound on an island near Hong Kong. Salvadorean and Guatemalan refugees pray to God that their torment will one day soon come to an end.

Many men, fed up with the mind-numbing and degrading existence in these camps where they are unable to work, strike out on their own to seek a better life for themselves and their families. Often they must abandon their families for long periods or even permanently. Many make their way, by whatever means they can, to Europe, the United States and Canada.

The signs are painfully visible. They scream out from the graffiti scrawled in black spray paint on the walls of run-down slums throughout Western Europe. "Foreigners go home!" Some threats are far more menacing: a graffito scrawled on the wall of a derelict building in central Paris reads "Il faut blanchir les bronzés avec une lance-flammes." Translation: The dark ones must be whitened with a flame-thrower.

The message behind these angry scrawls is brutally frank: Europe has grown tired of the seemingly endless waves of Third World refugees and illegal immigrants crashing her borders in search of a haven and a better life for themselves and their families. A strong odour of xenophobia permeates the air in every major city in every nation of Western Europe, from the Mediterranean countries to Scandinavia. Many politicians, who prefer to speak about this particular issue in polite, euphemistic terms, attribute the growth of xenophobia to "compassion fatigue." But a growing, much more vocal group, less prone to mincing niceties, blames the backlash on downright racism and warns that this rising tide is spilling ominously into official government policy in several Western European nations.

Europeans from all classes and of all political stripes are fed up. They are afraid of increasing crime. They worry about over-extended welfare budgets. They fear their way of life is being threatened by alien cultures — a sentiment that is exploited by right-wing politicians and sensational media reports. Today's situation is a far cry from that of 40 years earlier when, at the end of the Second World War, Europeans opened their hearts and homes to vast armies of displaced persons cast adrift from devastated cities, towns and villages. For the most part, these displaced people were not perceived as a threat because they had a lot in common with their hosts. They shared similar cultures, religions and backgrounds — and they were white. While humanitarian concern was a major factor in the welcome extended to refugees, Europe also desperately needed workers to help rebuild its shattered nations. Even then, there was a backlash aimed specifically at refugees who had fled communist rule in Eastern Europe. Western Europeans feared these displaced people offered a serious potential for social unrest. Through intense international efforts, more than one million of these unwanted refugees were resettled in the United States, Canada and Israel between 1947 and 1951.

To satisfy the urgent need for labour in the post-war reconstruction effort, millions of manual labourers were recruited from southern Europe and from the former colonies. The major colonial powers— Britain, France and the Netherlands — looked to their dependencies for cheap, willing workers. Those without colonies, such as West Germany and Switzerland, relied upon "guest workers" from Turkey, Yugoslavia, Italy, Spain and Portugal. At first, the arrangement worked well; the economy was booming and times were prosperous. But as the post-war demand for labour began to fade in the early 1970s, moves against immigrants gathered force throughout Europe. Then came the crippling economic slide of the late 1970s and early 1980s. Unemployment was rampant. Crime was on the increase. Inflation galloped out of control. Europeans began looking for a scapegoat, someone to blame for their declining standard of living. Immigrants and refugees became the target of their discontent and were the first to lose their jobs and the last to be recruited for new ones.

During the 1960s and 1970s, the focus of the world refugee problem shifted away from Europe to the far-flung reaches of the Third World. Afflicted with war, revolution, civil strife and famine, the Third World unleashed wave after wave of refugees — people compelled to flee their homelands because of a well-founded fear of persecution. They came from distant lands with very different cultures, languages and habits — Sri Lanka, Cambodia, Vietnam, Ethiopia, Ghana, Afghanistan, Iran, Lebanon, Chile, Argentina, Haiti, Uganda, El Salvador and Guatemala. The Third World countries were far more seriously affected by the worldwide economic decline than were their wealthy neighbours. Their bursting populations, burgeoning deficits and chronic unemployment launched a massive movement of people in search of opportunities for a better life. These wanderers are often referred to as economic migrants, and it is currently estimated that 50 to 60 million "economic refugees" are on the move toward greener pastures. There is a distinct difference between genuine refugees and economic migrants. The latter flee stagnation and poverty, while the former seek a haven to escape persecution and possible death. An economic migrant does not wish to return home. A refugee does not dare.

From the late 1970s, the gates of Western Europe have been flooded by ever-increasing arrivals of tens of thousands of asylum-seekers and economic migrants. Just a decade earlier, the number of applications for asylum in Western Europe averaged between 15,000 and 20,000 a year. In 1982, the number reached 60,000. A year later, it was 80,000. In 1984, there were 103,000 refugee claims, and the following year the total was 179,550. In 1986, Western Europe was hit with 198,650 requests for asylum. West Germany got the lion's share with 94,500. France received 23,400; Sweden,

15,000; Denmark, 10,000; Austria, 8,650; Switzerland, 8,550; Belgium, 7,650; the Netherlands, 5,700; Norway, 4,000; Turkey, 3,900; and the United Kingdom, 2,100.

The acceptance rate of refugee applications in Europe is low. By the end of 1985, there were more than 174,000 refugees in France. The highest number of applications continued to come from Ghanaians, Sri Lankans, Iranians and Haitians, yet fewer than 40 per cent of all refugee claims were successful. In West Germany, only 16 per cent of all asylum applications were granted while Switzerland, which granted 90 per cent of asylum claims in 1980, allowed only 12 per cent in 1986. Most European countries do not expel people whose claims have been denied, especially if they happen to come from areas which are wracked by civil war. Instead they are left in a state of limbo. Most are eventually permitted to work and some may be granted permanent resident status, but it appears that many European nations are hoping that hostilities in those Third World countries may end one day and then they can order the refugees to return.

Recent actions of Western European governments toward asylum-seekers have been lamentable. The politics of the refugee crisis has brought about dramatic and rapid legislative changes in countries long accustomed to taking due process for granted. There has been a hardening of hearts toward asylum-seekers, and the doors to many countries have been slammed shut. Many Europeans no longer want to hear about the world's homeless, destitute and suffering. Even the Vietnamese "boat people," whose plight once captured the hearts and sympathy of the Western world, have become targets of apathy, cynicism and even hostility.

On April 11, 1984, Poul Hartling, former United Nations High Commissioner for Refugees, convened a meeting of prominent international figures in Geneva for a round-table discussion entitled "Refugees: Victims of Xenophobia." Mr. Hartling warned that if left unchecked, the xenophobic trend infecting Western Europe is likely to have a "particularly destructive effect on one of the most outstanding achievements of the 20th century in the field of humanitarian endeavour." Mr. Hartling noted that the international mechanism established to deal with refugee claimants "is in danger today of being seriously undermined, as the refugee is caught up in the wave of resentment against foreigners which appears to be so widespread in the modern world." The tragic result, he added, is that governments are increasingly reluctant to admit refugees. "When asylum-seekers are admitted they are frequently subjected to a less than sympathetic hearing and have to face serious obstacles to their integration into local communities. Numerous governments which have hitherto followed generous policies — and have strongly supported my office's humanitarian endeavours in favour of refugees — have in recent times demonstrated a most distressing tendency to apply stringent measures with the evident aim of stemming the flow of asylum-seekers." Mr. Hartling stressed that a warning signal must be sounded because misunderstanding the special position of the refugees "strikes at the very heart of international action on their behalf." The round-table participants issued an earnest appeal to the public, to the news media and to government authorities throughout the world to make every effort to combat xenophobic trends, to ensure that the plight of the refugee is not ignored and to treat refugees according to recognized humanitarian standards.

Since Mr. Hartling's plea, however, the situation has deteriorated dramatically. In that time, Europeans have demanded that their political leaders pass tough laws to turn back the tide of illegal immigration and limit the number of refugees who receive asylum on their doorstep. Most European governments have acceded in some form or other to the public outcry. Immigration controls at border points have been intensified, and immigrants and refugees already in these countries are under constant pressure. They are discriminated against in employment, housing, health care, education and social assistance. They are harassed by police who have been given the power to carry out identity checks of individuals thought to be illegally in the country. Visible minorities are prime targets. The West German and French governments have gone so far as to offer cash bribes to guest workers to get them to go home. Others have simply been ordered to leave the country.

Xenophobia has gotten a nasty foothold in even the most sophisticated European countries. Switzerland, the Netherlands and Sweden, long renowned for tolerance and racial harmony, have fallen victim to the ravings of racists who exhort their fellow countrymen to beware of the black, brown and yellow hordes. Britain and West Germany have for some time been sorry textbook cases in racial intolerance. France and Denmark have recently joined the fold of front-ranking examples in the negative dynamics of race relations. The flood of refugees and economic migrants and the widening gulf between rich and poor nations appear to have impaired previous national attitudes of compassion and unleashed a flood of resentment against Third World immigrants and refugees.

In France, political parties from the extreme Right to the far Left know that a full quarter of the population can be seduced by rabid anti-immigration and racist propaganda. Immigration and race relations are hot topics in this nation of Liberty, Equality, and Fraternity. About 4.5 million of the country's 54 million inhabitants are immigrants. Almost 2 million are Arabs from former North African colonies. The remainder include immigrants from France's former colonies in Africa, the Caribbean and the Far East. Many French appear anxious and exasperated by the presence of so many foreigners in their country, even though foreign residents make up a paltry 7 per cent of the population. In fact, the proportion of foreign population is about the same as it was in 1931.

The feeling of being swamped by outsiders is especially strong in southern France, where the majority of Arabs who left Algeria during the bitter 1954-62 Algerian War have settled. In some districts of Nice and Marseilles, parents have put their children in private schools because the public ones have been "invaded" by Arabs. This anxiety is grist for the mill of the likes of Jean-Marie Le Pen, a former paratrooper and veteran of the Algerian conflict turned politician. As leader of the extreme right-wing National Front Party, Mr. Le Pen has scored impressive gains in a string of elections with a clear anti-immigrant campaign, buttressed by slogans such as "France for the French" and "French jobs for French workers." For many French people, the notion of a multiracial and multicultural society is alien and unacceptable. Louis Pauwels, a columnist for France's largest newspaper, the right-wing *Le Figaro*, wrote: "The new anti-racism wants to create a multicultural society, in other words a Tower of Babel . . . with people living side by side in a cacophony." Mr. Pauwels argued that the presence of recent arrivals "in the midst of an old people poses problems. But it is forbidden to have these problems. There must be contentment or else you will be called a racist . . . if I am a patriot, I am a racist. If I care about a national identity, I am a racist."

Such intolerance has naturally led to violence. From 1981 to 1986, there have been more than 160 racially motivated killings in France alone. In November, 1984, two Turkish immigrant workers were gunned down in a café in Châteaubriand, southwest of Paris. The killer, an unemployed Frenchman, told police: "I don't like immigrants." A year earlier, Habir Ghemzi, a passenger on a night train travelling through southern France, was insulted, beaten and finally thrown off the speeding train to his death by two recruits of the French Foreign Legion. One of the more chilling incidents occurred in the Mediterranean port of Toulon in mid-August, 1986. The calm of a late Sunday night was shattered when a four-door sedan blew up as it was making its way along a dark narrow street. Its four passengers were killed and two floors of a nearby concrete apartment block were destroyed. Police said later that the men in the car were members of an extreme Right, anti-immigrant political group called SOS France. They had set out to plant a bomb in an Arab café but it blew up prematurely. The event was quickly linked to six other bombing attacks in May and June against Arab cafés in a run-down district of the city known as Chicago. At the funeral of the four bombers, which was attended by local dignitaries, the eulogy was delivered by Jean-Claude Pelou, a high-ranking Toulon police officer. Gazing at the coffins, he said: "Your example ought to be an example to follow. Soldiers you were, and soldiers you are, dead. Your combat is ours. We will continue." Mr. Pelou was immediately suspended by the French minister responsible for the police.

The 1980s sent waves of asylum-seekers into West Germany, triggering a volatile political debate and a tense human drama. Refugees have been attacked in the streets, and their camps and hostels have been firebombed by right-wing radicals. Guest workers, who make up 4.4 million of the total population, were also caught in the cross-fire. Hardest hit have been the Turks, who prefer to live in ghettos and shun integration into mainstream German life.

Some politicians latched onto the highly charged issue for cheap political gain, and public officials have been caught making racially inflammatory statements reminiscent of Germany's Nazi era. The mayor of a town in Bavaria was quoted by the news media in August 1986, as saying: "Today we are giving these asylum-seekers bicycles and tomorrow we may have to give them our daughters." In 1986, Franz Josef Strauss, Bavaria's Christian Socialist leader, spearheaded a campaign to amend the country's constitution which declares that "all victims of politicial persecution are entitled to asylum." Mr. Strauss wanted to see that article eliminated or modified. In response to criticism by moderates he shot back: "To anyone opposed to a change in the constitution, I would say, 'Then you put some of these Tamils in your house'." Heinrich Lummer, West Berlin's conservative interior minister, called for thorough reform of the country's asylum laws, arguing that after accepting and integrating more than 600,000 refugees since the Second World War, West Germany was now "morally entitled to discard its hair shirt."

A large part of West Germany's refugee flood poured through a gaping hole in the Berlin Wall. Each year tens of thousands of refugees entered the country via East Berlin:

Tamil tea-pickers from Sri Lanka fleeing the bloodshed of a civil war; teenage boys smuggled out of Iran to evade the draft and the savage war with Iraq; East Indians, Turks, Ghanaians, Bangladeshis and Pakistanis. Most arrived on special fares promoted by eastern-bloc airlines and landed in groups at East Berlin's Schonefeld Airport. Without visas, they were admitted into East Germany, herded onto waiting buses and, in a matter of hours, hustled through a checkpoint in the Wall. Once inside West Berlin, they requested political asylum. Because of its status as a free and open city under the protection of the United States, France and Britain, West Berlin refuses to shut its doors to anyone coming from East Berlin. The communist East German authorities had been trying for years to force Bonn to close the "open" border. In a crass effort to force West Germany's hand while at the same time filling eastern-bloc commercial airlines with paying passengers, East Germany made an exception to its strict entry procedures, knowing full well that these Third World travellers would become a thorn in the sensitive underbelly of capitalist Europe.

In 1986, West Germany's population was estimated at 61 million. That year the country had a backlog of 673,000 refugees, and the total cost of feeding, sheltering and providing medical care to them amounted to almost $600 million. To put the situation into a Canadian perspective, West Germany is one-quarter the size of Ontario, which has a total population of about 9 million, and in the seven-year period beginning in 1980, Canada's entire refugee backlog amounted to roughly 23,000.

Forced to respond to a growing public backlash, the West German government had decided in 1983 to get tough with asylum-seekers by making their stay in the country uncomfortable. Most new refugees were sent to camps and not permitted to work for at least two years after their arrival. Conditions in the camps were so degrading that in 1985 the United Nations High Commission for Refugees (UNHCR) sharply criticized the West Germans' handling of ayslum-seekers. In a confidential report, the UNHCR said camp conditions, which it described as "shocking and inhuman," caused "bitterness and disillusionment" among inmates, pushing several to suicide. At one such camp, six refugees died after setting fire to a mattress to protest living conditions. United Nations investigators said they firmly believed these conditions were deliberately designed to dissuade refugees from entering West Germany, and to persuade those already in the country to leave. That suspicion was confirmed when a confidential directive issued by the state Interior Ministry in Baden-Württemberg was leaked to the press. It stated unequivocally that the purpose of the camps "is to raise in the asylum-seekers the desire to return to their own countries" and "to dissuade potential new arrivals."

A sorry backlash against asylum-seekers has also developed in Switzerland, a country traditionally regarded as an island of sanctuary for exiles. In April, 1984, Zurich police took a 29-year-old Polish citizen who had been refused asylum to Kloten International Airport in handcuffs and put him aboard a flight to Warsaw. The man, who had asked for political asylum because he was being sought by Polish police in connection with his links to the independent labour union, Solidarity, was about to obtain a visa to come to Canada. On November 3, 1985, in an operation dubbed by human-rights groups "Black Autumn," 59 Zaireans, in shackles and under heavy guard, were put on board a flight to Kinshasa in a move which outraged church and human-rights groups. Swiss authorities have also expelled Tamils, Chileans and Turks, saying they were in no danger upon return to their homelands. The government maintained that the implementation of a tougher refugee policy only reflected the need to separate "real" refugees from "false" ones. Some political observers said they believed the action was a reflection of the public mood. Racial bias against Third World refugees and immigrants had gained a strong foothold in the country. A deep rift divided advocates of a more liberal, compassionate attitude toward asylum-seekers and the right-wing elements pushing for more restrictive measures. One extremist group announced in late 1986 that it would campaign on a platform to forbid the government from granting asylum to any Third World refugees.

In late 1985 the Swiss government revised its ordinance on asylum, making it more restrictive. It introduced a law under which immigration officers could turn back refugees at the border if they deemed their request for asylum to be manifestly unfounded. Those who entered the country but whose claim was later rejected had six to eight weeks to leave. But the problem of increasing arrivals continued, causing government officials to conclude that asylum-seekers, in an attempt to circumvent these new procedures, have been paying professional guides up to $1,000 (U.S.) to sneak them into the country illegally. Giovanni Chicherio, secretary of the Swiss League of Human Rights, described the revisions as "the final blow against the law on asylum. It is not an expression of political will. Rather, it indicates a legal shift. Our policies on asylum are becoming the business of the police." He lamented that the "arbitrary deportations short-circuit the established mechanisms, and expeditious methods such as these are unworthy of Switzerland's traditions of welcome."

In June, 1986, the upper house of the Swiss Parliament gave final approval to measures granting the Federal Council extraordinary powers in refugee matters, including the authority to close Swiss borders to asylum-seekers. The government contended that these measures were aimed at economic migrants and not genuine refugees. The new measures also called for the establishment of reception centres and detention camps, and for the jailing of individuals who refuse to leave the country after their request for asylum was rejected.

As public debate continued, the issue boiled down to one question: "Is the boat full?" The phrase came from the title of a 1970s Swiss film that had harshly criticized the country's policy of refusing to accept all the Jews who tried to enter the country during the Second World War. Denis van der Veid, a member of the Swiss Committee for the Defence of the Right of Asylum, said: "We are close to a situation of the Second

World War where the law was such that the Jews all had to be sent back [to Nazi Germany]. We're responsible for thousands of people having been killed because we didn't accept them. We are now in a very similar situation in spite of the fact that nobody in the world is as rich as Switzerland." On April 5, 1987, the Swiss went to the polls to vote in a referendum on government plans for a more restrictive refugee policy. Final returns from all 23 cantons showed an overwhelming majority in favour of the stricter regulations.

Britain has instituted the toughest immigration and refugee legislation and most stringent airport screening procedures in all of Western Europe. Britain's course on the immigration issue was set in 1978, when Prime Minister Margaret Thatcher said: "We must hold out the prospect of a clear end to immigration. . . . People are really rather afraid that this country might be rather swamped by people with a different culture. . . . If there was any fear that it might be swamped, people are going to react and be hostile to those coming in." In January, 1981, the controversial British Nationality Act, a principal feature of Mrs. Thatcher's election platform, was introduced in Parliament. Home Secretary William Whitelaw described the legislation as government's move toward a long-needed rationalization of the laws. "We are doing nothing new in suggesting our citizenship should be given a better idea of where people actually belong." Opponents called it a blatant racist attempt to keep the non-white "debris of the Empire" out of the British mainland. "The act will result in injustice, greatly increase the numbers of stateless men, women and children, create uncertainties and feelings of insecurity and exacerbate racial tensions," said the Archbishop of Canterbury, Robert Runcie.

The Act, which came into force in January, 1983, created three separate categories of British citizen, to replace the old Citizenship of the United Kingdom and Colonies statute. Only those who qualify for the category called British citizen have the automatic right to live in the country. There are 57 million of these British citizens, all but 2 million of whom are white. Excluded from the right to settle are some 4.5 million of Her Majesty's loyal subjects consigned to the categories of "citizenship of the British dependent territories" and "British overseas citizenship." Hong Kong's largely non-white population falls into the former category, and there are some 1.5 million "overseas citizens," mostly from former colonies. The Act also ended the seven-century-old legal tradition of *ius soli*, or "right of the soil," by which any child born in Britain was automatically eligible for citizenship. Like its European neighbours, Britain has also been plagued in the 1980s by racial violence, usually the outpouring of frustration by black youth unable to find employment in the country's depressed economy.

Like the larger European nations, the Netherlands, Belgium, Sweden, Norway and Denmark also came down hard on asylum-seekers during the mid-1980s, amid complaints about their drain on social welfare systems and the political instability they allegedly introduced. In 1986 alone, some 30,000 refugees and asylum-seekers landed in Scandinavia, and in each country the cries for a tightening of the laws governing entry came hard and fast. Adding to the global refugee problem, the United States has recently joined its European allies by toughening immigration procedures in an effort to stem the flood of "illegal aliens" along its southern border. Although the traffic is primarily Mexican, Salvadorean and Guatemalan, the U.S. government began to experience a new problem in 1985 as thousands of citizens of 80 different countries, mainly from the Middle East and Asia, were apprehended attempting to cross into the country illegally from Mexico and Canada.

For Canadians, the plight of refugees in Western Europe was poignantly illustrated in August, 1986, with the rescue of 155 Tamils found drifting toward the rocky coast of Newfoundland, having set out on their journey to escape harsh conditions in West German camps. The repercussions of their dramatic arrival, and the subsequent arrival of thousands of other asylum-seekers in Canada, have forced the federal government to rethink its policy toward people coming to this country claiming refugee status. Despite pronouncements in November, 1986, that Canada would be increasing its annual immigration levels significantly over the next several years, indications were that the Canadian government was rapidly moving to a policy of tougher immigration enforcement and control. In large part, the policy was aimed directly at plugging the refugee flow.

Compounding the refugee dilemma are a number of confusing definitions and phrases. This complex issue has taken on a jargon all its own. Uprooted people are known or classified by various governments and agencies as refugees, Convention refugees, *de facto* refugees, political refugees, exiles, mandate refugees, asylum-seekers, displaced persons, humanitarian cases, expellees, returnees or economic refugees. At the root of the confusion are the United Nations 1951 Convention and the 1967 Protocol Relating to the Status of Refugees which fail to deal with the political realities of the 1980s. The convention was the first attempt by the international community to respond to the refugee problem in a more coherent and organized fashion, particularly in the aftermath of the Second World War. In 1967, a protocol was prepared by the UN in response to the emergence of new refugee situations. Both accords set out the definition of a refugee as a person who has a "well-founded fear of being persecuted for reasons of race, religion, nationality, membership of a particular social group or political opinion." The convention and protocol also enunciate the minimum standards for the treatment of refugees, and the principle of "non-refoulement" which protects them from being forcibly returned to a country where their life and liberty would be at risk. Article 33 of the convention states that "no contracting state shall expel or return (*refouler*) a refugee in any manner whatsoever to the frontiers of the territories where his life or freedom would be threatened. . . ." About one hundred nations, including Canada, have signed the international accords. The Eastern European nations are not signatories.

The problem with the UN definition is that most refugees today cannot prove that they personally have a "well-founded fear of being persecuted." While they may not as individuals be the target of deliberate persecution, they may well become the hapless victims of random violence or roaming death squads. To put it more crudely, for a person to prove he was individually persecuted, harassed, tortured or imprisoned for his beliefs, he would have to establish that the bomb or missile that devastated his village, killing 650 people and wounding another 1,500, was meant *specifically* for him. (In 1969, the Organization of African Unity expanded the refugee definition to include those fleeing "external aggression, foreign occupation, foreign domination, or events seriously disrupting public order." This definition describes the backgrounds of most asylum-seekers fleeing to the sanctuary of Europe and North America in recent years — people from Afghanistan, Sri Lanka, Iran, Iraq, Ethiopia, Chile and Lebanon.)

Needless to say, most refugee claimants fail to prove their case, and are rejected. The high rejection rate, based on a narrow and mean-spirited interpretation of the UN definition, gives politicians, immigration officials and bureaucrats the statistics to dismiss unsuccessful claims as "frivolous" and the claimants as "economic refugees" who are simply using the refugee process as a means to improve their lot in life. Yet a 1986 study by the United Nations High Commission for Refugees (UNHCR) concluded that the number of "manifestly unfounded claims" made in Western nations amounts to no more than 10 to 15 per cent of the total.

In an effort to keep refugees away from their shores, the rich and powerful nations have resorted to a wide range of restrictive measures. Most have imposed strict visa requirements on specific nationalities, without regard to whether they may be coming from refugee-producing countries. Many have imposed on international airline carriers stiff fines of up to $1,000 for every improperly documented person who arrives claiming to be a refugee. Airlines are also responsible for the return of passengers denied entry to the point of embarkation or to any other country where they might be accepted. In an editorial in the January, 1987, issue of *Refugees* magazine, the UNHCR warned that this "dangerous practice . . . will result in refugees not being able to reach a country of asylum."

The plight of refugees is an international one. It is massive in its proportions. Over the past three decades, more than 700 people a day have been forced to flee their homelands and become refugees, and there is nothing to suggest that this trend will be reversed in the immediate future, particularly in the Third World countries. The combination of social tensions, civil strife, military aggression, economic stagnation, acute poverty, large-scale environmental destruction and burgeoning populations is almost certain to push more and more people into the overflowing refugee pot. In spite of alarmism in the Western nations, the cold, hard reality is that the overwhelming burden of the global refugee crisis falls not on the shoulders of the rich and powerful nations, but on some of the poorest and most deprived countries in the world. UNHCR statistics indicate that the combined total of refugees and asylum-seekers in all of Western Europe represents less than 5 per cent of the estimated world refugee population. The governments of these so-called developed nations must realize that they cannot legislate their way out of this serious predicament. Desperate people fleeing war, tyranny and abject poverty cannot be, and will not be, prevented from seeking safe refuge in another country. Said UNHCR head Jean-Pierre Hocke during a 1986 visit to Ottawa: "Trying to be very practical and not philosophical, this is the reason I insist on this basic attitude of accepting the fact that the world is faced with a real problem . . . that it has to do with the root causes that are not of UNHCR responsibility but which have to do with the whole North-South issue of economics, trade, debt, unemployment . . . and as long as these problems are not dealt with in concrete terms, the consequences will be the erratic movement of large numbers of people looking for better prospects."

Durable solutions will not be found until the root causes, which are tangled in a web of political, sociological, economic and technical factors, are unravelled. There has to be a concerted international effort to prevent people from being forced to leave their homeland. Violations of human rights and the escalation of the refugee crisis will continue as long as the superpowers continue to fuel regional conflicts through military aid and arms sales. Nations with clout and influence must stop supporting repressive regimes. They must work at eliminating the crippling foreign debt facing many Third World nations. To date, these issues remain low on the international political agenda. A careful, thoughtful and balanced global approach to the issue of solutions is desperately needed, not one that places the interests of one country or groups of countries against another. Not one that leaves refugees stranded in camps for years and years, while the rich nations cleanse their collective conscience by throwing money into the coffers of the UNHCR to ensure that the refugees stay put. Refugee camps have their place in the overall scheme of protection but they are only a *temporary* solution. Sadly, there is an ever-looming threat that hundreds of thousands of these people will remain confined to camps forever. There are people in the world today, like the Palestinians, who have known nothing but the degrading life of a refugee camp. They were born in them and they will die in them — brutally and without dignity.

7 A MATTER OF PREFERENCE

IN A PACKED WAITING ROOM IN CANADA'S
immigration office in Vienna, a young man stood by a door-
way smoking one cigarette after another. Occasionally he
cast an impatient, worried glance at his wife who was bottle
feeding their eleven-month-old daughter while at the same
time trying to keep their four-year-old son from annoying the
others in the room.

The family had fled their native Poland eight months earlier and had been living in a turn-of-the-century army barracks while waiting to hear if a Western country, preferably
the United States or Canada, would accept them as refugees.
The effects of months of waiting, of filling out countless
forms, of interviews and questions, of hoping and praying,
were etched deeply into the faces of the young couple. On
this day, they would learn whether they would be accepted
to go to Canada. When their family name was called out, the
woman lifted her eyes to the ceiling and whispered a short
prayer. Her husband butted his cigarette on the floor and
gathered up his son. The foursome disappeared behind a
heavy, electronically controlled door. When they reappeared
45 minutes later, their smiles and laughter revealed the outcome. They were four of the lucky ones. They had been given
a chance to start a new life in Canada.

In waiting rooms in numerous cities around the globe where

100

Canada has immigration offices, and in tents, mud and bamboo huts in far-off, hard-to-reach refugee camps, the same human drama is replayed many times a day. Canada is a major player in the international refugee sweepstakes, providing sanctuary, hope and a new lease on life every year to thousands of individuals and families in the world's ever-growing ragtag army of an estimated 15 million refugees. There is no Statue of Liberty on the Canadian coastline to provide a beacon for the world's "huddled masses yearning to breathe free," yet since the Second World War more than 500,000 refugees have found a safe haven here. From 1945 to 1952, about 186,000 displaced persons in Western Europe were accepted as landed immigrants. Canada accepted more than 37,000 Hungarian refugees, who fled when Soviet tanks invaded their homeland in 1956. And when Soviet tanks pushed into Czechoslovakia in 1968, Canada opened its doors to 12,000 Czechoslovakian refugees. Other large refugee flows include 7,000 Ugandans in 1972; 17,000 Chileans since 1973; and more than 10,000 Lebanese from 1976 to 1978. The compassion and humanitarian tradition of Canadians toward refugees was put to the test in the aftermath of the fall of South Vietnam in 1975. The sad spectacle of thousands of "boat people" adrift for days and weeks on the treacherous South China Sea, clinging to anything that could float, captured the sympathy of many Canadians, as of people the world over. Since that time, Canada has accepted more than 72,000 Vietnamese refugees.

In 1980, Canada was again called on to help out in another world crisis when the communist government in Poland succumbed to intense pressure from the Soviet Union and imposed martial law on its citizens who were rallying behind the popular Solidarity union. More than 12,000 Polish refugees who fled the crackdown eventually settled in Canada. Since 1980, Canada has been called on to give sanctuary to a steady flow of refugees from Latin America, several Middle Eastern countries, Afghanistan and Sri Lanka.

From 1980 to 1986, the federal government has selected more than 130,000 refugees from abroad for resettlement in

Canada — more per capita, Canadian bureaucrats and politicians boast, than any other country in the world. "In recognition of the major and sustained contribution made to the cause of refugees in their country and throughout the world over the years," Jean-Pierre Hocke, head of the United Nations High Commission for Refugees (UNHCR), awarded the Canadian people the Nansen Medal in a ceremony in Ottawa on November 13, 1986. The medal is named after the famous Norwegian scholar and explorer Fridtjof Nansen, a pioneer in the field of international humanitarian aid who became League of Nations High Commissioner for Refugees in 1921. It was the first time since the medal was created in 1954 that it had been bestowed upon an entire nation.

The Canadian people have a lot to be proud of. The country has a long and distinguished record in assisting refugees fleeing persecution and oppression. Yet Canada also has some reason to be ashamed of its treatment of refugees, both in the past and in the present, and a frank recognition of our shortcomings could lead to a more cohesive and compassionate policy in the future.

Canada's long-standing policy toward refugees is to select them from abroad on the basis of their ability to settle successfully in the country. Oftentimes, it appears that in our quest for refugees who will not be a burden on the Canadian economy, economic considerations far outweigh humanitarian concerns. The government's policy of selecting refugees abroad is largely supported by our geography. Two vast and treacherous oceans to the east and west, the frozen, barren tundra to the north, and the United States acting as a buffer to the south are formidable barriers to large-scale flows of refugees from far-off countries in turmoil. Because of this isolation, Canada's international obligation to refugees has been chiefly to provide a country of resettlement rather than a country of first asylum. Canadian immigration officials prefer it that way. They prefer to send teams of immigration officers to refugee centres and camps around the globe to hand-pick refugees. That way, Canada knows what it is getting.

While Canada's international role in refugee resettlement has been applauded by many, its selective approach has its critics. In 1984, Ed Ratushny, a special advisor to former employment and immigration minister John Roberts, noted in a government report called *A New Refugee Status Determination Process for Canada* that some critics have described Canada's policy of limited resettlement as a "clean hands" approach to humanitarianism that "lacks the unconditional commitment typical of first-asylum countries of permanent settlement." Critics have also charged that the federal government's preferred policy of selecting refugees abroad has been made as an expression of self-interest, in order to enable Canada's selection apparatus to pick and choose those refugees who fit Canadian views of who deserves our help.

In a paper delivered to a seminar on refugees at York University in Toronto in late May, 1986, Raphael Girard, director of the refugee determination task force for Employment and Immigration Canada, countered that the latter view does not pay "due attention to the scope of Canadian involvement in all aspects of refugee relief — involvement on a scale that far exceeds what could naturally be expected as Canada's share among nations." In a speech on March 10, 1987, Gerry Weiner, minister of state for immigration, pointed out that the Canadian government would select 12,000 refugees from camps abroad in 1987 at a cost of some $110 million for adjustment assistance and language training. "We also provide some $4.9 million in grants to refugee and immigrant aid groups for settlement purposes. This year alone we will give $50 million to the United Nations High Commission for Refugees. We will give $16 million in food aid for refugees."

The UNHCR views resettlement as the third of three pillars upon which the international refugee-relief system is based. The first, which is the most desirable and most difficult to achieve, is repatriation. This can only be accomplished when war or civil strife has ended, and the winning side is willing to let the refugees return without carrying out some form of reprisal against them. The second is settlement in a neighbouring country of first asylum that shares local customs, traditions, lifestyle and climate.

Notwithstanding Canada's generosity, first-asylum countries, which receive the brunt of the refugee flows, have complained long and vociferously that the selective resettlement approach leaves them with the less desirables after immigration teams from such countries as Canada, the United States and Australia have skimmed off those refugees with marketable skills.

In designing a national refugee policy to reflect our preference, Canadian politicians and bureaucrats did not take into account the sheer will and determination of people who were not going to wait around in refugee camps in enforced idleness hoping that the war would end, or that maybe in a year or two or three, some Canadian immigration officer might pull up like a messiah in a jeep and bestow landed-immigrant status on them. As the jet age landed on the runways of the Third World, more and more refugees discovered that Canada, that distant land of freedom, democracy and prosperity, wasn't all that difficult to get to any more. Only two things were needed: money for the airline ticket, and valid travel documents. The latter, if impossible to obtain through legal channels, could easily be purchased on the international black market.

The unexpected and increasing arrival of refugees at Canadian borders since 1980 threw the federal government's refugee process into a tailspin. It had never been foreseen that so many people would land at Canada's international airports claiming to be refugees. In 1980, about 1,600 people claimed refugee status upon arrival in Canada. That figure more than doubled a year later. In 1984, the number of refugee claimants jumped to 7,100; a year later, it leapt to 8,400. In May, 1986, the backlog in the refugee determination system exceeded 23,000 claims. Immigration officials estimated that it would take more than $50 million and about ten years to clear it. In 1986 alone, the number of refugee claims made by people arriving in the country jumped to 18,280 with more than 13,000 arriving in the last six months of the year. January, 1987, began with a large arrival of refugee claimants from El Salvador, Guatemala, Chile, Sri Lanka, Ghana, Iran, Lebanon and Turkey. In the first three months of the year, more than 10,000 people claiming to be refugees entered Canada.

In the overall context of global refugee movements, these figures are a drop in the bucket, but the volume presented enormous problems for the bureaucracy designated to deal with the spontaneous arrival at Canadian borders of people seeking refugee status. The government's entire refugee determination system was quickly brought to a state of near collapse. The foundations had been crumbling for years. Successive dithering federal governments had failed to design and implement a fair and firm refugee policy, although significant problems were first flagged for the attention of senior immigration officials and politicians as far back as 1980.

The development of a refugee policy, in general, and the concept of a United Nations Convention refugee, in particular, are recent phenomena in Canada. Prior to the end of the Second World War, refugees represented a small and very sporadic portion of newcomers to Canada. However, in the post-war years the government recognized the need to establish special programs permitting large groups of refugees or displaced persons to settle in Canada. This settlement of groups was organized by international cooperation and expedited through official channels. In both the international and the Canadian context, the existence of a procedure for dealing with individuals arriving spontaneously and unassisted to ask for asylum or refugee status is therefore still quite new.

Canada signed the United Nations Convention and Protocol on refugees in 1969, after more than a decade of debate on the issue. Our signature thereby committed us to a refugee policy based upon the needs of people in distress rather than those of the Canadian economy. In setting out Canadian immigration policy, Section 3 (g) of the 1976 Immigration Act recognizes the need "to fulfil Canada's international obligations with respect to refugees and to uphold its humanitarian tradition with respect to the displaced and the persecuted." The Act also prescribes the procedure for determining refugee claims. The Green Paper, the federal government policy paper which preceded the 1976 Immigration Act, looked at the refugee question almost solely from the perspective of resettlement. There was no discussion of the asylum question, no evaluation, no critique. It was taken for granted that Canada's role would be that of assisting front-line refugee-receiving countries by supplying them with financial, material and technical aid, and by selecting certain numbers of refugees annually for resettlement in Canada. That the issue of unsponsored refugees coming to Canadian shores would eventually command a spotlight on the Canadian political stage was never considered.

The Immigration Act's rules of admission distinguish only two classes of people: immigrants and visitors. Refugees cannot be visitors who come to the country to see family, friends or play tourist, then decide to stay on. Prospective immigrants must apply for and obtain a visa before they can legally immigrate to Canada, although individual exceptions are made from time to time. Those who arrive seeking refugee status have not met the legal requirements of the Act, and as a result become entangled in a web of removal proceedings from the moment of their arrival. This does not mean that Canada automatically deports refugee claimants because they are not properly documented as bona fide visitors or immigrants. The Immigration Act guarantees individuals, regardless of how they get to Canada, a hearing on their claim for refugee status.

Canada established in 1973 its first formal administrative structure to deal with individuals claiming to be refugees. Claims were considered by an interdepartmental committee of civil servants from the Department of Manpower and Immigration and the Department of External Affairs, and their findings were submitted to the minister of manpower and immigration, who ultimately decided whether each claimant would be allowed to remain in the country. However, the procedure very soon began to bog down in red tape and procedural wrangling. In September, 1980, the minister of employment and immigration, Lloyd Axworthy, established a task force which made a wide range of recommendations to improve and streamline the process. The first of three major proposals was to set up the Refugee Status Advisory Committee (RSAC) as an independent body, distanced from the policy considerations of External Affairs and Immigration. The second proposal related to attempts to ensure that the definition of a Convention refugee was applied in *spirit* as well as in accordance with its letter. The third was the task force's central recommendation, echoing the views of non-governmental groups involved in refugee issues, that claimants be given an oral hearing in the determination of their claims. The oral hearing was established in May, 1983, but only as a pilot project in Montreal and Toronto. While all these recommendations were implemented, Mr. Axworthy underlined on several occasions that the most effective contribution by Canada to the world refugee crisis was in providing assistance abroad rather than in attempting to settle massive numbers of refugees in Canada.

In June, 1983, W. G. (Gerry) Robinson, a special advisor on immigration, presented Mr. Axworthy with a hefty report entitled *Illegal Migrants in Canada* urging that "procedures for the determination of refugee status within Canada be modified by comprehensive legislative amendment to the Immigration Act at the first opportunity." In the report, Mr. Robinson noted that Canada's refugee determination process is a feature of Canadian immigration policy in which Canadians can take pride. "However, it has outgrown its legislative garment. Moreover, it must be given the capacity to deal effectively with abusive claims. Otherwise, our resources will be squandered in fighting a rearguard action in Canada, when they could be so much more effectively deployed in attacking refugee problems at their source."

A year later, Ed Ratushny completed his study for new Liberal employment and immigration minister John Roberts. In *A New Refugee Status Determination Process for Canada*, Mr. Ratushny concluded that the present system of determining the validity of refugee claims within Canada is riddled with anomalies, inconsistencies and shortcomings which have demonstrated that it is both cumbersome and susceptible to abuse. He noted that while the process "does not affect a large number of people, it does affect a small number of human beings in a very intense and dramatic way. . . . An erroneous refugee determination could, in effect, result in a death sentence if the applicant is returned to the country of persecution." Mr. Ratushny also stressed that Canada's international obligation to refugees must be fulfilled in tandem with immigration enforcement. "Every sovereign state also has an obligation to itself and to its citizens to maintain the integrity of its borders." Nevertheless, he argued, the existing refugee determination process in Canada had serious flaws "which must be addressed as quickly as possible." What was required, Mr. Ratushny said, was to crystallize the specific form legislative changes should take and generate sufficient public support to establish the political will to act.

Mr. Roberts subsequently initiated another study, headed by Rabbi W. Gunther Plaut, to look into the direction the federal government should take in implementing a new refugee determination system. Meanwhile, on April 4, 1985, the Supreme Court of Canada came down with a major decision that dramatically affected the way refugee claimants would be dealt with in Canada. The court ruled that all individuals seeking refugee status from within Canada must be granted an oral hearing. Up until that time, except on a pilot basis in Montreal and Toronto, claimants recounted their stories into a tape recorder before an immigration officer. The transcript was sent to the Refugee Status Advisory Committee and, if the decision was negative, to the Immigration Appeal Board for a redetermination. The individual never got to tell his story in person to the people making the decision on the case. Immigration advocates applauded the Supreme Court ruling. Barbara Jackman, a Toronto lawyer who represented the Canadian Council of Churches before the court, described the decision as a "huge step forward in constitutional law." Ms Jackman noted that it was the "first case where the Supreme Court of Canada has commented on the application of the Charter of Rights and Freedoms to aliens, and they have decided that the Charter does apply to aliens."

Flora MacDonald, the new Tory minister of employment and immigration, said her department would adhere to the decision; however, the department was not geared to cope with the impact of the Supreme Court ruling. One senior immigration official calculated that with oral hearings, it would cost $3,500 to process one claim. At the time, there were 13,800 claims in the refugee backlog.

In mid-April, 1985, Rabbi Plaut presented his 221-page opus to Flora MacDonald. The study, which culled opinions of dozens of individuals and organizations involved in refugee issues, provided the government with a variety of suggestions, recommendations, measures and quasi-judicial models from which to design a new refugee determination system for Canada. From the outset, Rabbi Plaut stressed in his report that the refugee determination process must be "seen and designed as an act of welcome. It must be forever responsive to our humanitarian impulses and obligations and wary of any encroachment that would seek to impose other considerations and concerns upon it." Two months later, Ms MacDonald tabled the document in Parliament and in a brief interview outside the House of Commons angrily dismissed a suggestion that it would gather dust on a shelf in some bureaucrat's office. She said the Progressive Conservative government would study the report and act decisively, adding caustically that the Tories had inherited the refugee mess from the Liberals. Ms MacDonald said the government would deal with the issue in "a comprehensive package" and vowed that legislation for a new refugee determination system would be introduced in Parliament by November and certainly no later than Christmas 1985.

By the summer of that year, the existing refugee procedure had become a source of continued anguish and suffering for thousands of legitimate refugees caught up in the maze. It had also become a bonus for bogus claimants to use to their advantage. The Supreme Court ruling on oral hearings had thrown the Immigration Department into a tailspin. The bureaucrats found themselves unable to cope with the sheer volume of work ahead of them. Giving an oral hearing to every refugee claimant in the current backlog was a monumental and expensive task. But the problems stemmed not only from the Supreme Court ruling. They were part and parcel of the entire refugee determination process which was complex, confusing and clogged with inquiries, examinations, applications, hearings, determinations, redeterminations, appeals and reviews.

Under the existing process, an intricate and costly bureaucratic machine sputtered into action when an individual arrived in Canada and an immigration officer determined that the person was not a legitimate visitor or immigrant. First, an inquiry was scheduled to determine whether the person should be ordered to leave the country. Just to get an appointment for an inquiry could take several weeks and sometimes months, depending on the backlog. If during the inquiry the individual uttered the phrase "I want to make a refugee claim," or something like it, an entirely different set of gears shifted into motion. The inquiry was adjourned and an "examination under oath" was scheduled; because of backlogs, up to six months might pass before it was held. It then usually took several more months before the transcript was typed and sent to the minister of immigration who in turn forwarded it to the Refugee Status Advisory Committee for consideration and advice. Once RSAC had reached its decision, the case file was sent back to the minister, who decided on the claim. If his decision was negative, the case was referred to the Special Review Committee (SRC), a committee of senior departmental officials, for consideration on humanitarian and compassionate grounds. Again, this process could take several months.

If the SRC did not decide in the claimant's favour, Section 70 of the Immigration Act provided for an application for redetermination of the claim to the Immigration Appeal Board (IAB) within 15 days after receipt of the written decision by the minister. The process of redetermination before the IAB could take up to a year. The matter could then be taken to the Federal Court of Canada on an application for the case to be reconsidered by the IAB. If the application was granted, it could take up to a year for the board to rehear the case because of persistent postponements, adjournments, and scheduling problems. There was also a chance, although slim, for the individual to take his case by special leave to the Supreme Court of Canada. However, like the Federal Court, the Supreme Court could not determine the claimant to be a refugee. It could hear no evidence. All it could do was to set aside the IAB decision for a failure in law, fact or natural justice, and refer the matter back to the IAB for reconsideration.

In his report, Rabbi Plaut described the delays as intolerable, especially for the refugee "who suffers continued displacement and insecurity in addition to the considerable trauma and suffering he/she has already undergone." He added: "Delay also has another significant drawback in that it provides a vehicle for use by persons who wish to remain and work in Canada for a few years, persons who otherwise would not be eligible for such benefits under our existing immigration policies. The length of the process acts as a magnet for those who are not Convention refugees." Once an individual claimed refugee status, he was entitled to work, receive health care and welfare benefits and put his children into the public school system. Individuals who came to Canada with the hope of somehow attaining landed-immigrant status would not be entitled any of these benefits. They would have an inquiry and, in most cases, be ordered to leave in a short time. It was obvious that the very unwieldiness of the refugee system was an open invitation to abuse by bogus claimants who exploited it as a means of remaining in the country and getting work.

In late August, Ms MacDonald, who for months had been under a constant barrage of criticism over the refugee issue, finessed the troublesome immigration side of her portfolio to Walter McLean, who had been appointed minister of state for immigration in a minor Cabinet shuffle. Ms MacDonald stressed that she was still the lead immigration minister. Mr. McLean, the junior minister, would tend to the nuts-and-bolts operations of immigration , Ms MacDonald added, and she would keep an active interest in the development of the upcoming legislation still due before the end of the year. Nevertheless, it was Mr. McLean, brimming with pomp and circumstance, who announced the details of the government's proposed new refugee determination system in the House of Commons on May 21, 1986. "There is agreement that claims to refugee status should be treated fairly, humanely and expeditiously," Mr. McLean said in the House. "I want to assure you today, that this government has given very careful consideration to all of the views expressed by refugee aid groups, church groups and ethnic organizations across the country."

The package of proposed reforms would comply with Canada's international legal obligations, the Charter of Rights and Freedoms and Canada's humanitarian tradition, Mr. McLean stressed. The highlights included a non-adversarial setting for hearings; independent decision-making by a specialized refugee board; two-member panels which would offer the benefit of the doubt to the refugee claimant; and an appeal by leave to the Federal Court of Canada. He promised the long-awaited legislation would be tabled in September, 1986, but in the interim, he said, he wanted the proposed system to start up "without the inheritance of a case backlog." In order to make this possible, Mr. McLean announced an "administrative, case-by-case review" of the more than 23,000 backlogged refugee claims. The "administrative review" would examine each case according to humanitarian criteria, family ties or other strong links to Canada and ability to establish successfully. Anyone — legitimate and bogus claimants alike — trapped in the refugee backlog as of midnight on May 21 would be eligible for the program. Sensitive to public opinion, Mr. McLean was at pains to emphasize that this process was not an amnesty.

Before the ink was even dry on the government copies of the proposed refugee determination system, the critics were attacking it. Barbara Jackman, representing the immigration section of the Canadian Bar Association, rejected Mr. McLean's assertion that the new system would comply fully with Canada's international and legal obligations, the Canadian Charter of Rights and Freedoms and Canada's humanitarian traditions; she said the system failed "on all three grounds." She noted that Canada's obligations under its international legal commitments are "to consider every person who claims to be a refugee" and to give them a full hearing before a competent body. No one should be excluded from that process, she said. However, the government proposal did not contain a universal-access provision. It excluded from the right to an automatic hearing people recognized as refugees in countries that have signed the Geneva Convention. It also excluded those who had exceeded the time limit of six months for making claims after having entered or been admitted to Canada; those who had unsuccessfully claimed refugee status in Canada before; and those who were under a deportation order from Canada.

Michael Schelew, a lawyer and representative for the Canadian section of Amnesty International on refugee issues, argued that questions of access should be dealt with by the very body that decides refugee claims, the proposed refugee board, and not by an immigration officer at an airport or border crossing. He pointed out that in some countries in Western Europe, where immigration officers have the power to deny access, "this has led to arbitrary decisions" that have put "at risk certain individuals."

The heaviest criticism was levelled at the appeal procedure. Under the government's proposal, refugee claimants would be granted leave on discretion to appeal a decision to the Federal Court of Canada solely on questions of law. There would be no appeal on the merits of the case. Refugee-aid groups and Immigration Department officials locked horns in a lengthy and heated public debate over the appeal mechanism. The department held fast on its appeal procedure while the critics battered away at it, arguing vociferously that refugee cases are primarily matters of fact and credibility, which are not really legal questions; the Federal Court, which is limited to legal technicalities, would simply not have the jurisdiction to review a refused claim on its merits. Refugee advocates maintained that an appeal mechanism must be automatic and capable of dealing with the merits of a refused refugee claim if it is to be meaningful. David Matas, a Winnipeg immigration lawyer who has long been involved in refugee issues, stressed in a paper in July, 1986, that the appeal procedure in the proposed refugee system "is a violation of international standards." He pointed out that the executive committee of the United Nations High Commission for Refugees has recommended guarantees for refugee determination procedures. One of these recommended guarantees is an appeal that involves a formal reconsideration of the refugee decision. "The Canadian proposal violates the recommended guarantees because there would be no formal reconsideration available on factual issues."

Mr. Schelew of Amnesty International went so far as to put forward a compromise which garnered the support of most groups involved with refugees. Known as the Amnesty Model, it called for a centralized paper review of any claim rejected by the refugee board. In a brief to the minister of immigration in August, 1986, Mr. Schelew stated that a "centralized review should have the authority to reverse a negative decision on points of law, on the facts of the claim and on questions of mixed fact and law. In other words, if a local panel of the Board has erred in its interpretation of the Convention refugee definition, then the centralized review can reverse the decision. Of course, it goes without saying that the centralized review can agree with a negative decision of a panel of the board." Mr. Schelew also pointed out that in order for the review to be expeditious, "it is imperative that refugee claimants appeal within a prescribed period of time." The Amnesty Model suggested 30 days as an appropriate period. Anything after that would constitute undue delay. While the Canadian section of Amnesty International had no idea what resources would be necessary to establish a centralized review, it suggested transforming the Refugee Status

Advisory Committee into the review body. "We believe that a well-trained appellate body could handle the review mechanism we have suggested in a manner that would be expeditious and would not require many decision-makers," Mr. Schelew said.

In his thoughtful brief, Mr. Schelew stressed that Canada "is facing a historic moment" regarding the formulation of refugee policy. "We believe it is important that the government do what is right." Any refugee determination process that lacks an appeal on the merits, he suggested, is "fundamentally flawed. . . . It is imperative that we offer the highest degree of procedural protection to a group of people who will face arbitrary detention, torture and/or execution upon their return home for activities that Canadians take for granted."

Another major concern voiced by many individuals and groups involved in refugee issues was the method by which appointments were made to the quasi-judicial bodies hearing, reviewing and deciding on refugee claims. In a brief to Rabbi Plaut's study, William H. Angus, a professor at York University's Osgoode Hall Law School, noted that governments of all party stripes have used appointments to administrative agencies to dispense patronage. "As a result, such appointees not infrequently possess limited qualifications on merit for the demands of the position. It is therefore not surprising that the performance of these appointees leaves something to be desired."

The quality of the decisions on refugee cases made by the Immigration Appeal Board has come under attack over the years. One particularly appalling ruling involved a Chilean welder, Hector Eduardo Contreras-Guttierez, who was denied refugee status in Canada in March, 1981, despite arrests and torture in his homeland. The basis of the IAB's rejection was that it was "reasonable" to expect the Chilean military authorities to "exercise control over dissidents on . . . national political anniversaries. As a union activist who surfaced . . . it was perfectly reasonable to expect [Mr. Contreras-Guttierez's] detention at such times," the board wrote in its judgement. When the decision reached immigration minister Lloyd Axworthy's desk eight months later, he swiftly issued a minister's permit allowing the man to remain in Canada.

During the summer months of 1986, the Tories announced a spate of partisan political appointments to the Immigration Appeal Board, the existing refugee determination review body. These appointments were, for the most part, of individuals with excellent connections to the Conservative Party. Unfortunately, most of the appointees lacked solid expertise and in-depth experience in refugee matters. Such political patronage, critics maintained, has no place in a forum where the life and liberty of individuals are at stake. They argued that if these same political cronies were appointed to the proposed refugee board to hear cases under the proposed system, and the only avenue of recourse on a negative decision was a discretionary appeal limited to legal technicalities, then the refugee claimant would not have much hope of reversing an unfair ruling in the Federal Court.

The debate raged throughout the summer, fall and winter months, but the Tory government ultimately failed to bring in the legislation. Meanwhile, there were revelations in the news media about thousands of bogus refugee claimants flooding the system, in particular Portuguese and Turkish citizens who had no legitimate right to make a refugee claim but who were using the refugee system as a means of circumventing regular immigration procedures. These stories further eroded public faith in the beleaguered immigration system. Unfortunately, they also tarred genuine refugees with the same brush as bogus claimants.

When the government made its announcement on May 21, 1986, it hoped that the administrative review program would alleviate the backlog problem and give the temporary "fast-track" refugee process the ability to handle new claims quickly. Ironically, the so-called fast track, with a beefed-up Immigration Appeal Board, still had to face the same delays, roadblocks and legal wrangling that crushed the existing system. The fast track was nothing more than a smoke screen

deployed by desperate civil servants trying to show the public that something concrete was being done to stem the flow
of bogus refugee claimants; in less than eight months, the
second refugee backlog was approaching the total of the old
backlog which had taken more than five years to accumulate.
Canadians were becoming increasingly alarmed by government announcements and news reports of the mounting
numbers of people claiming to be refugees — 1,580 in October; 1,810 in November; 3,377 in December; 3,693 in January,
1987; 4,268 in February; and 2,090 in March. By mid-January,
1987, Employment and Immigration Minister Benoît Bouchard (Ms MacDonald had become communications minister in a Cabinet shuffle in early July, 1986) was so unnerved
by what he described as blatant abuse of the system in Montreal by Turkish citizens making bogus refugee claims that he
vowed he would bring in decisive legislation to curb, once
and for all, the influx of illegitimate claimants.

The minister's tough talk led refugee-aid groups to worry
that "enforcement minded" officials in his department were
gaining the upper hand in the battle over future refugee
policy. They firmly believed that certain immigration officials
had deliberately gone out of their way to cloud and confuse
the issue of bogus claimants. Refugee advocates feared that
the result would be the imposition of a very restrictive refugee policy that was far tougher than that announced on May
21. Their only difficulty was finding out just what the Immigration Department was proposing to Cabinet. On February
20, 1987, they got a hint of what was on the horizon. Mr.
Bouchard and the junior minister, Gerry Weiner, jointly
announced a series of "administrative measures" to increase
Canada's "ability to help genuine refugees who need our
protection by deterring abuse of the refugee determination
system." The most drastic move was an attempt to shut down
the overland route through the United States used by refugee
claimants from El Salvador and Guatemala, two refugee-
producing countries that the Canadian government had
acknowledged to be rife with human rights violations. (In
spite of the political persecution and terror in these two

countries, the former Liberal government had imposed a visa requirement on El Salvador on September 28, 1978, and on Guatemala on March 14, 1984.)

According to a secret Cabinet document, numbered 2-0018-87CR(01) and obtained during research for this book, the government proposed returning most Salvadorean and Guatemalan refugee claimants to the United States pending an immigration inquiry in Canada. The document, dated January 21, 1987, and entitled "Refugee Determination: Control Strategy," noted that the measure would be "highly visible" and the delay "should deter many" from coming to Canada to apply for refugee status. Another measure announced on February 20 was the immediate imposition of a transit visa on all countries whose citizens already required visas to visit Canada. However, the Cabinet document indicates the measure, which would "cut at least 2,000 claims a year," was primarily aimed at stopping Chileans who were using flights with refuelling stop-overs in Toronto and Montreal to disembark and make refugee claims in Canada. (On December 28, 1979, the short-lived Tory government of Joe Clark had imposed a visa requirement on Chile, another legitimate refugee-producing country.) A third measure cancelled a blanket policy on automatic admission and non-deportation to what was referred to as the B-1 list of 18 countries: Afghanistan, Albania, Bulgaria, Cuba, Czechoslovakia, Democratic Kampuchea, El Salvador, German Democratic Republic, Guatemala, Iran, Laos, Lebanon, North Korea, People's Republic of China, Romania, Sri Lanka, U.S.S.R. and Vietnam. The move meant that the automatic issuance of minister's permits, granting refugee claimants from these countries the right to remain and work in Canada for up to one year, would cease. The claimants would now be shoved into the existing refugee determination system, which was already crippled by a massive backlog.

Many immigrant-aid and refugee-aid groups wondered why the government would deliberately further clog a system that had for all intents and purposes broken down under the sheer volume of numbers. The one foreseeable immediate consequence, which would further enrage public opinion, would be a heavy, short-term demand on local and provincial welfare rolls because claimants would not be allowed to work until after their examination under oath — and just getting an appointment for an examination could take up to three months. Refugee advocates were unaware at the time that Cabinet had approved another "administrative review" to clear up the more recent and growing backlog, to coincide with the implementation of the new refugee determination process. A second Cabinet document obtained during the research for this book, stamped "secret" and numbered 2-0018-87RD (01), recommended that "the Minister of Employment and Immigration be authorized to implement a second backlog clearance by extending the present administrative review to include the estimated 23,000 refugee cases which will accumulate during the transition period between May 21, 1986 and the implementation of the new refugee determination system."

The document, prepared and approved by the Cabinet Committee on Priorities and Planning on February 12, 1987, noted that the second clearance is to commence when the new system is in place and stressed that it "not be specifically announced." In other words, there would be no press release or public announcement. Claimants in the backlog would simply receive notification to come in and be assessed for landed-immigrant status. The merits of the refugee claim would become secondary; the ability to establish successfully in Canada would be the overriding consideration. The irony was that such a "review" would serve only to reward many of the queue-jumpers who indignant Tory politicians and senior immigration officials had lamented were responsible for the abuse and the backlog. But the Tory Cabinet, realizing that there was no way they could clear this second backlog without a large infusion of money and personnel, secretly opted for the second administrative review.

Meanwhile, the measures announced on February 20 enraged refugee advocates from Montreal to Vancouver who charged that they were draconian, contrary to Canada's traditional humanitarian readiness to help refugees, and a sign of widespread indifference to the world's persecuted. The Canadian Conference of Catholic Bishops said the measures "may well serve to reinforce a fortress mentality in this country." A coalition of Montreal-based refugee-aid groups and churches went so far as to call on the United Nations to strip Canada of the Nansen Medal. In their unswerving attack, many refugee advocates recalled the words of Prime Minister Brian Mulroney who on August 19, 1986, in an attempt to quell a nasty public backlash over the arrival of the Tamil "lifeboat people" off the coast of Newfoundland, said: "And if we err, we will always err on the side of justice and on the side of compassion."

Rabbi Plaut, deeply concerned by the course being charted by the government, wrote in the *Canadian Jewish News* on March 12: "We have instituted measures which are effective practically, and defective morally. We have signalled a return to a former practice which made Canada all too often inaccessible to those most in need of succour." In a House of Commons debate on March 24, David Berger, Liberal Member of Parliament for the Montreal riding of Laurier, chided that the government's measures would even bar "Jesus of Nazareth." Mr. Berger lamented that February 20, 1987, would go down in Canadian history as "a day of shame, for it is the day that our government closed its doors to refugees. It was the day when this government announced a series of cruel measures that go against the humanitarian tradition established in Canada forty years ago. It was on February 20 that the government erected a barrier, not just on the U.S. border but across the world."

Mr. Bouchard angrily countered that with global population increases, strife in many regions of the world and reduced immigration opportunities, more and more people "are looking to Canada for a new home. We want a positive immigration program that permits the orderly entry of immigrants and refugees, but we cannot maintain such a program if we allow abuse of our refugee program to continue. . . . These measures reflect the government's commitment to provide genuine refugees with protection. To do so, we must prevent the refugee system from being undermined by abuse."

In an interview with the author in early April, 1987, Joe Stern, chairman of the government's Refugee Status Advisory Committee, said he firmly believed that senior immigration officials were out to poison public opinion over the issue of refugee determination in Canada. "There has been an effort [by these officials] for as long as I have been involved, since 1980, to delegitimize the whole process of refugee determination in our country, to characterize this movement as abusive. Of course the immigration officials regard this entire movement as abusive, even the one-third [RSAC] accepts as [genuine] refugees, on the grounds that they didn't come to Canada with proper documents, that they didn't apply for visas abroad. Their view is that anyone who comes to Canada without the prior permission of the Canadian government has abused our process." Mr. Stern also charged that these same officials deliberately manipulated statistics to "create a sense of crisis, a sense of being inundated by unscrupulous people who see us as patsies." This disinformation along with the "way the system has bogged down and the way the backlog has been characterized," he added, has created a "very sad and cynical situation" in Canada.

Mr. Stern said Canada's problems resulted not from the spontaneous arrival of genuine refugees fleeing persecution and strife but from delays in processing claims and an unwillingness on the part of the government to deport phony claimants. "I believe that bogus claimants will cease as soon as we demonstrate that we can deal with abusive claims quickly, and we'll remove [deport] people who have no right to be here. In order to have an effective refugee policy we have to remove people from Canada who obviously aren't refugees. If we don't remove them, we will continue to encourage abuse."

Winnipeg lawyer David Matas said the entire issue revolves around the Immigration Department's desire to be in total control of the refugee flow. "The department isn't against refugees. What it is opposed to is the notion that somebody can choose Canada rather than Canada choosing the person. So it is trying to set up a system where it decides who enters, and in effect, it is taking advantage of public concern about abuse to get its way." Mr. Matas maintained that when refugee-aid groups began dealing with Gerry Weiner, they found in him a man who understood the issues and truly sympathized with the concerns of people working with refugees. He noted that at first, when senior Immigration mandarins realized they weren't about to have their way with Mr. Weiner, who was handling the development of the refugee legislation, they turned to Benoît Bouchard, the senior minister, "who was never following or even interested in the refugee issue. Bouchard has only got one perspective on this issue, the department perspective, and he overruled Weiner. That's the way I see it."

On May 5, 1987, the Mulroney government finally tabled a bill to establish a new refugee determination process for Canada. In a statement to the House of Commons, Mr. Bouchard stressed that the proposed system "ensures that no genuine refugee will be returned to a country where they may face persecution. It also ensures that refugee claims will be processed fairly and quickly. It will now take only months to process a claim, not years."

The bill would set up a new body, the Convention Refugee Determination Board, to deal only with refugee claims. According to Raphael Girard, head of the refugee task force for the Immigration Department and one of the chief architects of the bill, the new streamlined procedure for screening refugee claimants would be reduced from eight steps to three. The most controversial section of the proposed legislation was a pre-screening process which all claimants would be required to go through. This first step would require claimants arriving in Canada to go through an initial hearing before an immigration adjudicator and a member of the Convention Refugee Determination Board to determine whether the case warrants referral to the board. The two officials would determine whether there was a credible basis for a claim. They would also establish if the claimant had the protection of another country or if he had the opportunity to make a refugee claim while in a "safe country" prior to coming to Canada. Mr. Girard said that this process would ensure that only arguable cases would go before the board. He estimated that upwards of 50 per cent of the claims would be rejected at this level and added that, "based on projections," only about one-third of those who make it past the pre-screening process and get a hearing before the new board would eventually be accepted by Canada as genuine refugees.

The Refugee Determination Board would be an independent, quasi-judicial body. Cases would be argued before a two-member panel; the hearing would be non-adversarial; the claimant would have a right to counsel; and only one board member must find in favour of the claimant. Negative decisions, which must be unanimous, could be appealed with leave to the Federal Court of Canada on matters of law only.

The critics lambasted the bill, describing it as "draconian" and a repudiation of Canadian standards of justice. Liberal Immigration critic Sergio Marchi said the bill was flawed: "There is a trading off of the safety of human life for an expeditious hearing." He vowed that the Liberal Party would fight for modifications in the bill "to change the course of what appears to be a dangerous piece of legislation." Mr. Marchi argued that the Conservative government "failed to honour the requirement for full accessibility to the refugee system which was advocated in the Plaut report, the report by the all-party Parliamentary Standing Committee on Labour, Employment and Immigration, and numerous submissions by non-governmental organizations involved in refugee issues."

New Democratic Party MP Michael Cassidy called the bill "a blot on Canada's achievements in giving safe sanctuary to refugees." He suggested that Canada return the Nansen Medal. Mr. Cassidy was particularly concerned with the provision for returning people to so-called safe countries. "Central Americans coming to Canada from the United States would be deported from Canada without a right to a hearing of their claim and told to claim refugee status in the U.S., even though the acceptance rate there is only 2 per cent as opposed to 50 per cent in Canada. Although it is technically correct to say that we will not be deporting genuine refugees back to torture and death, we will be letting the United States do our dirty work for us."

Michael Schelew of Amnesty International condemned the decision to block universal access to the proposed system and again lashed out at the lack of any meaningful appeal procedure. "These measures are designed to keep refugee claimants out of the country as opposed to ensuring that genuine refugee claimants are given protection." Barbara Jackman, representing the immigration section of the Canadian Bar Association, said the legislation did not meet the three principles advocated by the bar association: a hearing for every claimant before an independent body; oral hearings for every claimant; and a right to an appeal on the merits of the case. "The reason the bar association has supported these principles is because they comply with international standards of protections and rights guaranteed to persons under the Canadian Charter of Rights and Freedoms." In a written statement, the Inter-Church Committee for Refugees noted that after so many delays "it is incredible that such draconian legislation should appear in the face of an alternative humane, just, workable and expeditious procedure supported by church leaders, members of Parliament's own Standing Committee and other humanitarian groups." The Inter-Church group concluded angrily that "the human rights and standards of justice previously associated with the Canadian people have been sold short to immigration control preoccupations. The ripples will go far. This legislation can only further undermine international protection. It is a sad day for beleaguered refugees seeking a safe place to begin new lives who look to Canada to uphold the humanitarian tradition as a symbol of hope in a dark world."

David Matas, senior counsel for the Institute for International and Governmental Affairs of B'nai B'rith Canada, compared the Mulroney government's bill to Canadian policy in the 1930s and 1940s which barred Jews fleeing the Nazi terror from coming to Canada. "We have come full circle. . . . Of all the countries in the Western world that could have saved Jewish refugees fleeing the Holocaust, Canada had the worst record," Mr. Matas said.

Nobel laureate Elie Wiesel, who was in Toronto for a speaking engagement when the legislation was introduced, described the bill as regrettable and unnecessary. Mr. Wiesel, the 1986 winner of the Nobel Peace Prize, said he believed "a society can be measured and judged by its attitudes toward strangers. . . . I would hope that Canada would like to be measured according to these lofty rules." He maintained that the government should not simply respond to polls that show high approval rates for tougher measures against refugees. "If the polls are against refugees, it is up to the government to educate them, not to give in to the polls."

Junior Immigration Minister Gerry Weiner fired a salvo at the critics, arguing that the current refugee system was "chaotic." "We tried to put some fairness into the system. This is not a theoretical world. It's a real world. It requires realistic solutions, not naiveté. We need objective criteria, not subjective opinion." Mr. Weiner boasted that he was "very proud to be a co-sponsor" of the legislation and stressed that a real refugee will "never be sent back to face death or torture."

Rabbi Gunther Plaut said he regretted the bill. "I think the government is pandering to those forces that would like to close down our borders and maybe build a Berlin Wall around the country. Instead of zeroing in on abusers, they are zeroing in on the true refugees." Rabbi Plaut argued that the government could have developed a fair and quick procedure granting all claimants universal access and a meaningful appeal, a procedure that could have a claimant in and out in three to six months. He pointed out that abusers would not spend $2,000 to come to Canada only to be deported in a few months.

Rabbi Plaut also had some stinging words for the junior immigration minister. "I have one distinction from Mr. Weiner and that is that I was a refugee and I know what the soul of a refugee is like. . . . I'm really saddened that Mr. Weiner would confuse idealism and principles with being unrealistic. I'd like to think that the most realistic principles in this world are those that take full cognizance of the humanity of our fellow human beings."

In anticipation of the criticism, the Tory Cabinet developed a strategy to quell the opposition as the bill neared passage sometime toward the end of 1987. In a "secret" Cabinet committee document, a single, legal-size sheet of paper entitled "Sweeteners" dealt with possible measures that would make the government's approach to a new and more restrictive refugee determination policy more palatable to the public. In the document, uncovered during research for this book and never before made public, the Cabinet committee suggested increasing the refugee levels from overseas to 100,000 over five years — a net increase of 40,000 since the normal intake over that period would be 60,000 — because it "would improve public perceptions of government's commitment to the refugee issue" and "neutralize criticism that this government does not care about refugee protection." However, the document warned, the announcement of 100,000 refugees will create public unease "on the basis that new arrivals will take jobs away from Canadians. Concern will be expressed by some ethnic groups that refugees are being given preference over family reunification." Moreover, the costs for the scheme were estimated at $351 million for settlement services and $67.5 million for overseas operations for a total of $418.5 million.

Another suggested sweetener would be to increase the annual levels for immigration to Canada to 150,000, including a proportional increase in the refugee plan. An increase in the level of overall immigration would appeal to those supporting family reunification and other interest groups such as those concerned for refugees, those in favour of business immigration and those wishing to sponsor assisted relatives, the document said. But it again warned about "the negative side." Any announced increase will bring "some comment that jobs for Canadians will be taken up by immigrants." It noted that settlement costs will increase to $118 million per year for income support and language training programs and stressed that timing would be crucial. The increases "should not be announced until legislation on the new refugee system is tabled and some prior consultations are held with the provinces."

Lastly, the document said that once the Cabinet committee's preferred refugee determination process was in place and working, visa requirements on Portugal and Turkey could be removed. Citizens of both countries flooded Canada's refugee process with thousands of bogus claims before the federal government got around to imposing visa restrictions on Portugal in July, 1986, and Turkey in January, 1987. Any effort to restart the traffic in bogus refugees "could be immediately deterred by the new system," the document pointed out. It also noted that there would be no need to impose additional visas to deter claimants from countries with no significant human rights problems such as "Spain or Greece" because the fast return of initial applicants would deter others.

Ironically, the document said that visas would remain a "necessity to control arrivals from countries where human rights problems exist. They can make a *prima facie* case for a refugee claim even though they often are only economic refugees." Telling words, and the list of just some of the countries which require visas graphically illustrates that they are countries racked by violence and war, countries to which the federal government has considered it too dangerous to deport refugees — Lebanon, Iran, Afghanistan, Sri Lanka, Kampuchea, El Salvador. They are countries that few Canadians would want to live in and most would think twice about visiting. Refugees from these countries are often lucky to escape with their lives. Yet out-of-touch External Affairs and Immigration bureaucrats have convinced their political masters that if refugees in these countries feel they are truly being persecuted, they can simply apply at a Canadian embassy or consulate and claim refugee status. This approach, the bureaucrats maintain, will keep the process orderly. The hard, cold reality of refugees is that their flight is not an orderly process. They cannot afford the luxury, in the vast majority of cases, of going through bureaucratic procedures. They consider themselves extremely fortunate if they have the time to pack a bag before they run. In many of these countries, the Canadian embassies are under constant surveillance by secret police. Simply showing up for an appointment puts the individual at grave risk. He may face immediate arrest, interrogation, imprisonment, torture and even death.

Beatriz Eugenia Barrios Marroquin, a 26-year-old law student and mother of two boys, was abducted, tortured and killed on the eve of her departure from Guatemala to Canada. Ms Marroquin had decided on the advice of friends to leave Guatemala after she had been abducted by right-wing supporters of the government and held for three days in early November, 1985. On November 29, she filed an immigration request with the Canadian Embassy in Guatemala City. On December 6, she was given a ministerial permit, which was issued in response to the urgency of her case. She was forced to wait, however, until December 10 for a passport and a U.S. visa, which were necessary for her departure and a brief stopover in the United States. On the day she received these documents, she was abducted by four armed men. Her body was found three days later 40 kilometres from Guatemala City. Her hands had been cut off, her face was disfigured and there was evidence of blows to her head.

Michael Schelew of Amnesty International angrily argued that if Ms Marroquin had not needed a visa to be accepted as a refugee in Canada, she could have fled the country within hours or days of her first abduction. Since March, 1984, when Employment and Immigration Minister John Roberts imposed a visa requirement on Guatemala, citizens of that country have needed a tourist visa to enter Canada. Mr. Roberts said in a statement that while the number of Guatemalans seeking refugee status was still small, he was worried about the increasing number coming forward. In 1983, 453 Guatemalans claimed refugee status in Canada, the vast majority of whom were accepted as bona fide. The Tory government has also refused to rescind the visa requirement for citizens of Guatemala.

A serious flaw in Canada's requirement that persecuted individuals apply for refugee status from within their homeland is that frequently there is no Canadian embassy in the country, and when refugees arrive in a country where there is an embassy they often cannot get by the security guards for an interview. If they manage to get an interview, their cases are reviewed without many of the legal safeguards and standards they would be entitled to in Canada. No lawyer is present. There is no appeal and the decision is handed down by an External Affairs foreign service officer who may have no competence whatsoever in refugee matters. These very important issues are not even considered in any of the Cabinet documents dealing with a new refugee determination system.

For years it has been clear to anyone involved in this issue that Canada's refugee determination system needed to be revamped from scratch. The system had obviously become the target of abuse by people with no legitimate right to make a refugee claim, people who simply wanted to immigrate to Canada but who didn't want to bother going through proper immigration procedures. They were out to beat the system. It was equally clear that unscrupulous lawyers and consultants were deliberately jamming the refugee system with manifestly unfounded claims because they knew the system was a shambles.

The fact is that the debate over the so-called refugee invasion has been deliberately distorted by government exaggeration. Although the number of people claiming refugee status has been growing, compared with the thousands accepted by much smaller European nations, the Canadian wave is more like a cresting stream; compared with the front-line Third World countries, with millions of refugees confined to camps, it is a trickle. What must also be remembered is that most of the people who make refugee claims, despite what immigration officials continually report, have a legitimate fear of returning to their homeland, a real fear of being arrested, imprisoned, tortured and possibly executed.

Joe Stern of the Refugee Status Advisory Committee acknowledged that in virtually every year since 1980 about 65 per cent of the claimants are rejected by his committee, and it is the RSAC rejection statistics which government officials trot out to buttress their argument for tighter controls. However, Mr. Stern stressed that anyone who would describe the 65 per cent rejection rate as abusive would "show very little understanding of the experiences that these people relate in their testimony." He said that while RSAC is guided by the UN definition of a Convention refugee, his experience has shown that since he has been chairman those claims he would classify as "manifestly unfounded" run about 10 per cent. The remainder are stuck in the grey zone. That is, they cannot prove their case within the narrow UN definition of refugee but they do come from areas of the world shattered by war and violence. "The typical kind of person is someone who has owned a shop in Lebanon, for example, but the random violence, the killing, the uncertainty was so oppressive that he fled. Perhaps a relative of his was killed on the street while shopping for groceries. Perhaps he is someone who has tried very hard not to become involved in any of the political factions, tried not to be identified with any groups and finally fled in fear and belief that his children may not survive the bloodshed. Maybe he saw the inevitability of his children being given a gun and being killed. This person would not meet the definition of refugee but his claim certainly cannot be regarded as abusive or manifestly unfounded," Mr. Stern said.

In this tragic era of refugees, Canada can, and should, take more of these unfortunate people. Obviously Canada cannot accept them in unlimited numbers, but the majority of the world's refugees don't want to come to Canada or the West. They want to stay close to home, close to their culture and environment, in the chance they may be allowed to return to their homelands. It is also understood that Canada must maintain sovereignty and effective control of its borders. It would be irresponsible to suggest that Canada keep an "open door" policy, granting refugee status to anyone and everyone who makes a claim. Such a policy would render meaningless the international humanitarian concept of refugee status. But Canada should and must keep its doors open for people fleeing persecution or indiscriminate violence in their homelands, especially for refugees from countries like Chile, El Salvador or Guatemala for which Canada is a likely country of first asylum.

Canada's current refugee procedure is inadequate to deal with the contemporary situation of refugees. A fair, firm, efficient and streamlined system must be developed and implemented. The system must not restrict access; it should offer the hope of alleviating human distress. It must eliminate the incentives for those bogus claimants whose motives are purely economic. Claimants found to have made truly frivolous claims should be quickly deported. These measures alone will curb the abuse, and will act as an effective deterrent, making potential abusers think twice before spending hundreds of dollars on an airline ticket to come here, and then several hundreds of dollars more to pay an unscrupulous lawyer or consultant to weasel them through a process meant for genuine refugees.

If Canada wants to be truly compassionate, it should consider a policy which will allow Canadians to sponsor relatives — brothers, sisters, cousins, uncles, aunts — living in countries going through dangerous times. It is a double tragedy when an individual living under a constant threat of violence has a family member in Canada who is willing to assist that person but is not able to do so. A Lebanese-Canadian, for example, should be told that if he has a brother in Beirut who desperately wants to leave and the Canadian resident is prepared to undertake the responsibility of sponsorship, then Canada will make it easy for that person to come here.

Mr. Stern said such a proposal was made to Lloyd Axworthy when he was minister of employment and immigration in 1980. Obviously it was never implemented. "If it was, at least you would give some power to Canadians to do something," Mr. Stern said. "That way they wouldn't feel impotent. They wouldn't have to face the loss of their relatives and the guilt they would suffer later. I know that the Jews feel that profoundly. Many of the Jews who died in the Holocaust had very close relatives in Canada. But the Jews here could do little to save their relatives by getting them into Canada."

The government's approach toward refugees places too much power in the hands of the Immigration Department and immigration officers who work for External Affairs in foreign postings. Again, the issue goes back to the department's long-held preference of being able to choose refugees rather than refugees choosing Canada. Yet that preference flies in the face of the whole notion of a refugee. Frightened people flee and become refugees because of circumstances beyond their control, not because they are looking for greener pastures. The government's preference also contravenes Canada's commitment to refugees as a signatory to the UN Convention and Protocol. The Convention exists for no other reason but to ensure that its signatories will accept bona fide refugees arriving spontaneously at their borders and will not return them forcibly to their homelands. The Convention takes out of a government's hands the right to exercise sovereignty in its own interests and it gives individuals the right to seek safe haven. It may be true that some of these people would never be selected by Canada as immigrants, but that is not the issue. Every country which is a signatory to the Convention automatically becomes a country of first asylum even though, like Canada, it might also be a country of resettlement. Under current political conditions in Latin America, Canada *is* a natural first country of asylum for refugees from countries like Chile, Guatemala, Nicaragua and El Salvador.

Canada should develop a policy in line with this reality, one which acknowledges the concept of international responsibility sharing, and the federal government should declare by its actions that it accepts that burden by, for instance, lifting its visa requirements on countries whose citizens are likely to seek protection here. If every Western nation imposed a universal visa policy aimed at keeping out people from refugee-producing countries and also turned away asylum-seekers at its borders, then the UN Convention would be rendered meaningless. Canada should show some leadership by demonstrating to the rest of the world that while its door isn't wide open to every country in the world, it is prepared to remain open to those near by who have nowhere to go.

It is unfair to cast the Canadian government as the sole villain in the refugee fiasco. Part of the blame belongs to the nations of Western Europe and Scandinavia whose democratic governments have been systematically cutting off avenues of escape for so many genuine refugees. Part of the blame goes to the United States and its immigration bill, signed into law by President Ronald Reagan on November 6, 1986, which sent thousands of Salvadorean and Guatemalan refugees scrambling northward to Canada for safe haven. The bottom line is that most so-called First World nations are abrogating their responsibilities toward refugees, and Canada has been getting the spillover.

As imperfect as Canada is, there is hardly a country that has matched our commitment to refugees abroad. That is why it is especially disconcerting when the government reacts to the spontaneous arrival of refugees in a manner that makes it become part of the problem rather than the solution. By implementing overly restrictive measures, Canada is saying to the United States, to France, West Germany, Britain, Belgium, Holland, Sweden, Denmark, Switzerland: "If you're going to violate the UN Convention on refugees, then so are we." That response only serves to cut off yet another of the dwindling avenues of escape for refugees. This is a time when countries should begin to work together to solve the problem of large refugee movements and that can only be achieved if each nation holds foremost in mind the safety of the refugee. Canada should be a leader in this regard, not a follower.

On September 17, 1986, Carmen Gloria Quintana, a 19-year-old Chilean university student, was flown to Canada for treatment at the burn unit of Montreal's Hôtel Dieu Hospital. When she was well enough to travel, Ms Quintana went to Geneva, Switzerland, to testify before the United Nations Human Rights Commission. The following is part of her chilling testimony before the commission on March 5, 1987.

"On July 2, 1986, I was participating in a national strike [in Santiago] called by the National Civil Assembly. That day, Rodrigo Rojas De Negri was also present, a 19-year-old man, photographer, resident of the United States, son of an exiled Chilean woman, who had returned to his country to find his roots. I mention him in modest homage to his life, which he lost in his homeland.

"As we were walking toward a demonstration in our neighbourhood, a patrol of heavily armed soldiers in combat gear and with their faces painted black followed us in a civilian truck. They detained Rodrigo and me and we were insulted with obscenities, physically searched and brutally beaten. Two other vehicles with soldiers and two persons in civilian dress arrived on the scene, bringing the number of our assailants to 30 people. One of them carried a can of gasoline. Rodrigo was already semi-conscious on the ground, bleeding profusely from the brutal kicks, punches and blows from the butt end of the rifles. They continued beating me. The leader of the patrol began to douse us from head to foot with the gasoline despite my pleas that they stop because it was entering my mouth. The soldiers just laughed at us. As I was wiping my mouth with my hand, they threw something which exploded between us and we began to burn like human torches. I began to jump and roll on the ground to put out the flames, when a soldier hit me with the butt of his rifle in the mouth and I lost several teeth. Witnesses to the act said later that they left us in flames for several minutes.

"Almost unconscious, I remember we were wrapped in blankets and thrown into a vehicle as if we were sacks. Afterward, we were thrown into a ditch 23 kilometres from the place where this occurred, in the countryside. I woke up to feel myself being shaken by a man who was totally disfigured, with his face carbonized, his lips ashen and his nose bleeding. It was Rodrigo. We climbed out of the ditch like zombies with our arms and legs outstretched, and we began to walk with great difficulty to find help. Several cars, upon seeing us, swerved away frightened until a man assisted us and called the police. They took approximately two hours to bring us to a public hospital."

At the hospital, Ms Quintana and Mr. De Negri were diagnosed as having deep second- and third-degree burns over more than sixty per cent of their bodies. On July 6, Rodrigo died as a result of the injuries from the burning and severe beating, as well as being denied adequate medical care. During his funeral, police used water cannons and tear gas to disperse the mourners, which included the American ambassador to Chile. During the following weeks, the armed forces, including the country's military dictator, General Augusto Pinochet, denied any participation by the army, despite an abundance of evidence to the contrary. Eight months after the attack, only one officer, Lieutenant Pedro Fernandez Dittus, had been charged with negligence and was released by a military court after paying $25 (U.S.) bail.

Ms Quintana now lives in Montreal with her family and is undergoing long-term medical treatment.

8 THE LIFEBOAT TAMILS

SKIPPER GUS DALTON WAS OUT ON THE *Atlantic Reaper* searching for cod and flounder when he thought he heard a strange, muffled sound emanating from the light fog blanketing St. Mary's Bay. He dropped the heavy fishing net he was hauling in and scrambled to the bow of the longliner to investigate. For a brief instant, Gus thought he saw something on the gentle swells about half a kilometre away. He strained his eyes through the grey mist and, as a bank of swells subsided, he saw it again. There, bobbing in the perilous waters of the Atlantic Ocean less than ten kilometres from the jagged south-east coast of Newfoundland, were two lifeboats crammed with people. Arms were flailing frantically and frightened, excited voices were shouting in a foreign language. The skipper and his three-man crew abandoned the nets and raced to the rescue.

Squeezed like sardines into two fibreglass lifeboats, each designed to hold no more than 35 people, were 155 brown-skinned, black-haired people — 145 men, four women and six children. "You couldn't see between them, they was so crowded," Gus Dalton later recounted. "All I could see was these heads of black hair. At first I thought they was from a shipwreck but after they got on board, one of the fellows who spoke a little English told us they was cast adrift. He asked us if this was Canada and we told him they were near Newfoundland. Then he asked if Newfoundland was near Montreal."

Once the lifeboats were secured to the starboard side of the 15-metre-long *Atlantic Reaper*, Dalton radioed the crews of three other longliners fishing in the area for assistance. It was 1:30 p.m., Monday, August 11, 1986.

The tale the lifeboat people spun of their incredible hardship on the high seas sparked instant international headlines. The castaways said they were Tamils fleeing persecution and civil war in their native Sri Lanka. Under the cloak of darkness, they said, they had boarded a freighter off the southern coast of India some 25 days before and had been forced to remain huddled together in the ship's hold in abominable conditions for the duration of the journey. They were fed meagre rations of boiled rice and stale, mouldy bread. Then early one morning, the captain, who was described as a mean and ruthless German who shouted orders and never smiled, ordered them over the side and into the lifeboats. When the captain had discharged his miserable human cargo, he pointed into the fog and shouted: "Montreal is that way."

The crews of the Newfoundland longliners listened intently to the pitiful story, but Gus Dalton had a feeling in his belly that all was not as it appeared. A 56-year-old veteran fisherman, Gus Dalton knew the sea. He knew what it could do to those left to its mercy. "They told us they had been in the water five days. I'd say it was not more than probably 24 hours judging from the way they looked. They were too bright-looking to have been in the sea five days." He also said the castaways also appeared to be in unusually good condition after such a horrific voyage, and their clothes were remarkably dry considering, as they claimed, they had survived a torrential downpour and battering waves on the second day of their five days adrift on the ocean. Mr. Dalton also recounted that late the night before he noticed a large blip on his radar scope which he made out to be a ship about 200 to 300 feet long. It was "a deep load, a freighter about five and a half mile off."

Once the castaways were safely on board the fishing boats, Mr. Dalton radioed the Canadian Coast Guard and informed a disbelieving radio operator on the other end of his incredible catch. "We was told to stay put and not to bring the people to land." Five hours later, a federal Fisheries patrol vessel, the *Leonard J. Cowley*, arrived to take on the castaways.

Early the next morning, 12 hours after the dramatic rescue, the *Cowley* steamed into port. Officers with the Royal Canadian Mounted Police and the Immigration and Health Departments boarded the vessel for a quick examination before hustling the Tamils onto buses and taking them to RCMP headquarters to be photographed and fingerprinted. They were then bused to Memorial University where they were billeted in two vacant student residences. Meanwhile, word of the rescue had reached shore and scores of journalists began to converge on the port city of St. John's to await the arrival of the lifeboat people. Later that evening, before a battery of television cameras and whirling tape recorders, the Tamils recounted the story of their harrowing flight to freedom — a heartwrenching saga of desperate people fleeing bloodshed and persecution.

Acting as spokesman for his fellow refugees, 46-year-old Wijayanathan Nalliah said the group had fled their homeland because the Sinhalese-dominated government of Sri Lanka was "trying to eliminate" the Tamil minority in that country. He said that he, like the others, was spirited to India aboard a fishing trawler and shortly after arriving on the subcontinent was contacted by "a broker" who asked what kind of help he was looking for. The broker had asked Mr. Nalliah if he wanted to leave India. The soft-spoken accountant, who had worked for a hotel in his homeland, said yes. He had brought some jewellery which he then sold on the black market for hard currency, and within a few days the arrangements were firmed up. Under cover of darkness, he was led to a ship which he was told was destined for Canada. Mr. Nalliah said he knew that what he was doing was illegal, but he had attempted on several occasions to get a visa to come to Canada through legal channels and realized there was no way one would ever be issued to him.

The high seas voyage began on July 7 and life for the next 25 days in the ship's dark and stuffy cargo hold was a living nightmare, Mr. Nalliah said, wincing from memories of the recent experience. Food consisted of pitiful rations of watery rice in oil, served by an Oriental crewman, the only crew member he said he saw throughout the voyage. The two barrels of drinking water in the hold quickly became tainted and sanitary conditions were so foul that many of the passengers became nauseated. No one was permitted to leave the cargo hold. One morning, without the slightest warning, they were jostled onto the deck, ordered over the side and stuffed into two small boats. On the second day, drifting aimlessly in the vast ocean with no land in sight, the lifeboats were battered by an unrelenting rainstorm. Mr. Nalliah told the hushed entourage of reporters that he had feared the end was near, that the lifeboats would overturn and everyone would drown. He prayed and prepared himself for his fate. The accountant said he did not know the name of the ship because it was "foggy and night-time" when he boarded and when he disembarked.

It was a great news story, and the small army of reporters lapped it up. Then Gus Dalton, now a local hero and an overnight national celebrity, arrived in port to meet an anxious throng of press hounds who wanted a first-hand colour account of the dramatic rescue. The fisherman, nervous under the glare of television lights, planted the seeds of doubt in the minds of some reporters that eventually led to the unravelling of the Tamils' story. "They said they never washed since July 7. They didn't seem like people who didn't wash since July 7," Mr. Dalton said. "They also didn't look like people who had been on the sea in lifeboats for four or five days. Their clothes were dry." Inspector Jack Laver of the Royal Canadian Mounted Police also speculated aloud about the validity of some of the Tamils' statements. "I found it remarkable that in five days of fog and rain, they would remain so dry."

Gerry Weiner, minister of state for immigration, popped up that night in front of televison cameras in Ottawa to tell the Canadian public that 155 people "were saved from the cruel Atlantic Ocean." He said he understood that the boat people were citizens of Sri Lanka. "We don't know how they arrived. We're waiting for further examination to take place. You'll understand that we were most concerned about their health and safety and looked after that first." This was precisely what his senior officials and political advisors had instructed him to say, and in hindsight he should have stuck to the script, at least until the story of the Tamils was checked out thoroughly. But the newly appointed junior immigration minister got caught up in the glitz and glitter of his first national news media event and prematurely announced that the refugees would be given minister's permits that would allow them to live and work in Canada for a year, and that they would be moved at government expense to Toronto or Montreal, where established Tamil communities would be helpful in getting the group settled. Although he was already out on a limb, Mr. Weiner was not about to stop there. After all, he was a new face in the Tory Cabinet and he wanted to show the public that he had heart. "The very fact that they arrived by boat brings back a memory of people that left other countries at other times, even immediately after the Second World War," Mr. Weiner intoned, "and we must be very careful about people who leave countries in boats and seek a safe haven on our shores."

Back at the Immigration Department headquarters in Hull, across the river from the Parliament buildings, some of the minister's aides were beginning to feel somewhat uneasy. By the next morning, Wednesday, the story of the Tamils had begun to come apart at the seams. A team of reporters with the *Toronto Star* and the Canadian Press news wire service broke headline stories suggesting the lifeboat people came from West Germany and not India as they had claimed. Social workers who worked with refugees in West Germany said they had recognized some of the Tamils when the sea rescue drama was broadcast on German television.

In a move to squelch the contradictory reports, the Tamils hurriedly called a news conference. On the CBC's *The Journal*, a visibly upset Wijayanathan Nalliah insisted: "We are telling the truth. Why don't you believe us?" *The Journal's* Bill Cameron asked Mr. Nalliah where the Tamils had bought their Western-style clothes. He said they had been purchased on the black market in Colombo, Sri Lanka, where "you could buy everything but a father and mother." The foreign currency, including the German money that some Tamils had in their possession, was also purchased on the black market, he said. Mr. Cameron also asked how the Tamils managed to be so remarkably dry after five days at sea in lifeboats, especially after the drenching they received on their second day out. Mr. Nalliah replied that body heat had dried their clothes.

The *Toronto Star* news team dug deeper and by Thursday the newspaper broke another story contradicting the Tamils' version of events. West German police had told *Star* reporters that there was evidence indicating that many of the lifeboat people had been living in refugee communities near Hamburg and that their ship had sailed from a tiny port on the coast of West Germany in late July. The police also said they were investigating a tip that the Tamils had paid a professional smuggling ring $3,450 each to take them to Canada, where, they were advised, they would find it easy to claim refugee status. In a press conference in Ottawa, Employment and Immigration Minister Benoît Bouchard, the senior immigration minister, announced that the government would review its generous refugee policy if there were any more episodes of the kind of "adventure" used by the 155 Tamils to come to Canada seeking refugee status.

That evening the Tamils were divided into two groups; 61 were flown to Toronto, where they were taken into the homes of fellow countrymen, and the remainder went to Montreal, where they were put up at the Queen Elizabeth Hotel. Leaders of the Tamil community in both cities begged reporters to leave the refugees alone. "These people are tired and scared," said Gnana Thevathasan, president of the Tamil Eelam Society of Toronto. "Please give us some time alone with them; we must assure these people."

On Friday, Mr. Bouchard stunned reporters by revealing

that Canada had been warned well in advance of plans to smuggle the Tamils into the country from West Germany. No action was taken because the tip could not be verified. "We were informed in the course of the summer," Mr. Bouchard said. "We asked for confirmation from the government of West Germany. They confirmed to us that no known ship was leaving West German territory for here." The tip-off was received in Hamburg three days before the ship sailed. Dennis Baker, Canadian consul general in Hamburg, confirmed he had received an anonymous phone call on July 25, apparently from a disgruntled Tamil who was left behind. He immediately informed Hamburg authorities and notified the Department of External Affairs in Ottawa.

By now, the original outpouring of compassion by Canadians toward the Tamils had turned to bitter disdain, leaving the refugees to face yet another obstacle: a tempestuous public debate over their right to remain in Canada. A strong backlash toward the lifeboat people and the manner in which the Tory government had handled the entire affair had surfaced with a vengeance. On radio phone-in shows, in an avalanche of letters to newspapers, in protests to Members of Parliament, thousands of Canadians lashed out at the Tamils for short-circuiting normal immigration channels. Many Canadians were irate because they felt they had been duped. The castaways had lied about their voyage. People complained that they were not legitimate refugees but cheats, economic immigrants who had jumped Canada's immigration queues.

Many Canadians were particularly critical of the federal government's quick decision to allow the Tamils to remain in Canada for one year under a minister's permit, especially amid the mounting conflicting evidence about their journey. Several federal MPs said their Parliamentary and constituency offices were inundated with phone calls from outraged Canadians lambasting Mr. Weiner and Mr. Bouchard for their fast moves. Don Blenkarn, a Tory MP for Mississauga South, said many of his constituents questioned the government's decision to grant the ministerial permits before it was established whether or not the Tamils were bona fide refugees.

Mr. Bouchard countered that "personally, as [immigration] minister, I would not have accepted that human beings be left on boats for days on the pretext that we had not finished the inquiry into whether they were telling the truth or not." That comment further incensed Canadians, because no one had expected or demanded that the Tamils be left on the lifeboats while immigration officials checked out the stories. Moreover, with Mr. Bouchard's revelation that the government was informed well in advance that a shipload of refugees might be on its way to Canada from Germany, many Canadians wondered why it had been necessary to stage a melodramatic and hurried display of political compassion.

By Saturday, the evidence dug up by the *Toronto Star*'s investigative team strongly indicated that the Tamils were lying. Leaders of Tamil communities in Montreal and Toronto began to worry about the growing wave of public resentment. In private meetings, they urged their countrymen to clear the air and tell the truth. That evening, at a packed press conference in Montreal, Wijayanathan Nalliah, looking sheepish and drawn, finally admitted he had lied, and apologized to the Canadian public on behalf of the Tamil group for concocting the tale of the month-long sea voyage. "We deeply regret misleading the Canadian public. We pray for forgiveness, not only from the Almighty but from the Canadian public as well." Mr. Nalliah said that organizers of the smuggling ring and the ship's captain had "pressed" the Tamils not to reveal any details about their journey. They were specifically instructed not to say they had left from West Germany because if Canadian authorities learned of this they would be deported immediately to Sri Lanka. "We were frightened," Mr. Nalliah said. The Tamils, he continued, decided to confess because they felt ashamed. The Canadian public had received them with kindness and compassion. The Tamils did not want to continue the lie any longer. "We didn't want to be liars to Canadians. That is why we are now telling the truth."

The dramatic arrival of the Tamil boat people graphically illustrated to Canadians that Canada's policy for dealing with people who arrive unexpectedly in the country claiming to be refugees is nothing short of confusing, chaotic and ridiculous. It demonstrated the glaring weaknesses, inadequacies, inconsistencies and contradictions of that policy. The event also showed bureaucratic bungling at its worst, and cheap political opportunism at its most blatant.

Mr. Weiner and Mr. Bouchard rushed headlong into the glare of television lights without the facts and issued ministerial permits to the new arrivals without even a minimum investigation into their identities. Both men had grabbed at what they believed was a golden political opportunity to show the country that the Tories had heart. Mr. Weiner went so far as to liken the Tamils' boat journey to the arrival in Halifax in 1939 of the 900 Jews who had fled Nazi Europe aboard the liner *St. Louis*. Mr. Weiner's pathetic attempt at reaching for the quotable quote angered many Canadians, particularly Jewish Canadians, who felt his analogy was an affront to the memory of those who perished as a result of the government's decision to turn away the *St. Louis*. Many other Canadians wondered what Mr. Weiner was driving at. There certainly was no public expectation that the federal government should order the Tamil castaways to turn their lifeboats around and start rowing back to Sri Lanka, and unlike the Jews on the *St. Louis*, the Tamil lifeboat people initially encountered a genuine outpouring of sympathy and support.

After a six-day silence on the Tamil affair, Prime Minister Brian Mulroney finally stepped onto a podium in Ottawa to bail out his fumbling junior immigration minister and to try to stanch the flood of public indignation. Mr. Mulroney made an emotional plea to Canadians to treat the Tamil boat people with compassion. Canada, he said, was built by immigrants and refugees, and "it's not the presence of [these 155] frightened human beings searching for freedom and opportunity that's going to undermine Canada or our immigration policies, and to suggest that is not to understand the magnificence of our country." Mr. Mulroney should have stopped there but, like Mr. Weiner, he ventured further into the absurd. "My government will do anything but allow refugees in lifeboats to be turned aimlessly around in the ocean and turned away from our shores," he proclaimed with bravado.

While Mr. Mulroney was to be applauded for his firm stand and noble words about immigrants and refugees, the bitter irony was that they were inconsistent with the approach his own government was taking in developing a new policy on refugee determination. In May, 1986, his Cabinet had approved a proposal that moved Canada in a direction which would restrict entry to asylum-seekers arriving in the country and make it far more difficult for them to remain. Either he was headline-grabbing or Mr. Mulroney was not aware of his own government's policy direction.

Being an astute politician, the prime minister realized that the Tamil affair was hurting the Tories — not because of the benevolence bestowed on the castaways but because of the bungling of his two recently appointed Cabinet ministers. It was obvious to even the most inexperienced Ottawa observer that both Mr. Weiner and Mr. Bouchard were unfamiliar with the policies of the department they purported to head. Political insiders said the prime minister was particularly enraged at the ineptness of his junior immigration minister, and a tersely worded edict to put Mr. Weiner on a very short, tight leash was issued. Any outflow of information on the Tamil affair henceforth would be controlled by the Prime Minister's Office.

Even with Mr. Mulroney's advisors pulling the strings, the puppet still managed to trip over them. Just as the story was being pushed onto the back pages of newspapers and the tail end of newscasts, Mr. Weiner held a press conference and declared that he was considering dismantling the government's policy of not deporting persons if their homeland was embroiled in war and civil strife, as was Iran, El Salvador or

Sri Lanka. His comments flew in the face of Mr. Mulroney's eloquent defence of refugees just two days earlier. Thus the transparent and ill-advised attempt by the Immigration Department to appear to be toughening up had backfired and only served again to highlight the confusion over Canada's refugee policy.

Another problem poignantly illustrated by the Tamil voyage was the hopelessness of asylum-seekers facing the international system designed to protect them by offering sanctuary. It was noted repeatedly by those critical of the government's response that the lifeboat people had asked for and were in fact receiving protection in West Germany, and that their flight to Canada proved they were not legitimate refugees but economic migrants attempting to circumvent normal immigration procedures. In other words, they chose to jump the queue. "The debate is over Canada's role in accepting people who have already been given protection in another country," said Michael Lanphier, director of the Refugee Documentation Centre at Toronto's York University.

Professor Lanphier noted that the Tamils' situation was especially complex because they were granted asylum in West Germany but not refugee status. Their lives were not in imminent danger; Canada was therefore not obliged to accept them and would have been within its rights to send them back to West Germany. However, their flight from that country provided disturbing and revealing testimony about the treatment they and other Third World refugees receive throughout Western Europe: treatment that drove 155 men, women and children to risk their lives on the open seas; treatment that compelled destitute people to seek out smugglers and forgers to provide illegal escape routes to perhaps a more hospitable country like Canada; treatment that has resulted in so many suicides in European refugee camps and hostels. The sad and brutal reality demonstrated by the arrival of the Tamil boat people was that most Western European nations treat refugees with disdain. Life for refugee groups like the Tamils, Afghans and Iranians is made deliberately uncomfortable by their European hosts in order to encourage them to leave. Although the situation for Tamil refugees in West Germany or in any other European country is a far cry better than the squalor, misery and degradation of a refugee camp in southern India, the humanitarian and compassionate welcome they had anticipated had been long worn out by the problems posed by the thousands of refugees already living in Europe. Instead, they faced a hostile population that hurled a seemingly endless barrage of racist epithets at them. Many Tamils were placed in camps in West Germany, Austria and Italy, where they whiled away months and even years doing nothing. In some countries, their movement was restricted. In others, they were not permitted to work. Life was a constant uncertainty spent fearing that one day they would be deported to Sri Lanka.

Yet while Canadians were being told by politicians that Canada prefers refugees to arrive here in an orderly fashion through its overseas refugee-selection process, the prospect of refugee groups like the Tamils, Afghans and Iranians getting a fair shot at Canada's refugee selection sweepstakes was nothing short of bleak. Mr. Weiner and Mr. Bouchard boasted to Canadians about Canada's generous refugee selection process abroad, but they omitted to mention in their verbal backslapping during the lifeboat affair just how many Tamil refugees from the estimated 150,000 living in camps in southern India were successful in their bid to be selected by this procedure. Aruls Arulliah, an executive with the Tamil Eelam Society of Canada, noted that in 1984, only eight Tamil refugees were accepted. In 1985, that number jumped to twelve. In that same two-year period, Canada accepted almost 25,000 refugees from abroad.

Mr. Nalliah, spokesman for the rescued lifeboat people, told reporters that Tamil refugees often approach Canadian embassies in Colombo, New Delhi, and capitals throughout Europe requesting they be considered under the refugee selection process. "We are routinely turned away," he stated. The only chance they have of survival, he added, is turning to illegal channels to make good their flight to freedom.

The arrival of the Tamils should have been an occasion for

compassion and understanding and, at first, it was. Unfortunately it turned into an unsavoury controversy with some observers saying that much of the public backlash was racist. The good will of Canadians toward refugees was severely tried, and the incredible bungling of Ottawa politicians and bureaucrats left many people who work with refugees wondering whether perhaps the incompetence hadn't been deliberately used to further Ottawa's plans to crack down on refugees. There had been several attempts by Canadian immigration officials to tighten the screws on Canada's outdated and cumbersome refugee determination procedure by making it tougher for claimants to gain access to any newly created process. Mr. Weiner's later musings about tightening up that policy drew sharp criticism in late August from members of more than 20 human-rights, church and refugee-aid organizations who convened an emergency meeting in Toronto to voice concern that the public outcry could undermine Canada's humanitarian policies toward refugees. Anne Squire, newly elected moderator of the United Church of Canada, said: "The reason people use the back door is that the front door gets them into so much bureaucratic hassle."

The unsettling racist undertone of many critics naturally caused alarm in ethnic communities throughout the country. Dan Heap, Immigration critic for the federal New Democratic Party, said: "Anger properly directed at our immigration system is being dumped onto the Tamils because of their brown skins. It might not have happened if they had white skins." Many observers steered away from the racist arguments, preferring instead to blame much of the fallout on a widespread misunderstanding of the Tamils' situation. Immmigration lawyer Barbara Jackman said that if Canadians realized how difficult it is for refugees to find a country of resettlement, "we would not have a backlash."

Much of the public rage, critics suggested, emanated from angry and frustrated Canadians who have been battling for years to bring family members to Canada through the normal immigration route. Calgary West Tory MP James Hawkes, chairman of the Parliamentary Standing Committee on Labour, Employment and Immigration, said, "It has become clear that Canadian immigration policy is a mess. There are many people who had to fight like the devil to get here" only to be thwarted in their attempts by a rigid and contradictory immigration policy. Mr. Hawkes suggested optimistically that maybe one positive aspect of the Tamil fury would be a long-overdue public debate on Canada's immigration and refugee policies.

9 THE PORTUGUESE SCAM

IN THE LATE SUMMER OF 1985 IMMIGRATION officials at Toronto's Lester B. Pearson International Airport began to notice that flights from Portugal were packed with people who could little afford the airline ticket, let alone a vacation in Canada. An unusual number of the arrivals came in large family groups. But what most triggered the suspicion of customs officers was that many of the so-called visitors were lugging five and six large suitcases packed with virtually all their worldly possessions — family portraits and heirlooms, jewellery, personal papers and documents, crocheted bedspreads, embroidered tablecloths, silverware and enough clothing for a dozen six-week vacations. Individual after individual, and family after family, were referred by customs officers to the immigration section for further investigation. During routine questioning, many of the new arrivals spluttered a sentence in belaboured English that at first took immigration officers by surprise: "We wish to claim refugee status."

That single magical phrase changed the entire direction of how these people would be dealt with by Canadian authorities from then on. Normally, they would have been channelled into the immigration inquiry stream to determine whether they were entering the country as bona fide visitors or attempting to circumvent proper immigration procedures and remain in Canada illegally. If the inquiry had determined they were not bona fide visitors but had other motives

150

in mind, they would have been classified as inadmissible and asked to leave within a specified period of time, or they would have been held and deported back to their homeland on the next available flight. By claiming to be refugees, the Portuguese travellers bypassed that straightforward procedure and automatically became entitled to a hearing under the refugee determination process.

The difference between the two procedures was that an immigration inquiry could be held at most within a couple of weeks. A refugee hearing, because of a massive backlog built up over years of political fence-sitting by the federal Liberal and then Conservative governments, could take anywhere from three to five years to complete, and during that period refugee claimants could remain in the country and be free to work. Even if the individual failed to be accepted as a bona fide refugee after exhausting all the appeal procedures, he still stood a good chance of being allowed to remain in the country. The policy of the Immigration Department was to consider each case favourably on humanitarian and compassionate grounds, since the individual would surely have established himself in the country by that time and it would be cruel to send him back to his homeland.

Over the following weeks, one flight after another arrived, and more and more Portuguese citizens were referred to the immigration section where they announced their wish to claim refugee status. "I took a double-take and asked these people to repeat what they had said. I thought I was hearing things," recalled an immigration officer at the Toronto airport. "I hadn't heard of any human rights violations or persecution of any kind in Portugal." The story these self-styled refugees narrated was that they were Jehovah's Witnesses persecuted for their beliefs in a country dominated by Roman Catholics. Yet a representative for Amnesty International, the Portuguese ambassador to Canada and a spokesman for *The Watch Tower of Canada*, a major publication of the Jehovah's Witnesses, said they knew of no persecution of the faith in that country. The refugee claims were manifestly unfounded, they concluded.

Adding a seedy undercurrent to this bizarre drama was the fact that the Portuguese arrivals were virtually all represented by a tight clique of immigration lawyers and consultants. Enforcement officers at the immigration offices on University Avenue in downtown Toronto quickly realized that they had stumbled onto an international operation designed to deliberately circumvent Canada's normal immigration process. The ploy was to use religious persecution as a ruse. A faux pas by one of the key players in the scam added a comic note. In the first few months, one consultant herded scores of Portuguese claimants into immigration offices around the city. Each client, the consultant announced with a voice of feigned concern, was a Jehovah's Witness. Yet most of his clients sported gold crucifixes around their necks and some of the older women were clutching rosaries in their hands.

Memos about the mounting Portuguese influx were fired off from the immigration section at the airport to the department's Ontario regional headquarters and from there to national headquarters in Ottawa. Again and again the problem was detailed in writing, but the only instruction from senior bureaucrats in Ottawa and their political masters — then Employment and Immigration Minister Flora Mac-Donald and junior Immigration Minister Walter McLean — was to continue to monitor the situation. By December, 1985, Portugal, which had not even been on the list of the top 20 countries whose citizens were seeking refugee status in Canada, now led the list. No other group of foreign nationals came close to the number of refugee claims initiated by Portuguese visitors: in less than six months, more than 1,000 claims were made by Portuguese citizens.

Concerned about the stories of religious persecution involving members of his faith, Walter Graham, a spokesman for *The Watch Tower*, contacted Canadian missionaries in Portugal for an update on their activities. The report was terse and unequivocal: "There is no persecution of Jehovah's Witnesses in Portugal. . . . Our work here is going very well." Moreover, not one of the so-called Portuguese refugees had made contact with the Jehovah's Witnesses church since arriving in Canada. Michael Schelew, a Toronto lawyer and Canadian representative on refugee affairs for Amnesty International, checked with his organization's headquarters in London, England. The international human rights group told him they had no evidence of any religious or political persecution, arbitrary detention or torture in Portugal. Yet the "refugees" kept coming.

The *Globe and Mail* launched an investigation after hearing from frustrated immigration officers that Ottawa was simply turning a blind eye to this flagrant abuse of Canada's refugee determination system. The trail quickly led to a number of immigration consultants, lawyers and travel agents operating in Portuguese communities in and around Toronto and in Portugal. Several Portuguese community workers and immigration officers pointed the finger at specific consultants and lawyers who had virtually cornered the market on bogus refugee claimants. These unscrupulous counsellors were charging a starting fee of $1,500 per customer. The scheme involved bringing in people from impoverished areas of Portugal, in particular the Azores. They were hooked by assurances that they could get landed-immigrant status in Canada without having to go to the trouble of lining up outside the Canadian embassy in Lisbon. Many of the hopeful immigrants were unsuspecting, but just as many had latched onto the scheme with their eyes wide open. They knew full well that what they were doing was illegal, but they were convinced that the ultimate prize of landed-immigrant status was worth the risk. Upon arrival in Toronto, they were instructed to claim refugee status and to say no more until they saw their lawyer or consultant, who would handle the case from there.

In an investigative story for the *Toronto Star*, reporter David Greenberg interviewed several consultants and a lawyer who represented many of the Portuguese refugee claimants. Larry Simones, a consultant, told the *Star*: "I am not advising anyone to claim to be a refugee." He maintained he showed them the grounds on which refugee status could be obtained and "they look into it and right away they come to the religious part. Everyone who comes to my office knows about it. It's nothing new. I don't know if he is or is not [a Jehovah's Witness] and I couldn't care less." Immigration consultant José Rafael of Rafael and Associates angrily refused to discuss his business dealings with the *Star*, saying only that "I am doing everything in the law. I do my job." When asked if he had ever counselled a client to lie to an immigration officer, he screamed into the telephone: "I'm going to find you and I'll smash your f—g face." Lawyer R. A. Sainaney, who has one of the busiest practices in Toronto's Portuguese community, told the *Star* that he had many clients who made refugee claims, but pointed out that they had come to him with the proposition. "I don't tell them anything," Mr. Sainaney said, when asked by Mr. Greenberg if he advised them to claim refugee status. "[The client] gives me a story and that's his story and that's that."

Joe Stern, chairman of Canada's Refugee Status Advisory Committee (RSAC), said that as far as he was concerned the influx of Portuguese refugees was nothing short of "an organized assault on the immigration system . . . organized by very unscrupulous travel agents and immigration counsellors." The difficulty facing his committee, he said, was that according to the law each claim *must* be heard. "One cannot assume a case is without merit until it is looked at. But I'd be very surprised to find any of these cases to be bona fide." What troubled him most was that such blatant abuses "are so terribly demoralizing" to genuine refugees who are forced to live "in a state of tremendous anxiety and uncertainty . . . because their cases are delayed by the administrative burden of dealing with spurious cases."

Under pressure for a response to the assault on the integrity of Canada's refugee determination system, Mr. McLean, the junior immigration minister, complained that "genuine refugees are now in great jeopardy due to deliberate and persistent abuse of the refugee determination process in Canada." He pointed out that Canada "has a generous refugee system which allows any individual arriving on our shores to make a claim for refugee status." However, he continued, "this process cannot be sustained under a systematic attempt to subvert it by claimants whose basis for coming in is designed to circumvent normal immigration requirements and is not related to fear for their safety."

But the pressing question was, what was the government going to do about it? In order "to minimize abuse," Mr. McLean replied, he was urging community and church organizations and refugee- and immigrant-aid groups to watch out for and denounce "those who promise guaranteed Canadian residence in return for large sums of money. These people are con artists who are taking ruthless advantage of innocent people." He also warned that if the abuse continued, he may be forced to take "more stringent measures," such as imposing a visa requirement for all Portuguese wishing to visit Canada. It was a typical political non-reply.

Concerned by the negative image cast on the community by news reports of the refugee scam, leaders of Toronto's Portuguese community fought back by attacking the questionable lawyers and consultants, the federal government's refugee determination process, the Immigration Department's family reunification program and the news media. Ed Graca, chairman of the Portuguese Interagency Network, an umbrella organization representing more than 60 member groups and individuals, charged that his community was being "scapegoated by the federal government" and the news media. While admitting that the news reports were factual, he pointed out that Portuguese refugee claimants made up only 5 per cent of 20,000-plus claims in the process, and argued that his community should not be blamed for a problem "that has been created by the inaction and indecision of the federal government." Mr. Graca said the main reason so many Portuguese citizens were opting for the refugee route was that they could not get their applications to immigrate to Canada processed under the family reunification program. He said the Canadian embassy in Lisbon routinely rejected applications and often, because of a heavy demand, simply did not bother to process many of them.

"There are many Portuguese families here who desperately want to be reunited with their brothers and sisters. They got fed up of waiting and invited them to come here anyway."

In a paper on the activities of immigration consultants, Frederika Rotter, a lawyer with Parkdale Community Legal Services in Toronto, touched on the issue of why otherwise law-abiding Portuguese citizens are so willing to defy the laws of Canada in respect to immigration matters. She noted that most of the Portuguese visitors of which her office is aware have made or were considering making false refugee claims "after exploring every legal alternative for remaining in this country. Generally these people have family members in Canada, but because our family reunification program is so restrictive, these people have no other recourse for reuniting other than to do so by illegal means. Such persons are extremely vulnerable as they are desperate to reunite with their families and accordingly more susceptible to the false promises of immigration consultants." Ms Rotter suggested that if Canada were to adopt a more humanitarian family reunification policy, these people would not have to resort to making false refugee claims.

Nancy Nicholls of the Inter-Church Committee on Refugees similarly argued that the Portuguese claimants were really victims of Canada's inadequate refugee procedure. It is a process, she said, that is "backlogged, that has become so cumbersome that it gives unscrupulous counsellors an opportunity to create a scam. If there hadn't been a backlog and there was a process that was just and expeditious, it wouldn't have been worth anybody's while to try to abuse it."

Portuguese community leaders challenged the government to crack down on the immigration counsellors who were perpetrating the scam, rather than going after the "innocent victims." Mr. McLean shot back that he had ordered immigration officials to begin tracking suspected cases of phony refugees and again reiterated his threat of imposing a visa on Portugal. That was in late January, 1986. Mainly because of the cold weather and in some part because of the publicity, the number of Portuguese refugees dropped off markedly in the first two months of the year. But immigration intelligence officers knew they hadn't seen the last of this scam. They had word that some of the key Canadian players in the scheme were in Portugal drumming up more business.

In early March priests at several Roman Catholic parishes serving the Toronto Portuguese community delivered stinging rebukes from their pulpits to all those who had lied and shunned their faith by professing to be Jehovah's Witnesses. They urged their parishioners to come forward and confess. The guilt and shame were too much for many of the devout Catholics to bear; almost four hundred answered the call and came forward. They gathered in a church basement and recounted their stories to Toronto lawyer Richard Boraks. Mr. Boraks said the community wanted to show the federal government that it was eager to cooperate in stamping out the flourishing traffic in illegal immigrants. In turn, the community sought assurances from Ottawa that it would take firm and decisive action in doing something about the Immigration Department's faltering family reunification program.

Not everyone in the community agreed with Mr. Boraks's approach. Mr. Graca felt that anyone who responded to this call to come forward would "be led to slaughter." He reiterated that the problem was twofold: "a mismanaged refugee determination system and a restrictive family reunification procedure." If the government cleaned up its act on both fronts, there would be no influx of illegal immigrants from Portugal, Mr. Graca said. Mr. Boraks countered that if Ottawa did not take decisive action quickly, the number of phony Portuguese refugees would soon begin to rise to alarming proportions. He warned of "back-alley politicians in the Portuguese community who are going around saying that the government is about to collapse on this issue and grant a general amnesty."

Cesar De Morais, an executive of the Federation of Portuguese Canadian Business and Professionals, met with Mr. McLean and urged him to push the refugee claims made by Portuguese citizens through the system as quickly as possible. "Our suggestion was that if there are no bona fide grounds for their claims, those people should be returned to Portugal. I know it is a difficult position to take, but it's realistic." Noting that he was sympathetic to the hardships faced by many of the Portuguese newcomers, Mr. McLean maintained that there would be no amnesty for any of them. His paramount concern, he said, was the integrity of the immigration process, adding that the Tory government could not be seen as rewarding queue-jumpers while thousands of applicants stood patiently in line overseas waiting for their chance to immigrate legally.

In early April, 1986, immigration officers at the Toronto airport compiled a report on Portuguese arrivals for the month of March. There was a doubling in the numbers over the combined first two months of the year. One immigration officer joked that there were now more Portuguese Jehovah's Witnesses in Canada than in all of Portugal. The situation was on the verge of being out of control and senior immigration officials in Ottawa knew concrete steps had to be taken to stem the tide. They fired off a strong recommendation to Mr. McLean urging the government to impose a visa requirement on all visitors from Portugal. "We see it as our only mechanism to control the situation," Ralph Mousaw, a policy advisor with the Immigration Department, said. In response, an order-in-council to impose a visa requirement on Portuguese visitors was prepared for Cabinet—and sat gathering dust while more and more Portuguese refugees arrived throughout April and May.

On May 21, Mr. McLean announced in Parliament a program to clear the refugee backlog, which had grown to almost 23,000 claimants since about 1981. It was not an amnesty, he repeatedly stressed, but "an administrative clearance." The minister strongly urged reporters not to interpret the new program as an amnesty. He was concerned that such an interpretation would have a negative impact on the integrity of Canada's immigration process, but whether he would admit it or not, the administrative clearance translated into a general amnesty for almost every person in the refugee backlog. Nine months after it was announced, slightly more than 85 per cent of the people in the refugee backlog were granted landed-immigrant status. The bona fides of a refugee claim never even entered the equation. The main criteria of the clearance program were whether the individual in question had family ties to Canada, and whether he had been able to demonstrate successful establishment in the country by having a job. Senior immigration officials confirmed that most of the Portuguese claimants, whose numbers eventually reached 3,363 in 1986 alone, would easily qualify.

Mr. McLean said the case-by-case administrative review was ordered because the refugee process had been crippled by the massive backlog. But in an effort to stanch any criticism, the government also announced an interim refugee process to handle any new claims being made after May 21. The interim process, which he dubbed "fast track," would function until an improved refugee determination system was put in place, and legislation for that new system was expected to be tabled in September, 1986.

Reporters in the national press gallery were unaware that the minister had also been planning to announce that Portugal would be removed from Canada's list of visa-exempt countries but had changed his mind at the last minute. A well-placed government source later confirmed that up until late that morning the imposition of a visa on Portugal had been part of the announcement. No senior Immigration Department official would confirm this intention for the record. A political faux pas on the part of the minister revealed the government's earlier plans. Out of courtesy, Mr. McLean had dispatched an advance copy of the statement he was to deliver in the House of Commons that afternoon to Liberal Immigration critic Sergio Marchi and New Democrat Immigration critic Dan Heap. The last paragraph of that statement said: "I am also announcing that effective May 26, 1986, Portugal will be temporarily removed from Canada's visa-exempt list of countries."

Asked by a reporter why the last paragraph was subsequently dropped in his speech to Parliament, Mr. McLean, looking sheepish, said the decision was made after discussions with the Tory caucus and because he had not been able to discuss the issue with External Affairs Minister Joe Clark. A top official in the Immigration Department later said, not for attribution, that the decision was made after an abrupt phone call to the minister just before lunch from a key political aide in the Prime Minister's Office. Several Tory MPs from the Metropolitan Toronto area had voiced serious concern that the Progressive Conservative Party would be seen as "anti-ethnic" in the large immigrant community in that city. This was an image the party dearly wanted to shed in its campaign to steal votes from the Liberals and NDP, who traditionally received immigrant support.

It soon became obvious that the "fast track" system would have virtually no effect in stemming the numbers of Portuguese citizens arriving and claiming refugee status. The system was supposed to ensure that an inquiry into a refugee claim was initiated within a few weeks. Mr. McLean said the temporary measure was designed "to expedite the [refugee] procedure," but within three weeks cases were already backlogged into November. Consultants and lawyers were openly telling clients that the temporary measure was doomed to failure because all the appeal processes and the right to request postponements in order to prepare a case were still in place. By mid-June, the immigration office in downtown Toronto had registered more than five hundred new refugee claims. Every morning there were line-ups stretching two blocks around the University Avenue building. Immigration lawyer Lorne Waldman said it had become obvious to anyone involved in refugee issues that many lawyers and consultants were "deliberately encouraging phony refugee claims" in an attempt to "overload the government's new fast track system and force Ottawa into announcing a general amnesty." An exasperated Walter McLean ordered his officials to prepare a full report on what local immigration officers were describing as a chaotic and confused situation at the Lester B. Pearson International Airport and at immigration offices in Toronto. The minister then conceded that the fast track was not going as fast as anticipated. "Maximum speed right now is about six months. It could be longer," he admitted.

Several honest immigration lawyers and consultants fell victim to sharp verbal attacks from some of their clients. Martin Bjarnason, a Toronto immigration consultant who refused to have anything to do with the Jehovah's Witness scam, said the government's announcement of the administrative review rocked his credibility. In a letter dated June 19, 1986, to James Bissett, executive director of immigration, Mr. Bjarnason noted that while there were no easy solutions to the problem of "frivolous refugee claimants" who have effectively backlogged the refugee system, he could not even begin to express his astonishment and extreme disappointment at the decision by the government to deal favourably with this group through an administrative review.

"There are consultants and lawyers who do not become involved with claimants who clearly have no reasonable refugee claim and who would blatantly abuse both the letter and spirit of the law. There are others who have no such scruples. What the Commission has done is to reward these latter counsel and their clients for their dishonesty and, perhaps even worse, have extended the credibility to unscrupulous counsel who continue to promote schemes to circumvent the intent of Canada's generous refugee policy," Mr. Bjarnason wrote. "At the same time reputable counsel and their clients, who work within the law, lose out because they have the integrity not to become involved in abusing and corrupting immigration policy. Place yourself in my position. What shall I say to the many prospective clients I advised not to make frivolous refugee claims, who accepted my advice and who are now left out in the cold? What do I tell clients I counselled to leave Canada and apply abroad who now learn that their 'refugee' friends still in Canada are to be landed? I believe I speak not only for myself but also express the feelings of reputable counsel in the immigration consulting field, and their clients, who feel betrayed. No matter what the pressure of their numbers, how can it be that the Commission's solution to this problem is to reward the dishonest and in effect punish the honest?" (In an interview with the author, the consultant said he had sent one client back to Portugal, convinced him to follow the rules and apply to immigrate to Canada from there. "He has been refused even an interview in Lisbon, and all his friends are going to be landed immigrants. Who serves these people better? Me or the scoundrels? It's a pretty hard thing to explain to your clients.")

Mr. Bjarnason suggested to Mr. Bissett that the department "must consider the unthinkable" and declare a more extensive review program. "I hesitate to use the term amnesty, but the Commission can only right this obvious injustice and redeem itself by affording equal opportunities to those who had the basic honesty not to go refugee merely as a matter of convenience." He added that while he does not endorse special programs which in effect deal with illegal immigrants who have deliberately broken the law to avoid the selection process abroad, he felt that he could find no other equitable or practical solution but to allow everyone in Canada, legally or illegally, one last chance to apply within Canada. "Thereafter, the Commission should have the fortitude to insist without exception that all applicants, other than legitimate refugee claimants, apply abroad, that enforcement practices within Canada be supported, and that the law be rigidly enforced." He noted that he hoped such a policy would in turn be accompanied by the introduction of less rigid immigration selection criteria abroad.

In early June, 1986, Mr. McLean flatly ruled out any possibility of amending the administrative review program and added sternly that if the continuing abuse went on "much longer, we'll be forced to do something." Nevertheless, later that month an urgent appeal went out to immigration officers in all parts of Metropolitan Toronto and points beyond: plenty of overtime money to be earned on weekends at Lester B. Pearson International Airport. The number of flights from Portugal had *increased*. Fully booked special charters were now coming at the rate of four per weekend bringing with them more and more Portuguese "refugees." In the first two weeks of the month, more than 250 Portuguese visitors indicated when questioned by immigration officers at the airport that they would be applying for refugee status. Immigration officers suspected that when the final tally was in, more than double that number would apply for refugee status once they contacted the lawyers and consultants waiting in the airport lobby.

Senior immigration officials met in yet another emergency session to discuss the options. They all knew there was only one: impose a visa restriction on Portugal. Once again the paperwork was set in motion, and this time it was approved by Cabinet. The announcement was set for June 29 or 30, but once again an abrupt phone call came from a political advisor in the Prime Minister's Office and the plug was pulled. Mr. McLean was left to ramble on to the news media about the many encouraging meetings he had had with leaders of the Portuguese community and how much that community had contributed to building Canada. Imposing a visa on Portugal would be a slap in the face to these hardworking, industrious Canadians, he claimed. That last remark prompted sharp reaction in some quarters since no one had disputed the contribution of Portuguese Canadians, and the last thing the controversy needed was to be muddied with racial overtones. The issue was clear: Canada's refugee determination process was being abused by phony refugee claimants who happened to be from Portugal. The government had the authority and the responsibility to do something to stop it and was not responding.

One ironic aside was that while Tory politicians and political hacks were flapping about and holding meetings with leaders in the Portuguese community in an effort to avoid the backlash bound to occur when the inevitable visa requirement was imposed, not once did any of them meet with leaders of the Dominican Republic community in Canada to discuss the imposition of a visa on visitors from that country in late November, 1985. The decision was made, the order-in-council signed, and that was that. There were no vociferous appeals from Tory MPs urging Cabinet to rescind its decision. The reason for the visa: "To control an obvious source of illegal migration [from the Dominican Republic] into Canada," an Immigration Department news release stated. After all, the government noted in its defence, in all of 1984 about 300 citizens from the Dominican Republic submitted claims for refugee status, compared with 16 in 1983. "There is no indication persecution is currently taking place in that country," the press release said. Similar arguments have been put forward since 1978 by previous Liberal governments for imposing visa requirements on more than a dozen countries including Chile, Guatemala, El Salvador, Sri Lanka, India and Bangladesh. Yet many of these countries are sources of legitimate refugees fleeing persecution and the threat of death.

Senior immigration officials unanimously agreed that past influxes of so-called illegal migrants from other countries paled in comparison with the three-thousand-plus Portuguese onslaught, but they would not venture an on-the-record comment over the failure of the Tory government to take decisive and firm action. However, several individuals involved with refugee-aid groups unabashedly ventured into the realm of speculation. Said Richard Boraks, who ran unsuccessfully for the Tories in the 1984 federal election in what is considered an ethnic riding in Metro Toronto with a large number of Portuguese-Canadian voters: "Unfortunately, the party suffers from an image of being anti-ethnic and if we slam a visa on Portugal, some Toronto [Tory] MPs feel we'll be stuck with that label." Lawyer Barbara Jackman said that the only possible conclusion to draw from the government's lack of resolve over the Portuguese dilemma was that they had other motivations. "To put it directly, I think they have a sectarian interest in not imposing a visa, [which is] winning votes in Toronto. I mean, what other conclusion can you draw from it?" Ms Jackman said the Tory government simply had to overcome "its political perceptions" and act "responsibly toward Canadian citizens. Some kind of effective action is needed to control the problem."

Kathleen Ptolemy, who works on refugee issues for the Anglican Church of Canada, did not want to delve into the reasons behind the government's inaction on the Portuguese flood. Her concern was the damaging effect it was having on genuine refugees. Yet another enormous backlog was being created, which would mean added suffering for genuine refugees caught up in it. Ms Ptolemy was also worried that the abuse and lack of political will would "aid and abet a public distrust of the refugee system. Here we are on the eve of trying to put new refugee determination procedures in place . . . and the government refuses to do the obvious which is to control what is clearly a large number of people whose intention is to abuse the system. It just doesn't make sense. It's really scandalous."

On June 30, a beleaguered Walter McLean was unceremoniously bounced from the Mulroney Cabinet. He was replaced by Gerry Weiner, an MP from the West Island of Montreal who was the Parliamentary secretary to Employment and Immigration Minister Flora MacDonald. Ms MacDonald, who had kept a very low, almost non-existent profile on refugee and immigration issues, became communications minister, and Quebec MP Benoît Bouchard inherited her old portfolio. For two weeks, Mr. Weiner remained virtually underground. He said he was being briefed by his officials on immigration matters. On July 17, he surfaced to make his first major announcement: effective midnight, all Portuguese citizens wishing to visit Canada would require a visa to enter the country. The move was made, he said, to stop the flood of Portuguese who had been arriving in Toronto over the past year claiming refugee status. "We had a situation that was about to destroy the integrity of not only our refugee system but our whole immigration process," Mr. Weiner said. He added that the Tory government saw the visa imposition as a temporary measure that would be reviewed at some later date.

Reaction from leaders in Portuguese communities across Canada was predictable. Many described the action as regrettable, noting that the Portuguese community had contributed so much to the growth of Canada. Ed Graca of the Portuguese Interagency Network said that the government should have gone after the lawyers and consultants who were reaping enormous profits "counselling so many innocent victims to make false refugee claims." He warned that if the government did not take firm legal action to put these practitioners out of business, the problem soon would rear its head in other ethnic communities. He continued to urge the government to take firm action on the Immigration Department's slowness in dealing with family reunification applications.

Mr. Weiner also announced that after July 17 people arriving in Canada claiming to be refugees would no longer be issued work permits immediately after they have had their inquiry before the immigration authorities. Instead, they would be required to wait until they made their statements under oath at a refugee hearing, which under the current backlog conditions could take several months. That action came under swift and heavy criticism from individuals and groups involved with refugees. They argued that legitimate refugees would be the only people hurt by the move, while phony claimants would simply go underground and work illegally.

David Matas, a Winnipeg lawyer who specializes in immigration, pointed out that the federal government through its own inaction created the problem of abuse and the ensuing backlog in its new "fast-track" system. It did so, he said, by failing to respond quickly and effectively to a situation of wholesale abuse. Mr. Matas noted that had a visa been imposed when the problem was first highlighted by immigration officials late in 1985, there would have been no justification for the work permit deferment. The government, he said, "tainted the system they set up and created the justification for the delay in issuing a work permit. So in a sense, the government used the abuse to tighten up the system even more, and the only people who are going to suffer as a result are the genuine refugees." Mr. Weiner countered that his officials have found that once work authorizations were received, there was little incentive for non-genuine claimants to continue with the procedure since they were already in

Canada and had permission to work. "Inquiries may be adjourned repeatedly, thus slowing down the entire process. The feeling in the department is if we withhold the employment authorization until they give their statement under oath, there'd be a tendency to give that statement much quicker." Many refugee-aid workers said they would have no problem with the examination under oath if it was done within a few weeks. The difficulty was that because of backlogs, it took up to four months before an appointment could be made to see an immigration officer to get a report written, another two or three months to get an inquiry under way and finally another two or three months before an examination under oath was held. Despite the criticisms, the government refused to rescind its decision on work permits.

The once chaotic situation at the immigration lounge of the Lester B. Pearson International Airport quickly abated. There was still a constant trickle of people from various parts of the globe claiming to be refugees but imposition of the visa had effectively turned off the tap from Portugal.

Yet just as the Portuguese immigration scam was laid to rest, another was starting to surface. This time the scene was Montreal's Mirabel International Airport. It began, like the Portuguese scenario, with a trickle and ended with a flood as Turkish citizens tested the waters of Canada's beleaguered refugee determination system. Immigration officials in Quebec sensed something was amiss during the summer months. Again the memos began to fly. By September, with the arrival of 136 Turkish refugee claimants, their suspicions were confirmed. That number increased to 332 in October, 585 in November and more than 700 in December. The first two weeks of January indicated yet another record-breaking month. Again, the Tory government dithered until it was forced into action in early January, 1987. By then, however, 2,049 Turkish citizens, most of whom were conned by sleazy travel agents in their homeland into coming to Canada as legitimate immigrants, had applied for refugee status.

This time the political hot potato was juggled by Employment and Immigration Minister Benoît Bouchard, who said in early January that he would be reluctant to impose visa restrictions to stem the flood of Turkish arrivals. A week later, on January 8, in response to unrelenting blasts by the Quebec news media, the Tory government was forced to act. Mr. Bouchard announced a visa restriction on Turkey. "The Canadian refugee process has been overwhelmed, notably by Turkish citizens who come into Canada and claim refugee status rather than follow immigration procedures," the minister said. The visa requirement, he added, was imposed to protect "the integrity of our borders and the intent of our immigration and refugee policies." Mr. Bouchard announced visa requirements on four other countries — Tanzania, Sierra Leone, Mauritius and Gambia — because of "increasing evidence of fraudulent use of travel documents . . . to gain access to Canada."

The Portuguese and Turkish refugee rackets pointed to three serious problems plaguing Canada's immigration and refugee systems which demanded appropriate and decisive government action, not political fence-sitting and useless bureaucratic paper-shuffling. These three defects are: an unworkable and cumbersome refugee determination system that begged to be abused; convoluted procedures which played into the hands of unscrupulous immigration lawyers and consultants; and an immigration selection process overseas that adhered too rigidly to the narrow definition of family-class immigration.

What the Tory government should have done was move swiftly to design and implement a fair and speedy refugee determination system that discouraged people from making manifestly unfounded and frivolous claims. It also should have provided effective legal tools to deal firmly with immigration lawyers and consultants who abuse the system for profit. Lastly, it should have called for urgent reforms in the Immigration Act to allow for easier and more compassionate selection of immigrants abroad with close family ties in Canada. When the Progressive Conservatives came to power in

September, 1984, they blamed the chaotic state of immigration on the former Liberal government. They were right in doing so. They had inherited a fiasco, but in the three years since they have had the opportunity to show leadership and improve it. Instead, the situation has continued to deteriorate and public confidence in Canada's immigration and refugee policy, once a source of national pride, has been tragically undermined.

10 LIFE IN THE SHADOWS

JUST AFTER DINNER ON A WEEKDAY EVENING in late January, incessant knocking rattled the door of the two-bedroom apartment on its hinges. Carlos Ramos froze. He waved his thick hands at his six-year-old son Daniel, beseeching him to be quiet. His wife, Paula, cupped her hand gently over three-year-old Clarissa's mouth. The family stood rigid with fear in the living room, oblivious to the fact that the television was blaring the theme to *The A Team*. They had not expected any visitors and this was not the coded knock their friends used. After several stomach-churning seconds, the door shook again. Mrs. Ramos, her dark eyes wide in fear, fumbled for the tiny gold crucifix around her neck, looked up to the ceiling and whispered a short prayer. Her husband tiptoed to the door and peered cautiously through the peephole. Angrily, he pulled the bolt from the frame and yanked open the door.

"What do you want?" he shouted to a startled teenage boy standing in the dimly lit corridor.

"Do you want a subscription to the *Toronto Sun*? If you take a year subscription—"

"I do not want your newspaper. Please do not bother me with this. Do not come here again. Leave us alone. Go away." Mr. Ramos slammed the door in the boy's face.

For the next week, the tension created by that seemingly insignificant incident lingered. Only Mr. Ramos went out to work, and when he returned his wife left to do some grocery

170

shopping. The children stayed indoors. There were no family walks to the park or strolls along the neighbourhood streets. Since coming to Canada from Argentina in May, 1982, the Ramos family has lived under a state of siege, fearing that one day they will be found out, arrested and deported to their homeland. They are illegal immigrants.

Mr. Ramos, his wife and their son came to Canada to see what life was like here. They had heard from friends that the living was easier than back home. When they landed at Toronto's Lester B. Pearson International Airport they told a suspicious immigration officer that they were tourists wishing to see the country. The officer did not believe their story and ordered them to report for an immigration inquiry the following day. They ignored the request and nervously slipped into the vast underground network of illegal immigrants in Toronto. Now their biggest fear is getting caught. It has almost happened on two occasions, but through quick thinking and fast footwork they have managed to elude the immigration enforcement officers sent to check them out.

Like many illegals, Mr. Ramos lives and works under an alias. He has a stolen social insurance card purchased on the streets for $750 through a connection. His greatest sorrow is that Clarissa, his daughter, who was born in Canada, does not bear his family name. She was registered under the family alias. Mr. Ramos and his wife have had to endure abuse from various employers who know they are illegals. One employer pushed Mr. Ramos for a month straight on double-time shifts, promising him a hefty pay cheque at the end of the month. Instead, the employer made an anonymous phone call to the immigration enforcement unit telling them where they could find a "short, stocky, black-haired illegal South American at lunchtime." Two enforcement officers, wearing white trench coats, suddenly appeared on the loading dock where Mr. Ramos was sitting quietly eating his lunch. As soon as he glimpsed the two men, he bolted into the building, raced through a labyrinth of hallways and stairwells and emerged onto a busy street where he disappeared into the crowd. The officers lost sight of their man on the first stairwell and gave up the chase.

When she first arrived, Paula Ramos landed a job operating a sewing machine in a clothing factory . She earned 75 cents an hour below minimum wage but she didn't care. She had a job and that was all that mattered. One Friday afternoon as she was preparing to leave work, the floor manager asked her out. She gracefully declined the offer, saying she was married. The balding, middle-aged man told her that if she wanted to get paid for the previous two weeks and avoid the police, she had better rethink her answer. Mrs. Ramos agreed to meet him at a bar later that evening. She didn't show up and never returned to her job, a decision which cost her two weeks' pay.

Carlos and Paula are only two people in a nearly invisible army of illegal immigrants conservatively estimated to be at least 50,000 strong in Canada. Most Canadians know nothing about these people. They exist, for the most part, in the shadows, moving stealthily among the immigrant mainstream, always on the lookout for the authorities and trusting almost no one. The majority arrive in Canada as visitors with only one intention: to find a job and remain in the country. Few are actually smuggled over the border. Most can be found in Toronto, Montreal and Vancouver, where they can quickly melt into the multicultural backdrop of these cities. Many South-east and East Asians prefer to make their way to Vancouver. Haitians and Latin Americans gravitate to Montreal. Europeans flock to Toronto. But a sprinkling of these illegal immigrants can be found in every Canadian city from Halifax to Victoria.

To many Canadians, they are the cheaters who enter Canada through the back door rather than lining up at the front door of our overseas immigration offices like good law-abiding people. To others, they are desperate people from impoverished lands who simply want a chance to improve their lot in life. Many Canadians also see these illegals as job-stealers at a time when the labour market is suffering chronic unemployment. Organized labour has complained that illegal immigration results in adverse consequences in the work-place by encouraging lower wages and impeding improvements in working conditions. And many Canadians believe that these people are burdening already over-taxed health and social service schemes. Yet these concerns are not borne out in studies of illegal immigration. Most illegals do not steal jobs but take on positions that few Canadians are willing to fill: menial, mind-numbing tasks such as washing dishes in restaurants, sewing zippers on slacks and buttons on shirts in factories, cleaning offices and scrubbing hotel toilets. Moreover, taxes are deducted from their wages and they pay into benefit packages that most, even though they are entitled to them as taxpayers, are too afraid to use for fear of being found out. Despite these drawbacks, most illegal immigrants would not trade their existence in Canada for a free airplane ticket home.

One argument that rarely if ever enters the public debate over illegal immigrants is whether Canada — the country that many politicians boast was built by immigrants — has fallen victim to the same pernicious xenophobic trends that have besieged Western Europe over the past decade. Some observers will argue that Canadians are worried about this underground society because it is made up primarily of non-white faces.

In June, 1983, Vancouver immigration lawyer W. Gerry Robinson released a lengthy and detailed report called *Illegal Migrants in Canada*. The study was commissioned by the then minister of employment and immigration, Lloyd Axworthy. Mr. Robinson's report pointed out that the problem of illegal migrants in Canada "pales in comparison with that in many other countries throughout the world." He also noted that the problem is not simply one of immigrants looking for a better life for themselves and their families. Much of the movement is for family reasons, brothers and sisters wanting to reunite with family members in Canada. Many people with close family members in the country originally come here for a visit and then decide to stay. Because of their family connections, they get social insurance cards, quickly find jobs and live life in the illegal lane. Mr. Robinson concluded that he did not believe the problem of illegal migration in Canada "is of crisis proportions," but it is one, he stressed, warranting an immediate and coordinated response as well as increased attention on a continuing basis. He warned that although Canada has not experienced the serious degree of illegal immigration which other Western countries have, "we should not remain complacent. The pressure of illegal immigration may well increase world-wide, and we will not be immune."

Shortly after Robinson's report was made public, the Liberal government announced its long-term illegals program. The government wanted illegal immigrants who had been living underground for five consecutive years without coming to the attention of the authorities to now surface. The illegals were told they could apply anonymously and if they were rejected, no one would be the wiser as to who they were and where they lived. In response to criticism, the Liberals argued that this was not an amnesty or a political reprieve. It was a case-by-case review of individuals, who would have to show that they had established themselves in Canada in order to stay in the country as legal immigrants. They had to have good work records and no criminal convictions here or abroad. The program was to run for one year; however, it was extended several times, twice after the Tories came to power in September, 1984, and was finally put to rest in July, 1985. What these extensions accomplished was to give several hundred more illegals the opportunity to qualify with a full five years underground. Yet despite the so-called good will of the government, the program drew fewer than 4,000 people out of the underground. When all the paperwork was done, 3,764 applications were accepted and 157 were refused.

Amnesties, or partial amnesties, are nothing new to the Immigration Department. In 1973, the Liberal government announced a general amnesty which it dubbed Project 97 to deal with a problem described as "out of control." According to government estimates at the time, the population of illegal immigrants had reached a high of around 200,000. In announcing the amnesty, the immigration minister of the time told the House of Commons that: "This is a wide-open invitation to those who have lived in Canada since November 30, 1972, to come forward and apply for adjustment of their status. But it is also the last chance. . . . In plain language, . . . the choice facing all those eligible for adjustment of status is this: either to come forward . . . or to remain underground for the rest of their lives in Canada running the constant risk of detection and deportation."

Although the government's offer was open and generous, fewer than 18,000 illegal immigrants came forward, and when the program was dismantled, the government held firm that there would be no more amnesties for illegal immigrants. The reasoning was that to offer amnesty would discriminate unfairly against those who apply to immigrate to Canada in accordance with the law. When the Liberal government announced the long-term illegals program in August, 1983, it reiterated its position that there would be no more amnesties, stressing that this program wasn't really an amnesty but rather an adjustment of status; and when the Progressive Conservatives came to power in 1984, Flora MacDonald stated emphatically that her government did not believe in rewarding queue-jumpers and that once the long-term illegals program came to an end, there would be no more amnesties of any kind for illegals. But when the deadlines rolled around, Ms MacDonald acceded to pressures and twice extended the program.

In a smoke-filled tavern in downtown Toronto, a group of immigration enforcement officers sit down to quaff a few rounds of draft beer and commiserate over the state of their department. They're basically a good bunch, somewhat like the nice-guy cops portrayed on television. Mike Finnerty, who heads the central enforcement unit in Toronto, the busiest squad in the country, says that there is so much work that the pursuit of illegals is almost totally reactive. "We don't go knocking on doors, or stop people in the streets and ask for identification. We act only on information through filter agencies such as the police, citizens' complaints, landlords, employers, community groups and unions." Tips also come from jilted lovers, former friends and beleaguered relatives. "A man will call and say he invited his brother six months ago and now he doesn't want to leave. They'll say, 'Come and get him. I'll be the guy wearing the yellow sweater. Tell your men to give me a hard time so my brother doesn't think it was me who called you.'"

Another officer complains of cases where an employer "who has used an illegal domestic as a slave for a year or two calls us and tells us where to get her. Often we'll find the woman hasn't been paid for months. Unfortunately, she doesn't have much of a legal leg to stand on. In any case, she'll be deported before anything can be done about it."

"We've also had lots of cases where a sleazy lawyer or immigration consultant has taken hundreds, even thousands of dollars from these people, swearing they could get them landed-immigrant status. After they've milked these poor people for everything they could get, they tip us off, telling us where we could find them," a third officer interjects.

Throughout Canada, about 130 enforcement officers play the role of the heavy for the Immigration Department. They are the least appreciated cog in the entire immigration process. They are required to uphold the Immigration Act and they know what their job is: to apprehend people who are living and working illegally in Canada. It is a difficult and thankless job, but the officers' biggest complaint is that they are simply not given the tools or the moral backing by their superiors in Ottawa to do it properly. Their workload is so overwhelming that they don't get around to acting on most tips. In the Toronto office alone, bins laden with hundreds of anonymous tips gather dust. According to Mike Finnerty, many tips are simply purged at the end of the month, and his officers don't get around to responding to most until a second or third tip comes in on the same individual. Mr. Finnerty estimates that half the illegal population in Canada is living in the Toronto area. On any given day, he has no more than 16 enforcement officers on the street, making little more than a tiny dent in the numbers. They not only stuggle with scarce resources and manpower but are also subject to constant interference from political masters in Ottawa who change the rules to suit the voting patterns of their constituencies. Said one frustrated enforcement officer: "We are told to uphold the Immigration Act. That's our job. So we get a tip and apprehend an illegal. We set in motion the work to remove this person from the country. After all, he has broken the law. But while this procedure is in motion, this guy, either through a lawyer or some leader in his community, gets the support of the local Member of Parliament who in turn lobbies the minister of immigration. Before you know it, the guy, who knowingly came here illegally, who knowingly broke the law, is rewarded by being given landed-immigrant status.

"This political interference is so widespread and uneven, it's incredible. Whether an illegal will eventually be kicked out of the country depends on so many factors. You're in if your MP happens to be a member of the party in power, especially if your ethnic group generally supports that party or has some political clout. Let me tell you this, if you're Portuguese and you're an illegal, your chances of getting the immigration minister to clear you are far better than if you're a black from Jamaica or Guyana."

The problem of illegal immigration is a blight on the integrity of Canada's immigration program. Effective control of our borders is a fundamental obligation of the government. Our right to choose immigrants, according to fair selection criteria, is the basis on which the system must work. To control the traffic of illegal immigrants, Canada must adopt a much broader visa requirement. Immigration enforcement officers agree that this is the most effective control measure. Many also feel that visitors from every country, except United States citizens, should be required to obtain visitor's visas before coming to Canada. For those who manage to slip through the screen, Canada should maintain a policy of dealing with each case firmly. In other words, it should require the person to leave the country and apply from abroad. The government, however, must always leave room for discretion on humanitarian and compassionate grounds. If an individual comes here on a lengthy visit, falls in love and gets married, it would be ridiculous to require that person to return home and apply to immigrate to Canada from there. And what the government must avoid, at all costs, is an aggressive enforcement policy whereby immigration police are sent out in patrol cars with the power to stop, detain and interrogate anyone they might think is an illegal immigrant. Such a policy could easily turn into a direct assault on visible minorities. One effective way to curb the entry of illegals is to impose stiff sanctions on employers who knowingly hire them. That measure alone could have a significant impact on dramatically reducing the illegal immigrant population in Canada.

The government must avoid amnesties and pseudo-amnesties, which only serve to diminish the so-called integrity of Canada's immigration selection program abroad. Lastly, there should be a program for long-term illegals who, for all intents and purposes, have become de facto permanent residents of Canada. These are individuals who have been here for years and have established themselves reasonably successfully. They may be married and have children born in the country. To send them back would be, in a word, cruel. Most immigrant-aid organizations firmly believe that Canada's interests in such instances would be best served by the exercise of compassion on a case-by-case basis. If applied fairly but firmly, this type of program will not act as a magnet to draw hordes of immigration queue-jumpers into the country.

The Ramoses have managed to save a little more than eight thousand dollars in the past five years. The one thing they want most now is a chance to remain in Canada. "We have proven that we can work hard and be good Canadians," Mr. Ramos said. "We just want a safe and happy future for our children. Is that too much to ask? Soon I will approach the Immigration Department and ask if I can remain here. If God is with us, we will get our wish."

11 UNETHICAL PRACTICES

IN MID-APRIL OF 1985, PAMELA MOORE, A SHY-looking, Jamaican-born woman, was armed with a hidden tape recorder and a worst-case scenario that would make it virtually impossible for any immigration official in Canada to grant her landed-immigrant status either as a refugee or under the federal government's former long-term illegal-immigrant program. Ms Moore visited four well-known Toronto immigration consultants and three lawyers. The 28-year-old domestic wove a pathetic tale that, according to one senior immigration enforcement officer, would have her on an airplane bound for Jamaica within weeks of being apprehended or turned in. Ms Moore told the lawyers and consultants that she had been living underground in Toronto illegally for four years. She was single, had no immediate family here and had a spotty job record.

Only one lawyer told her flat out that she didn't have a chance and refused to take her case. The lawyer even refused to take his standard $75 consultation fee. All the others led her to believe that the chances were good to excellent that she would be allowed to stay. Most said they would file an anonymous application under the illegal immigrant program, which required a person to have lived underground and undetected by authorities in Canada for a minimum of five years. Ms Moore did not meet that basic but essential requirement. One immigration consultant said after a ten-minute talk, "I don't think you will have any problem getting into

180

Canada. You are going to make it." He took $100 for the brief consultation and instructed her to bring $350 and her passport on her next visit. Two other consultants said they would file a claim for refugee status for her. A consultant in east-end Toronto said bluntly that if the anonymous application under the illegal immigrant program "doesn't work, then we'll go for refugee status." He never asked the woman if she had any grounds to make such a claim. He asked for $600 to take on the case, in addition to the $100 for the 20-minute consultation.

Also posing as an illegal immigrant, Uruguayan Maria Ibarra went to a lawyer to see what her chances were of obtaining landed-immigrant status in Canada. The lawyer's clerk, who screened potential clients for her boss, told Ms Ibarra that she didn't meet the requirements of the illegal immigrant program since she had only been in the country for three years. Then without asking for any personal history from the woman, the clerk suggested she might want to try the refugee route. Ms Ibarra replied she had never had any trouble with authorities in her native Uruguay and was not a member of any political organization. The clerk suggested she give the matter some thought and if she wanted to claim refugee status, the lawyer would take on the case for $1,500.

In September, 1980, Lloyd Axworthy, Canada's minister of employment and immigration, established a task force to look into the practices of unscrupulous immigration consultants. He had been hearing about their scurrilous antics for far too long and he wanted action. In April, 1981, the task force presented Mr. Axworthy with a 19-page document called *The Exploitation of Potential Immigrants by Unscrupulous Consultants*, which began: "On a number of occasions over the past year, newspaper reports have referred to incidents of unscrupulous immigration consultants taking advantage of gullible immigrants." It went on to describe the following incidents: the payment of a $14,000 fee by two Hungarian sisters after a promise to bring their third sister to Canada; the payment of a $1,000 fee for representation "of a useless nature" before the Immigration Appeal Board; the payment of large sums of money to consultants on the understanding that they would be used to bribe immigration officers and police; and the payment of $1,000 fees for "scandalous advice" in relation to applications for refugee status.

The task force members stressed that they were particularly concerned with improper conduct by many of these so-called consultants, and that their concern was broken down into three categories: the charging of fees for incompetent services, where the consultant is actually ignorant of immigration laws, procedures and practices, or does not perform his work diligently; the charging of unduly high fees for simple services such as $100 for filling out a simple form or for a brief consultation; and express misrepresentation and fraud in the extraction of fees where the consultant states that an extra $1,000 will be required to bribe officials. The task force noted that while it was dealing specifically with immigration consultants, "it is not inconceivable that some lawyers might conduct themselves in the offences described above." However, they pointed out, lawyers are at least subject to professional rules, ethical guidelines and institutional controls through the provincial law societies.

Upon releasing the document a month later, Mr. Axworthy announced a number of initiatives he had personally started to implement to deal with the problem. A government press release, dated May 14, 1981, said that "the minister has already taken steps to initiate two pilot projects [in Toronto and Montreal] to develop community ethnic resources as an alternative source of advisory services for immigrants." The purpose of these projects "will be to educate ethnic communities about past exploitation and to develop expertise within these communities by providing instruction in immigration law, procedures and practices." Volunteers in the community would then make the information available to immigrants. Mr. Axworthy described the development of these two pilot projects as potentially "one of the most fruitful of longer-term solutions. The availability of expertise and reliable service within the community should reduce the incentive to rely upon unscrupulous consultants."

The press release went on to describe other steps outlined in the report and already adopted by Mr. Axworthy. Victims would be encouraged to report abuses and to cooperate in the prosecution of offenders; consultations would be held with the provinces and provincial law societies to determine the extent of existing and potential protection available through provincial consumer protection services; and immigration officials would begin to collect and maintain information on the number and location of immigration consultants, types of services provided, and fees charged, as well as to document incidents of misconduct. In spite of these good intentions, the situation had not improved by 1984, when the Liberals were voted out of office. In fact, it had deteriorated, and it was revealed that the Liberals, despite the flashy press releases and announcements, had done nothing. Meanwhile, the Tory government, which inherited the mess, would prove themselves just as ineffective.

In April, 1985, several prominent immigration lawyers, consultants, immigrant-aid workers and federal front-line immigration officers told the *Globe and Mail* that the activities of unscrupulous immigration lawyers and consultants had reached alarming proportions right across Canada. Hundreds of potential immigrants, they said, were being exploited every year by an ever-expanding and sophisticated network of lawyers and consultants, who promised desperate people new lives they knew they could not deliver. In interview after interview, lawyers and consultants working within the law recited the pathetic stories of the victims.

Most people who seek the advice of lawyers and consultants have entered Canada as visitors. At some point, they decide they want to stay but are afraid to approach immigration officials for fear of being ordered to leave the country or, ultimately, of being deported. These are people, said Toronto immigration lawyer Barbara Jackman, who "desperately want to believe that their situation will be straightened out. So when someone promises them the world, they grab at it."

Lorne Waldman, another immigration lawyer, said that every month dozens of people who have been victimized by shady operators come into his office. "The Immigration Department has known about this problem for years. They can do something about it but they don't even bother," he said. Toronto immigration lawyer Mendel Green recalled a case where a "very well-known Jamaican consultant had given bad and, as far as I'm concerned, very unethical advice" to two clients who eventually came to see Green for help. "Coincidentally, they came into my office back to back. One was a black man from Guyana. The second was an Indian from Guyana. [The consultant] convinced the Indian gentleman that since the prime minister of Guyana was black and there was racial prejudice against Indians, he should make a refugee claim. He then told the black man to make a refugee claim on the basis that the Guyanese minister of justice was an Indian and his rights could not be protected. For this advice, he received $1,500 from each of these men," Mr. Green recounted. Both refugee claims were eventually dismissed and the men were ordered deported.

As part of the *Globe* investigation, the then minister of employment and immigration, Flora MacDonald, agreed to an interview on the topic of immigration lawyers and consultants. Minutes before the meeting, she cancelled, informing her press aide that she preferred to read what the *Globe and Mail* had turned up before commenting. However, briefing notes prepared for Ms MacDonald by department officials for the interview were leaked to the reporter. They indicated that none of the key recommendations of the 1981 task force report were ever implemented by the Liberal government or by the Immigration Department. For instance, the key announcement on establishing two pilot projects in Montreal and Toronto, which the press release said had been initiated, was not acted on. The briefing notes said that in late 1981, the regions involved provided national headquarters with a preliminary breakdown of costs which were then passed on to Mr. Axworthy for consideration and direction. "The minister subsequently decided that in light of the resource constraints, it would not be desirable to proceed with the formal pilot projects as were initially envisioned" by the task force report. "Nevertheless," the notes continued, "the minister did express an interest in the regions doing whatever possible, in an in-house capacity, to accomplish the objectives set out" in the report. Several veteran immigration officers in local offices around the country said they could not recall any such in-house initiatives being undertaken.

Ms MacDonald's briefing notes also made reference to a recommendation that a colourful "flyer" be prepared warning potential immigrants in their own languages about unscrupulous operators. This flyer was never produced. As for collecting and maintaining information on consultants and their activities, the department made a feeble attempt at finding out how many consultants were working in the immigration field. It determined that as of 1981 there were 71 non-licensed immigration consultants operating in Canada. Most were found to be in Vancouver, Toronto and Montreal. That had been the full extent of the department's effort on gathering information on consultants to date.

Lastly, the briefing notes indicated that no real effort had been made to encourage victims to report abuses and cooperate in the prosecution of offenders. The department explained that persons who had fallen victim to unscrupulous consultants were frequently reluctant to report the details of such incidents to immigration officials. "Any action which these officials could have taken has, therefore, been constrained as a result. Immigration officials in Canada and abroad are most willing to receive any complaints made by persons who feel aggrieved by the consultant's practices." Said one senior immigration official in Toronto: "The fact is we were never instructed by headquarters to try to get victims to come forward."

Many Canadian immigration lawyers are sharply critical of the federal government's foot-dragging. They want to see consultants licensed and required to pass a test on immigration matters given by an appropriately qualified body, such as the Canadian Bar Association. They also want consultants placed under the auspices of a watchdog agency that could receive complaints from the public and revoke the licenses of unethical practitioners. The major problem is that at present anyone can hang out a shingle calling himself or herself an immigration consultant. For several years, Mendel Green has spearheaded a battle to get the federal government to do something about the antics of immigration consultants. "I have found incompetence, overcharging to the extent of gouging, and irresponsibility," he commented.

Martin Bjarnason is one of those few immigration consultants with a good reputation in the immigrant community and among lawyers. Mendel Green once described him as "the only reputable, competent and responsible immigration consultant in Toronto." Mr. Bjarnason, on the other hand, wasn't about to sit back and allow consultants to become the scapegoat of the legal community in its criticism of weaknesses in the immigration system. He launched into a vociferous counter-attack against immigration lawyers, saying that in his experience he has found that there are just as many unscrupulous immigration lawyers as there are disreputable consultants. Mr. Bjarnason pointed to the activities of a Toronto lawyer who after "running out of East Indians" began counselling Portuguese visitors to make phony refugee claims. "I mean, that's just a total scam, a total abuse of the system. These people are no more refugees than you or I." He noted that the Law Society of Upper Canada was well aware of the antics of this lawyer yet had never hauled the man before the disciplinary committee. "So much for the Law Society disciplining its own," Mr. Bjarnason commented.

Most consultants simply scoff when they hear lawyers professing that they are bound by the professional rules of conduct of the Law Society. According to the rules of the Law Society, an individual who feels he or she has been exploited or poorly served by a lawyer can lay a complaint with the society, but Mr. Bjarnason is skeptical. "Most immigrants don't even know the Law Society exists," he said, and many immigration lawyers agree with his observation. "Anyway, the Law Society exists for lawyers, not their clients," he continued. "Lawyers are always saying they're controlled, but in the twenty years I've been in this business, I can't recall hearing of any lawyer being reprimanded for not doing the proper thing in an immigration matter."

Barbara Jackman noted that even if an immigrant had a legitimate complaint about a lawyer, many would be too afraid to go to the Law Society. "They believe that if they complain, they'll get themselves into trouble." The heart of the problem, Ms Jackman said, is that the Law Society has not made any effort "to assure these people or to put out any kind of documentation within the immigrant community in other languages to explain what they could do if a lawyer is misrepresenting them or giving bad advice."

On the third side of the triangle, many immigration officers across the country had little good to say about lawyers or consultants. They wondered why anyone would bother paying for advice immigration counsellors dispense for free. "It's ironic," said a Vancouver immigration officer. "We could give them the same counselling services advice and the best thing is it doesn't cost them a cent. Yet these people continue to go to these shysters and get bilked for thousands of dollars, and most of the time they get bad advice."

But it is the poor quality of the free services from Immigration that leads thousands and thousands of immigrants and Canadians each year into the offices of lawyers and consultants across the country. The crux of the issue is the strongly held perception in the immigrant communities that over the years the federal bureaucracy has deliberately created a process that is unfeeling, incredibly complex and concerned more with keeping certain immigrants out than serving those who are qualified to enter. This has led to a deep-rooted distrust of immigration officers among ethnic communities across the country, and a consequence has been the proliferation of immigration lawyers and consultants.

Lorne Waldman said that in 1980 he would have instructed many of his clients to go to the Immigration Department on their own. "Today, just seven years later, I wouldn't give that advice to anyone." He noted that it is not the law itself that is complex, rather it's the immigration system as it has developed. "It's all the policies and administrative guidelines that go with it which make it very difficult for a lay person to understand what is going on." The once fairly straightforward immigration system, he said, has been transformed into a legal quagmire of regulations, procedures and policies that the average layman could not even begin to comprehend.

Martin Bjarnason recalled that when he hung out his shingle as a consultant 20 years ago, he could count the number of immigration lawyers and consultants on the fingers of one hand. Today, he cannot even begin to estimate how many people are making a good living specializing in advising clients on immigration matters. Part of the growth in this industry, he surmised, is because there are simply too many unemployed lawyers on the street and immigration is a wide open and easy field to get into. But the overriding reason, Mr. Bjarnason stressed, is that the immigration system "has become a jungle of contradictions. It just doesn't make any sense."

The consultant went on to cite numerous examples. Two of the most aggravating and contradictory situations he had ever experienced occurred on the same day in mid-April, 1985. "I took two people to Immigration. One client had been deported twice from Canada and re-entered illegally a third time. He doesn't have a hell of a lot to offer, but he did get married this time, and in spite of his previous deportations his case was approved. The other case is of a well-educated woman who has been here legally for five years and whose entire family is in Canada. Her mother, her brothers, a sister . . . I tried to make a case for her and was told it didn't look good. She didn't fit in the family reunification program because she was not a minor." Mr. Bjarnason said that what continues to anger and frustrate him is that those who know how to play the system — the cheats, the liars, the phony refugee claimants — somehow manage to get rewarded by a federal bureaucracy that eventually grants them permanent residence. Yet those people who come to Canada to visit family and friends and subsequently decide they would like to immigrate are ordered to leave the country by rule-bound, unfeeling civil servants. Many of these people, he pointed out, have a lot to offer. "They would make good Canadians. But because they want to do things right, because they aren't about to scream, shout and play the system right to the hilt, they are penalized."

One senior immigration official confirmed, in an off-record interview, that the system is enmeshed in regulations and procedures. "I think our biggest problem is that we're far too technical, too legalistic and far too enforcement-minded when we should perhaps be a little more understanding, more human and less rigid. We tend to verify, re-verify and triple-verify immigration documents and refer constantly to the procedures and regulations manuals instead of showing a little compassion and good will. Are we racist? No, I believe our officers will get *anybody* regardless of race, religion, creed, colour or sex," the official said.

Barbara Jackman said many of her clients are afraid of immigration officers. She said the department "has an image of being enforcement-oriented as opposed to a commission that facilitates situations." Her comment was supported by several lawyers and consultants who firmly believe that immigration officers are under constant pressure, whether direct or subtle, to reject a certain number of cases a month. Ms Jackman believes this attitude is "specifically cultivated at national headquarters. Although they're not saying 'send all these people home,' the atmosphere or the kind of scoring points these officers get is for sending people back and not trying to facilitate valid humanitarian concerns." Senior immigration officials in Ottawa flatly reject this notion. They maintain there are no quotas for acceptances versus rejections and that each officer has a job to do and does it to the best of his or her ability. On a more worrisome note, many lawyers stressed that a lot of immigrants believe immigration officers both in Canada and in Canadian embassies, high commissions and consulates abroad harbour strong racist feelings toward particular cultural and religious groups.

Another serious concern often raised by lawyers, consultants and individuals who work for refugee and immigrant-aid groups is the department's penchant for smothering its programs, procedures and directives in indecipherable bureaucratic bafflegab, or simply not sufficiently publicizing new programs or changes to existing ones. An embarrassing example came to light in late February, 1986. The department had established new guidelines for granting landed-immigrant status to people who have been living in Canada illegally for several years. But for some peculiar reason, the department didn't want the public to know about the significant changes to its special program for "illegal de facto residents," described by immigration manuals as "persons who have not previously come to our attention and who, although they have no legal status in Canada, have been here so long and are so established that, in fact, if not in law, they have their residence in Canada and not abroad." The department estimates that as many as 10,000 of the more than 50,000 illegal immigrants thought to be living underground in the country would meet this definition.

As the newly established guidelines for illegal *de facto* residents were being distributed to immigration officers across the country for inclusion in their thick manuals, Walter McLean, then minister of state for immigration, received a memorandum stamped "confidential" from Gaétan Lussier, deputy minister and chairman of Employment and Immigration Canada. In that memo, Mr. Lussier warned that if the guidelines of the program were publicized, they "could contribute to an increase in the numbers of people violating our immigration legislation in an attempt to eventually qualify under these provisions." The deputy minister also suggested that no press release be issued because the department wanted to avoid creating an impression that this was a new program. "These directives do not constitute a new program," Mr. Lussier wrote, "nor a replacement of the now defunct Program on Long-term Illegal Migrants, but rather a clarification of instructions which have, for years, formed part of the immigration manual. We believe that widespread dissemination of these instructions is not necessary since they are available to applicants at any stage of the [immigration] review process."

But *are* they readily available to applicants at any stage of the process? The guidelines, which Mr. Lussier's memo does not point out, state that immigration officers "are not expected to initiate an application but may do so if the details of the case indicate a review is warranted." In other words, if an individual aptly qualified for consideration under the criteria doesn't know about the program, the immigration officer is not obliged to tell him about it.

On January 7, 1986, in reaction to what he described as a "deliberate and persistent" assault on Canada's refugee determination process by shady consultants counselling clients to make bogus refugee claims, Walter McLean announced that he had instructed the department's Ontario region to set up a system to track obvious abuses. He said the information collected would be used for possible legal action against these counsellors and their clients. Three months later, the *Globe and Mail* asked what the new system had turned up. An official in the Ontario region said no procedure had been established because national headquarters in Ottawa had never instructed the regional offices. "But everyone at regional headquarters in Toronto read Mr. McLean's comments in the newspapers back in January," the official admitted.

Shortly after being sworn in as Mr. McLean's successor on June 30, 1986, Gerry Weiner came out of the Tory bullpen in a feisty mood. He served notice that the government was going to crack down on these unprincipled parasites who charge exorbitant fees to would-be immigrants for advice on ways to remain illegally in Canada. "We're going to lay charges and we're going to make them stick," he promised reporters after announcing on July 16 that visitors from Portugal would require a visitor's visa before coming to Canada for business reasons or on a vacation. The reason his government was imposing a visa, he said, was because in just one year more than 3,000 Portuguese citizens had made bogus refugee claims after arriving in the country. Mr. Weiner said he believed these people "have been improperly counselled about immigration laws by private entrepreneurs, and may have made misleading statements on their immigration documents pertaining to their status. Those individuals in Canada whom we suspect of improperly counselling these citizens of Portugal are now being investigated by the RCMP."

In early November, Mr. Weiner told *Toronto Star* reporter David Greenberg that the investigation of the "despicable" practices was over and charges were imminent. "My credibility is at stake. We have an issue where we have to lay charges and we will. Unscrupulous counsellors are going to have a very hard time in this country." Section 95 (i) of the Immigration Act states that every person "who knowingly makes any false or misleading statement at an examination or inquiry under this Act or in connection with the admission of any person or the application for admission by any person" is guilty of an offence and is liable on conviction on indictment to a fine not exceeding $5,000 or to a prison term not exceeding two years, or both; or on summary conviction, to a fine not exceeding $1,000 or to imprisonment for a term not exceeding six months, or both.

Mr. Weiner also said he would hold discussions with the Law Society of Upper Canada "to seek their cooperation in ending these abuses" and would contact provincial officials to see what could be done about licensing consultants. After all, the minister noted somewhat apologetically, the regulation of professions and trades falls in the provincial sphere. However, he was reminded that there is a provision in the 1976 Immigration Act (Section 115-1u) which gives the minister power to license and regulate "any person, other than a person who is a member of the bar of any province, to make application for and obtain a license from such authority as is prescribed before he may appear before an adjudicator or the [Immigration Appeal] Board as counsel in exchange for any fee, reward or other form of remuneration. . . ." Mr. Weiner appeared somewhat disconcerted that his officials had neglected to inform him of this wrinkle in the Immigration Act. "I wasn't aware of that. I'll have to check that with my officials," he responded. To date, no regulations have been enacted persuant to this section.

In an effort to counter the mounting criticism, several immigration consultants in Toronto got together to form the Association of Immigration Consultants. At a press conference in late fall, 1986, an ill-prepared board of directors told reporters that they had signed up 75 per cent of all consultants in Metropolitan Toronto. Yet they didn't know what the total membership was, or how many consultants were in the city. A board spokesman said the association would institute a code of ethics but was at a loss as to how they would enforce it. Suggested one of the directors: "As a last resort we could order that a member be expelled and the letters LMAIC [Licensed Member of the Association of Immigration Consultants] be expunged from his business card." The press conference quickly deteriorated when *Star* reporter David Greenberg pointed out that one of the directors had a criminal record for immigration fraud and was currently involved in the Portuguese refugee scam.

At the opening of a Canada Immigration Centre in downtown Toronto on April 10, Mr. Weiner was reminded of his tough words and his "credibility." In terse, measured words, the minister replied: "We've done our job. We've supplied the RCMP with information. It's now up to them to do their job."

On June 10, 1987, almost a year after the RCMP investigation into the Portuguese refugee scam was completed, a Toronto lawyer and five immigration consultants were arrested and charged under the Immigration Act with a total of 74 counts of "aiding and abetting Portuguese immigrants to remain in Canada by fraudulent and improper means, to wit: by the making of a false claim to refugee status." The maximum penalty on each count is a fine not exceeding $5,000 and a jail term not exceeding two years.

In a paper submitted to the Unauthorized Practices Committee of the Law Society of Upper Canada and prepared for Parkdale Community Legal Services, lawyer Frederika Rotter argued that immigration consultants are involved in the unauthorized practice of law contrary to Section 50 (1) of the Law Society Act which provides that: "Except where otherwise provided by law, no person, other than a member whose rights and privileges are not suspended, shall act as a barrister or solicitor or hold himself out as or represent himself to be a barrister or solicitor or practice as a barrister or solicitor." Ms Rotter maintained that consultants who advise clients in respect of their rights and status in Canada "are in fact acting and practicing as barristers or solicitors." She suggested that the Law Society use its influence to urge the federal Cabinet to amend the Immigration Act and the Immigration Appeal Board rules "so that parties may not be represented at immigration proceedings by unqualified immigration consultants charging fees for their services." Her conclusions were that immigration consultants should be prohibited from practising unless they work under the authority and supervision of a qualified legal practitioner, and that consultants counselling persons to make fraudulent refugee claims should be prosecuted.

In the final analysis, the power to do something concrete about the underhanded dealings of shady lawyers and consultants lies with the immigration minister and senior departmental officials. Immigration officials have seen the victims of these rip-off artists troop into their offices for years, yet they have dithered instead of acting firmly and decisively. They have not bothered to keep records on the activities of even the most blatantly unscrupulous operators.

As a first step, the department should institute a monitoring system whereby front-line immigration officers who see the abuses on a daily basis can flag their suspicions to regional headquarters. Immigration adjudicators hearing testimony at various inquiry stages should also be instructed to record their concerns. If a pattern of flagrant abuse by a particular consultant or lawyer emerges, then the information should be turned over to the Royal Canadian Mounted

Police for further investigation. The RCMP could then proceed with the federal Justice Department in laying criminal charges if the investigation finds strong evidence of deliberate misrepresentation. Only then can the department begin to restore a semblance of integrity to the immigration system.

12 NONE IS TOO MANY—AGAIN

ON DECEMBER 27, 1979, HEADLINES IN NEWS-papers around the world announced that tens of thousands of Soviet troops, backed by tanks, helicopter gunships and MiG jets had invaded Afghanistan. The Soviet propaganda machine steadfastly maintained that their action must in no way be construed as military aggression since they were invited into Afghanistan by that country's government to counter American imperialist forces who were attempting to topple the popular people's regime by subversive means. According to a report issued by the Political Committee of the European Parliament in May, 1986, about 1.5 million people had been killed in almost seven years of fighting, a very high proportion of them civilians. In addition, the committee calculated that almost five million Afghans had taken refuge in neighbouring Pakistan, Iran and India. Afghanistan's population, it said, had been reduced by as much as 40 per cent. The United Nations High Commission for Refugees estimated in 1987 that Afghans represented almost half the entire world population of refugees. Almost three million live in sprawling, makeshift camps in the North-west Frontier province of Pakistan while another 1.5 million have crossed into Iran, and another half-million are scattered around the globe.

Most Afghan refugees simply want to return to their villages and farms and get on with their simple lives. Instead, they are crammed into tents near the Afghan border, where

196

each passing hour they pray to Allah that one day soon the Soviet invaders will leave their homeland. But there are also thousands of men and women who do not fit into the life of the Afghan refugee camp. They come from the urban centres, and as middle-class, educated Afghans they are estranged from the tribal allegiances and ethnic affiliations that structure the camps. Living outside the camps, they are beyond the reach of organized refugee relief benefits. They gravitate to the larger cities of Rawalpindi, Islamabad, Karachi, Tehran and New Delhi, working at odd jobs. There are some 45,000 to 60,000 urban Afghans trapped in this dilemma who need and want desperately to be resettled in a third country. More and more, they strike out on their own — illegally and clandestinely — hoping to find a country that will give them not only refuge but a future. Many of these desperate people have knocked on and pleaded fruitlessly at the doors of every embassy of every nation in the free world whose political leaders have made eloquent speeches about the Afghan struggle for freedom. Among them we must include Canada.

Najib Tahiri, a founding member of the Afghan Association of Ontario, was particularly moved by remarks made by Stephen Lewis, a gifted orator and Canada's ambassador to the United Nations, who, at the UN in early November, 1985, delivered a scathing denunciation of Soviet genocide in Afghanistan. "Whatever the rationale," Mr. Lewis said, "explicit or conspiratorial — and not a word of it is believable in any event — the Soviet Union, in its war against the people of Afghanistan, has reverted to the ethics, the excesses and the excrescences of Stalinism." In the packed chamber, international delegates sat riveted to their seats in stunned silence at such an unusually outspoken speech from Canada.

Weeks later came the release of a chilling report on the war by Helsinki Watch, a non-profit organization set up to monitor the human rights provisions of the 1975 Helsinki Accord on security and cooperation in Europe. The report, entitled "Tears, Blood and Cries," condemned the actions of Soviet troops in Afghanistan. It said that after interviewing refugees in the Pakistan border town of Peshawar, Helsinki Watch investigators found that "just about every conceivable human rights violation is occurring in Afghanistan, and on an enormous scale." Among those violations, it said, were mothers being forced to watch as their children were being given electric shocks and men being forced to witness their wives being sexually molested in torture chambers. The report said that the "crimes of indiscriminate warfare" are combined with the "worst excesses of unbridled state-sanctioned violence against civilians." The "ruthless savagery" practised by Soviet and Afghan troops in the countryside, the report noted, was matched by "arbitrary arrest, torture, imprisonment and execution" in the cities. The investigators also learned of "bound men forced to lie down on the roads to be crushed by Soviet tanks" and "grenades thrown into rooms where women and children were told to wait." Several Red Army soldiers, captured by Afghan freedom fighters, and others who, fed up with the killing, deserted their regiments, told foreign journalists of their personal participation in such atrocities.

A year later in November, 1986, Mr. Lewis again stood at the podium addressing the UN General Assembly and accused the Soviet Union of exhibiting a "sickness equivalent to depravity" in its war against the Afghan people. He said the continuing "liquidation" of Afghanistan leaves no other conclusion than that the Soviet Union believes "nihilism is preferable to negotiation, that butchery is preferable to bargaining." Mr. Lewis countered Soviet Foreign Minister Edvard Shevardnadze's comment that the Soviet-installed Afghan government is the product of a national democratic revolution by calling it nothing more than a mask that "hides the brute face of oppression." He cited documented evidence that Soviet troops have used booby-trap bombs concealed in pens, soap, snuff boxes, matchboxes and bundles of bank notes, and he also noted that it had been known for more than a year that butterfly-shaped bombs have been dropped from helicopters in rural farming regions. The prime victims of these toy bombs have been children, whose hands and legs have been blown apart and whose faces have been disfigured beyond recognition.

For the eighth time, the UN General Assembly approved a resolution calling for the withdrawal of Soviet troops from Afghanistan. Canada was one of 122 countries voting for the non-binding resolution, up from 112 countries the year before.

In the first seven years of the war, Canada's overseas immigration officers selected only 781 Afghan refugees as landed immigrants. In that same period from 1980 to the end of 1986, Canada sponsored more than 130,000 refugees from around the world. In November, 1985, immigration officials set the government-assisted refugee quota for 1986 at 12,000 — an increase of 1,000 over the previous year. The group benefiting most were Eastern Europeans with a quota of 3,100, an increase of 900 over 1985. Latin America had its quota increased by 200 for a total of 3,200, and South-east Asia dropped by 500 for 3,200 places. The level for Africa remained at 1,000 and the Middle East got an increase of 100, to 900 places. "Other World Areas," which includes refugees in India and Pakistan, got 300, an increase of 100.

The November, 1985, announcement of refugee quotas cut through the heart of the tiny Afghan communities in Toronto, Montreal and Edmonton like a buzzsaw. Grateful for the eloquent and moving words of support from such prominent Canadians as Prime Minister Brian Mulroney, Joe Clark and Stephen Lewis, they were baffled at Canada's reluctance to go beyond rhetoric. They had expected a significant gesture of compassion in 1986. Instead, they got yet another slap in the face. To some observers, Canada's treatment of Afghan refugees bore an embarrassing resemblance to the country's apathetic response to the plight of the Jews fleeing the Nazi terror. In their book *None Is Too Many*, historians Irving Abella and Harold Troper revealed that the Canadian government found room for fewer than 5,000 Jews between 1933 and 1945, even in the face of mounting evidence of genocide.

In late December, 1985, at his austere apartment in north Toronto, Najib Tahiri and several members of the Afghan Association of Ontario talked into the night about the plight of their people and, more specifically, about Canada's deplorable response to their pleas. "For whatever reason, and we don't know why, Afghan refugees have not benefited from Canada's generous refugee programs," Mr. Tahiri said. "Our people are turned away from the Canadian embassies in Islamabad and New Delhi. We cannot get applications to apply to come to Canada. The receptionists hang up on us when we phone. Our letters are not answered. We cannot understand why we are treated like this. In Canada, we have not benefited from the Immigration Department's family reunification program. For more than two years, our letters, our phone calls and our meetings with immigration officials have ended with smiles, warm handshakes and promises for action, but so far we have seen nothing. Not one person here has been united with his family.

"We are not asking that Canada take every Afghan refugee," the 27-year-old stressed. "That would be ridiculous, and not every refugee in Pakistan or Iran wants to come to Canada. Most want to stay where they are because they feel they must fight, and they pray that one day they will go home."

Mr. Tahiri had taken his destiny in his own hands and fled the numbing, destitute life of a refugee camp in Pakistan. In 1980, he escaped from Kabul with the secret police hot on his trail. Having just graduated from university as a mechanical engineer, Mr. Tahiri was involved in preparing and distributing leaflets supporting the activities of the Mujahadeen resistance. For several months, relatives and friends hid him in cold, damp cellars, moving him only under the cover of darkness. Then in the fall of 1980, he slipped out of Kabul and trekked for 20 days on foot over treacherous mountains to safety in Pakistan. In his four years in that country, he approached several Western embassies in the capital city of Islamabad, including those of the United States, France, Australia, West Germany, Britain and Canada. "I couldn't get past the gates of the Canadian embassy. The security guards stopped me and ordered me to leave," he recalled.

The years of strife were taking their toll on the young Afghan. "I came to a point where it was either I save my life or I die. I was very depressed. There was death and suffering all around me. My brain and my spirit were dying in the camps. There was nothing to do. I never had enough food to eat, no proper clothes and I had to share a small tent with ten men." Through his family, he scraped together $2,000 U.S. and bought a forged Portuguese passport and an airline ticket to Canada. He landed at Montreal's Mirabel International Airport in the spring of 1984, and claimed refugee status. He was finally free. Mr. Tahiri said he knew what he did to get to Canada was illegal but the legal channels, he stressed, were virtually closed to him and thousands like him. "What is the use of knocking at the door of an embassy when no one will answer? Most of us know the only way to freedom, the only way to save your life is to cheat and to lie because no one cares about us."

In 1986, a little more than two hundred Afghan refugees arrived in Canada on forged travel documents. Most have similar stories of futile efforts spent trying to present their case to Canadian immigration officers at embassies in Pakistan and India. On several occasions over the past two years, the fledgling Afghan Association has approached immigration officials in Ottawa to ask that the door be opened wider, if only slightly, to Afghan refugees. Repeatedly, they were met with smiles, handshakes, solemn expressions of concern and commitments that "we'll be taking a hard look into this," but nothing has changed. Nothing has happened.

Frustrated and dejected, the association took its case to immigration lawyer Mendel Green. They trembled at what it might cost but they were desperate people on a desperate mission. Mr. Green was moved by Mr. Tahiri's account of buck-passing in Ottawa. He took on the Afghans' case for free.

Mr. Green prepared a thick brief outlining the situation and sent it to Walter McLean, then minister of state for immigration. In a letter dated November 29, 1985, the lawyer wrote: "Canada's record of accepting Afghan refugees is, with respect, deplorable, having in mind the vast numbers of persons already displaced." Mr. Green suggested that the Canadian government consider setting up a special program for Afghan refugees along the lines of those established in the past for Hungarian, Czechoslovakian, Ugandan, Polish and Vietnamese refugees. Such a program, he pointed out, might in some way "alleviate the suffering of the many million refugees."

In an interview with the author in late December, 1985, Mr. McLean appeared troubled when given the numbers of government-assisted Afghan refugees accepted by immigration officers overseas. Then, looking down at briefing notes provided by senior officials in his department, the minister read that Canada "wants to be generous, but our answer is to help with solutions in the region." He pointed out that Afghan refugees are welcomed in Pakistan where they receive food and shelter. He promised that he would nevertheless request a full review of the situation "with a view to increasing the quota for Afghan refugees."

In a separate interview late that month in Ottawa, Scott Heatherington, head of refugee affairs for the Immigration Department, recycled the thrust of Mr. McLean's briefing notes. The main factor behind the low quota for Afghan refugees, he said, revolved around the willingness of Pakistan to offer protection to Afghan refugees and not force them back into Afghanistan. "In the main, we have looked at it as a protection issue. Normally, when we are looking at a refugee issue our first concern is to ensure the protection of refugees . . . in the country of first asylum. Our second concern is to ensure that people are well cared for. Then we look at durable solutions such as local integration and voluntary repatriation. The last thing we look at is resettlement in most instances. However, if resettlement is required to ensure protection, then you know very well from our record we react very quickly."

Yet in an Immigration Department report entitled *Refugee Perspectives, 1984-85*, there was a fleeting paragraph on Afghans that stated that resettlement was not considered necessary for the vast majority of these refugees, "with the exception of those from the urban middle class who cannot benefit fully from local integration." No further discussion or recommendation followed. While arguing that Afghan refugees have protection and safety in Pakistan, Mr. Heatherington conceded that the number of refugees selected from this area "indeed could be higher and this is why we've been talking to the Afghan Association." Those conversations and entreaties must have fallen on deaf political and bureaucratic ears. When the government's 1987 refugee level was established in November, 1986, the Afghans did not even merit a mention. Their level remained virtually unchanged over the previous year's.

Shafiq Jasar, who replaced Mr. Tahiri as president of the Afghan Association in 1986, waited with anticipation for the announcement. He had met with Gerry Weiner, Mr. McLean's successor, in Toronto in October and left with the impression that things would improve. Now it seemed that Mr. Weiner had bought the departmental line that all Afghans are receiving sufficient protection in Pakistan. Peering intently through his black-rimmed glasses, Mr. Jasar wondered how any government official could state with a clear conscience that the millions of Afghan people trapped in crowded and vulnerable refugee camps are living happy, safe and relatively comfortable lives. During the Helsinki Watch team's visit to Pakistan in 1985 the Afghan air force, flying Soviet MiG jets, bombed a public market in a border town of Pakistan, killing dozens of Afghan refugees and Pakistani civilians. It was just one of a number of such attacks intended to signal that Pakistan is no longer a secure refuge. In the first three months of 1987, MiG fighters bombed

Afghan refugee camps inside Pakistan, leaving behind death, destruction and suffering.

A telling tale of Canada's reluctance to become seriously involved in the Afghan plight comes from an Edmonton woman. In the spring of 1985, Jane Thomas went to Pakistan on a five-month international development education exchange program and saw firsthand the miserable conditions of refugee camps throughout the North-west Frontier province. In a report prepared after her return home, Ms Thomas noted that foreign dignitaries are usually flown in by helicopter to inspect what are jokingly referred to locally as "tourist camps" maintained specifically to be shown to the foreign sources of funds. "These camps are in especially good condition and host a variety of international relief projects," she wrote. "The reality of most refugees is quite different than that painted in the tourist camps. Besides the horrors of what was experienced before leaving Afghanistan, often including the destruction of villages and crops and the deaths of family members . . . refugees suffer major problems with culture shock, malnutrition, disease, mental illness, idleness and unemployment, no access to higher education, bribery and coercion by Pakistani police, Afghan army air attacks and the martial law of Pakistan," Ms Thomas wrote. "There are very widespread complaints that material aid intended for Afghans ends up for sale in the local market. Rations are erratic, and those refugees determined to emigrate face incredible obstacles."

Ms Thomas said she came into contact with many Afghan refugees during her stay and the question she was asked most often was: Why is it so difficult to immigrate to Canada? "When this matter was being noticed by so many people in so many places, my curiosity got to me and I went to the embassy of Canada to ask." At the Canadian embassy in Islamabad, Ms Thomas spoke with an immigration officer and was shocked at his attitude toward Afghans. During the meeting, she diligently jotted the officer's remarks into her journal. "We have a lot of trouble with Afghans," Ms Thomas later quoted the officer as saying. "They lie through their teeth. They lie about their backgrounds, make up the most incredible stories." The officer added that the very fact that there is no sizeable Afghan community in Canada to assist them in settling into a new life is "their own fault for being so dishonest."

Ms Thomas wanted to be sure she hadn't caught the officer on a bad day and went back for two more meetings. "His consistently negative remarks and prejudice are borne out in the statistics he provided me. According to him thousands apply or try to go to Canada illegally but only nine Afghans immigrated to Canada last year [1984] from Pakistan." In fact, according to Immigration statistics, of the 64 Afghan refugees selected in 1984, only ten came from Islamabad, and of the 781 grand total since 1980, the Canadian High Commission in India selected the most: 444, followed by the Canadian embassy in Islamabad with 161, in a country inundated by almost three million Afghan refugees. Meanwhile, the Canadian embassy in Rome, where some Afghans manage to flee with stolen or forged travel documents, selected 112 Afghan refugees to come to Canada.

From conversations with Afghan refugees, Ms Thomas learned that most believed they were forbidden to approach the Canadian embassy in Islamabad. Refugees who managed to get to the capital city from Peshawar were usually stopped at the gate by security officers and turned back, she was told. And those who succeeded in obtaining a Canadian immigration application form were not given any assistance in filling it out. Most never received a reply to their applications; and those that did had them rejected outright without even the courtesy of an explanation.

Ms Thomas sent her report to David Kilgour, Tory MP for Edmonton Strathcona. He in turn forwarded copies to External Affairs Minister Joe Clark, Employment and Immigration Minister Flora MacDonald and junior Immigration Minister Walter McLean. Mr. Clark wrote Ms Thomas a letter in which he defended Canada's low intake of Afghan refugees, saying that life wasn't so bad for them in Pakistan, and with some exceptions, they should remain there until they are able to return home. "This position," Mr. Clark pointed out, "is supported by the United Nations High Commission for Refugees."

But the UNHCR in Pakistan, overwhelmed by the magnitude of the refugee situation there, has had its hands full just trying to shelter, feed, clothe and care for the Afghan refugees. It simply has not had the time to become involved in the issue of resettlement. Nanda Na Champasaak, a spokesperson for the agency in Ottawa, noted that the UNHCR has no resettlement officer in Pakistan or India because "Afghan refugees have freedom of movement and can travel from embassy to embassy on their own. They supposedly have free access to those embassies."

Shortly after her return to Canada in November, 1985, Ms Thomas met with Scott Heatherington, head of refugee affairs, in Ottawa. In an interview in the summer of 1986, the soft-spoken civil servant recounted to the author his meeting with Ms Thomas. He described her as a sincere and decent woman. "I think what she was really complaining about was the fact that [the immigration officer in Islamabad] had explained our policy in terms of who we select, who needs protection and the whole issue of durable solution, and I think perhaps the way he explained it was not as clear as it might have been, and I think she interpreted that as being antagonistic to Afghans."

It was pointed out that according to Ms Thomas the officer in question had made some disturbing and racist remarks about Afghans. "I talked to her about that," Mr. Heatherington replied, "and I don't believe that [the officer] is racist. I wasn't there. I don't have a transcript of the conversation and I don't know exactly what was said but I think she shaded it a little bit. I don't think he actually said those things. He may have said something similar to that and I'm not excusing it. But I think you would have to sit the two of them down and sort out what was said and reach some sort of conclusions."

Mr. Heatherington was reminded that Ms Thomas did

meet with the officer on two more occasions. "Well, when she came to Ottawa we spent two or three hours talking about various issues around this and there was a lot she didn't understand about our policies. I put it down more to the fact that the fellow just explained the situation in a very crude manner. But I don't believe he's a racist. I believe he's young, inexperienced, and perhaps not as sensitive as he might be. I also spoke to his officer-in-charge and gave him a copy of the letter and pointed out that if he held any of these views that this is unacceptable." What was the end result? Mr. Heatherington said he thought the officer had been spoken to but did not know what was said. "You see, I took it more as a fact that she had over-reacted to what he had said."

Most of the handful of Afghan refugees who have managed to reach the safety of Canada now share one all-consuming objective: to reunite with their families by bringing them to this country. The Afghan Association began its struggle to bring family members to Canada as far back as December, 1983, when it met with Raphael Girard, then director of refugee affairs for the Immigration Department, at a national conference on refugees. In a letter to Mr. Girard dated January 10, 1984, the association pointed out that immigration officials were refusing the requests of would-be sponsors "on the grounds of insufficient resources to care for their relatives." The association appealed to the immigration official "to help us to save our relatives and reunite our families here in Canada."

More than a month later, on February 21, Mr. Girard replied that the names and addresses of the family members supplied by the association had been forwarded to the offices responsible abroad. "We have, at the same time, requested our overseas offices to consider these applicants sympathetically, but realistically, taking into account the prevailing conditions in their current countries of residence, as well as the level of assistance that might be available to them on arrival in Canada, in order to ensure that any persons selected may actually benefit by their move to Canada." Nothing happened that year, and after a meeting with Mr. Girard on February 18, 1985, the association on March 29 sent him another detailed list containing the names, addresses and dates of birth of relatives. Mr. Girard replied on May 8 that the list had been forwarded to the responsible offices abroad. Mr. Tahiri wrote again on July 25, pointing out that "so far we have not seen any response from them [overseas offices], as we are informed by the members of the families in Pakistan and India."

The newly appointed Mr. Heatherington replied to Mr. Tahiri on September 16. His letter upset the association executive when he informed them, albeit in a roundabout way, that no correspondence had as yet been forwarded overseas. Mr. Heatherington indicated that the names and addresses of the individuals "you have mentioned *will* be forwarded to the responsible offices abroad" (emphasis added).

On November 8, the immigration official met with representatives of the association and Dr. Helga Kutz-Harder of the United Church, the only non-governmental organization that has responded with commitment to the Afghan situation, during which time they had what was described as a "frank and open discussion." Mr. Heatherington left promising the group he would attempt to resolve the situation. Three weeks later, exasperated and fed up, the executive of the association arrived at the Bay Street office of Mendel Green.

In his November 29, 1985, letter to Mr. McLean, the lawyer also dealt with the issue of family reunification. He pointed out that his clients had been attempting to obtain some effective response from the Immigration Department since their first letter in January, 1984. "Not one individual [from the list of 232 family members submitted to immigration officials almost two years earlier] has been contacted by your embassies abroad and in fact, when family members in Canada of refugees have approached those embassies, particularly in Islamabad, they have been turned away. This situation is shocking and deserves your personal intervention with an explicit direction to those visa officers to commence processing these individuals," Mr. Green wrote.

On March 5, 1986, Mr. McLean finally replied. He noted that four people on the list "have been issued visas in the last few months and 29 persons have been provisionally accepted and visas will be issued when they have met our medical requirement. Another 18 persons are to be interviewed in the next month, while efforts are underway to try to contact another 84 persons who for one reason or another have not responded to our requests to fill out application forms or who have not received their mail." Mr. McLean added that 47 applicants had been refused because they did not meet "eligibility and selection criteria and are only distantly related to residents in Canada."

He then expounded on "the more general question of the way in which Canada responds to emerging refugee situations and the plight of Afghan refugees in Pakistan." He noted that the United Nations High Commission for Refugees has programs which "provide care and protection for these refugees. . . . In the specific instance of Afghans in Pakistan, the government of Pakistan provides Afghan refugees with generous terms of asylum which allows them to participate actively in the economic and social life of Pakistan and protects them from refoulement to Afghanistan."

However, Mr. McLean conceded that in "any general situation there are a number of Convention refugees who cannot benefit from local solutions and for whom resettlement in Canada is a necessary and viable option." He added that it was for that reason that "my officials have maintained close contact with the Afghan Association in Canada and are attempting to facilitate the entry of Afghans" who meet the criteria. In an interview, Mr. McLean blamed the problems on the family reunification front on a breakdown in communication "in a sense that some of the people who had been making the applications were expecting that we would contact them, and we were expecting them to go to the embassy."

Mr. Tahiri countered that any such breakdown was not the fault of the Afghans. "We have written to our families and told them to go to the Canadian embassy in Islamabad and New Delhi, but when they get there they are turned away by the guards. They phone and the receptionist tells them they cannot get an appointment. They write and their letters are not answered, or they get a letter saying their case has been rejected but there is no explanation." Mr. McLean said Telexes had been fired off to immigration offices in Islamabad and New Delhi ordering immediate action on the family reunification cases. Concrete results, he added, would be seen within two months.

By the end of the summer of 1986, members of the Afghan Association were still waiting for their families. Mr. Heatherington said 72 people "have been approved or visa'ed and we have about another hundred people who we haven't been able to track down . . . and we have about 59 people who have been refused and of those who have been refused it's generally on the grounds that they don't meet the criteria as Convention refugees. I've asked the post to look at a couple of them where I've felt that perhaps there was room to take a more sympathetic view of the case. The problem you have with people coming out of Afghanistan is that a lot of people are displaced by the continuing turmoil and that doesn't always translate into being able to prove that you have been persecuted as an individual. So there are some people who are certainly deserving of assistance and are getting it from the international community but they unfortunately don't meet the Convention criteria." Mr. Heatherington also said he was generally satisfied that a lot of the cases had been acted on "and things are going better than, say, a year ago."

Mr. Tahiri shook his head when the numbers were recounted. "We are given these figures. They tell us 72 people have been approved. Where are they? It is already September. Why are they not here? And then they say they cannot find another hundred. Why don't they ask us? We know where they are. They are where we told them they are. I really, really cannot understand what is going on here.

"It is really shocking for Afghans to see how our people are being treated by Canada. We have gone through a lot and we have seen many tragedies before our eyes. When I see the way Canadian representatives in Pakistan and India treat our people and then hear how much Canada says it cares for peace and the suffering people in the world, I really have to wonder. I know people who have been rejected who can qualify under the immigration criteria as immigrants. Still the immigration officers in Islamabad and New Delhi will try to find a fault with their application. They never process an application of an Afghan on humanitarian and compassionate grounds. They can come only if they meet the criteria, if they fit the regulations.

"These are people who need to be saved. They are looking for a place to save their lives. I am sorry if when they arrive they are not wearing suits and neckties, but they are very poor, and I am sorry that they have not had the opportunity to remove the dust on their clothes from the miles of travel or that they had not taken a bubble bath before the interview. Maybe before sending officers to posts abroad, the External Affairs Department should send them for a walk along Yonge Street near the Eaton Centre to fully appreciate the appearance of the cultural mosaic of Canada," Mr. Tahiri suggested.

The numbers game continued into the autumn with a letter from Gerry Weiner stating that "progress is being made in effecting family reunification of close members" in the Afghan Association. He noted that more than one hundred persons contacted by Canadian posts have not returned their applications. "Nonetheless, at the end of May, 1986, of the 138 persons who have applied to come to Canada, 13 are already in Canada, 59 have been provisionally accepted after interview, seven are waiting interview, and 50 more have been refused as not having met eligibility criteria as Convention refugees," the immigration minister wrote.

Again the Afghan Association found serious discrepancies with what was being said and what was happening. Mr. Jasar had grown cynical of repeated letters from immigration officials saying progress is being made. "They supply us with statistics but not the people," he said, arguing that only two or three people had not returned their applications, not one hundred as claimed by immigration officials. He also noted that the 13 Afghans already in Canada were not from the association's original list and suggested that the Immigration Department was using that number to make it look as if something concrete was being done. But what really upset and baffled the association president was that the government had refused 50 Afghans because they did not meet the definition of a Convention refugee. Mr. Jasar stressed that all 50 are recognized as refugees by the United Nations High Commission for Refugees. He also said that two of his surviving brothers and his father were refused by Canadian embassy officials in Islamabad in early 1986 because they were not Convention refugees. "That is absurd. I was accepted by the Refugee Status Advisory Committee in Canada as a Convention refugee because two of my brothers were killed by the Red Army. My father and two other brothers had to flee Afghanistan because they, like myself, would have been executed."

Mr. Jasar said that after continuing his fight with the Immigration Department he got word several months later that his family had been refused a second time. "Their reason that time was because the Canadian immigration officials in Islamabad said they didn't have family in Canada. I called Mr. Heatherington immediately and said this is ridiculous when the request for them to come here was initiated by a son and brother in Canada on their behalf. He apologized for the stupidity of the embassy staff. He called it a misunderstanding and hoped he could straighten it out."

Mr. Jasar said he was delivered a stunning blow when Mr. Heatherington told him in October that he would have to sponsor his family if he wanted them to come to Canada. Trying hard to maintain his composure, he continued: "Originally, the government agreed to sponsor everyone on our list. Now they are pressing our members to sponsor their families. Most of us cannot afford it and the Immigration Department knows that. I will have to go to the bank and get a loan to bring them over. There is simply no humanitarian basis for that decision."

Mr. Jasar met with Mr. Weiner on October 29, 1986, to plead the association's case once again. The minister, he said, was sympathetic. "He told us that 75 people had been approved and will come soon. He then told us that he would not put dynamite under his officials like Mr. McLean threatened to do. He said he would take concrete steps to try to solve our problem. He also said he was really astounded that Canada can process thousands of refugees from all over the world each year, and yet only 250 people from our list cannot make it to Canada."

The association discussed five issues with the minister: family reunification; establishing refugee intake quotas for Afghans; permitting wounded Afghan children, women and men to come to Canada for reconstructive surgery; assisting Afghans in liberated areas of their homeland with food and medical aid; and putting political pressure on the Soviet Union to withdraw their troops from Afghanistan. "Mr. Weiner said he would discuss these items with his colleagues in Cabinet. We heard of one of the results a month later," Mr. Jasar said.

In mid-November, External Affairs Minister Joe Clark confirmed that Canada had dropped sanctions imposed on the Soviet Union in response to that country's invasion of Afghanistan in December, 1979. Those very sanctions were announced by Mr. Clark when he was prime minister of the Progressive Conservative government in 1980. Ottawa, Mr. Clark said, was completing talks with the Soviets on renewing cultural, educational, scientific and technical exchanges. "One of the unhappy realities about sanctions is that they do not always have the results that you seek," Mr. Clark told reporters in Toronto. "I think that clearly the cutting off of relations with the Soviet Union did not have the effect that we sought."

Responding to questions on Ottawa's apparently contradictory position on sanctions as they related to the Soviet Union and South Africa, Mr. Clark said different countries require different approaches. He said that Ottawa's limited sanctions on the Soviet Union did not work, so there was no reason to continue them. "We believe that in the case of the Soviet Union, it now makes more sense for us to put ourselves in the position where we might be about to influence their behaviour by our contacts with them. . . . Our purpose is to try to achieve changes in the attitude of countries that have repressive regimes, to have them stop the repression. In some cases, it may be that actions in the field of trade will help them stop the repression. We think it will in South Africa." The minister added that his government felt that one approach that has a better chance of changing Soviet repression is to draw that country's attention to the fact that Canadians will not buy Soviet goods, which will make it more difficult for Moscow to reduce its trade imbalance with Canada.

At the start of May, 1987, Mr. Jasar was still waiting for members of his family to arrive. He noted that from the original list of 250 people supplied to the Immigration Department by the Afghan Association in February, 1984, a family of nine arrived in November, 1986, and three individuals arrived in March, 1987. He shook his head in disgust. "I just cannot understand why we are being treated like this. What have we done wrong? I can't understand what is happening. I just can't."

13 VISAS FOR SALE

"CANADA IS OPEN FOR BUSINESS." PRIME Minister Brian Mulroney has repeated that very phrase on numerous occasions since taking office in September, 1984. And to show he meant every word, his government seized the Immigration Department's Entrepreneur Program, originally launched by the Liberals to lure rich immigrants to Canada, and charged into the fray. The requirements for getting permanent residence status under the program are impressive: the candidate must have a net worth of more than $500,000, the intention to make a substantial investment in Canada and a proven track record in business.

As soon as they had moved into the offices of power on Parliament Hill, the Tories invited executives from the Department of Employment and Immigration for a chat about the Entrepreneur Program. The bureaucrats trooped into various committee rooms in the House of Commons with documents, flow charts and graphs illustrating just how well the program had been doing since it was first introduced in 1978. At first blush, the scheme appeared to be a tremendous success — at least on paper. It appeared that thousands of wealthy individuals and their families from a host of countries had been coming to Canada each year, investing hundreds of millions of dollars and creating tens of thousands of jobs for Canadians. Scores of projects, large and small, had been established right across the country putting unemployed Canadians to work. In fact, many Canadian compan-

215

ies on the rocky road to bankruptcy were saved by the foreign capital, entrepreneurial spirit and know-how of these new-comers who weren't afraid to invest in Canada, supporters of the Entrepreneur Program boasted.

Given the graphs, charts and pages of statistics, the program could hardly be knocked. As a result, the Parliamentary Standing Committee on Labour, Employment and Immigration, headed by Tory MP Jim Hawkes, strongly recommended to the House of Commons on June 5, 1985, that the government "send a very clear signal to posts abroad that Canada needs jobs and is looking for their help in expanding the Entrepreneur Program. The clearest signal would be to raise the annual intake targets for entrepreneurs in 1986 to 5,000-7,000, and to 8,000-10,000 in 1987." In other words, swing open the doors to these rich immigrants and watch Canada prosper. The Parliamentary committee had caught the entrepreneurial fever and the top mandarins at the Department of Employment and Immigration applauded a job well done.

But just what was fed to these politicians that had them shouting for more? Facts and figures supplied by senior bureaucrats who put on their best dog-and-pony show to ensure that their program remained unsullied by impertinent questions and partisan tinkering. After all, it was a nice change for immigration officers to rub elbows with the rich and powerful instead of with impoverished refugees or ordinary immigrants, and the entrepreneur game brought in the high stakes and high rollers.

With colour-coded graphs perched on aluminum easels the civil servants showed the Parliamentary Standing Committee on Labour, Employment and Immigration that in 1984 alone, 2,094 immigrant entrepreneurs were admitted to Canada, investing $817 million and creating 8,271 jobs. According to flashy government press releases, more than 11,000 business immigrants have been granted landed-immigrant status in Canada since the program was launched in 1978. The charts also indicated that they had invested a little more than $3.4 billion, creating almost 25,000 jobs in the process.

Committee members were awed by these impressive figures. In November, 1985, buoyed by the support of the committee, the Department of Employment and Immigration announced that "in order to send out a clear signal of the government's desire to attract business immigrants," the quota for this category for 1986 would be set at 4,000, an increase of 82 per cent over the previous year's level of 2,200. "There is a strong consensus in Canada that the recruitment and selection of business immigrants should be fostered, because these newcomers provide significant economic benefits to Canada through increased capital formation and job creation," said the department's *Annual Report to Parliament on Future Immigration Levels*.

In the late autumn of 1985, the author asked a political assistant to Minister of State for Immigration Walter McLean and a top immigration official for the studies on which these figures were based. Repeated phone calls were not returned. Finally after almost two weeks of hounding, word came down that the figures highlighted by the federal government reflect "only the declared intention" of entrepreneurs. There were *no* reports or studies on the actual program itself. Clearly the Entrepreneur Program warranted a hard look, starting with the initial scribblings on an application form and ending with the arrival of these job-creators in Canada. Hong Kong was a logical starting point, since 51 per cent of 2,136 visas issued to business immigrants in 1985 came from there.

Visitors to Hong Kong soon perceive that almost everyone is suffering from what is known as the "1997 jitters;" in that year China formally takes the British colony back into the fold. The slightest rumour of impending hard times under the communist People's Republic of China sends fleets of Rolls-Royces and Mercedeses zooming off in the direction of Hennessey Road, where the Canadian High Commission has its immigration offices. There, in a separate waiting room away from the ordinary, clamouring hordes of prospective, run-of-the-mill immigrants, the red carpet is rolled out and the bureaucratic red tape is rolled up. While back home federal politicians wax eloquent that family-class immigration is the cornerstone of Canada's immigration policy, it is patently obvious which class gets the preferred treatment in Hong Kong. Of 13 officers working in the immigration section there, five were assigned to work solely on entrepreneurial applications.

William Sinclair, head of the immigration section in Hong Kong, said the main concern of his staff is to select entrepreneurs who will actually do what they say they are going to do once they arrive in Canada. The section does not want to be seen, Mr. Sinclair stressed, as selling visas to the wealthy, who will keep the documents tucked neatly away in a safety deposit box in case they need them late in the next decade. He had heard that many Hong Kong businessmen who had received permanent residence status in Canada subsequently returned to the colony to do business as usual while their families were safely ensconced in some posh Canadian suburb.

Yet surely anyone who doesn't fulfil his end of the contract would be deported? Mr. Sinclair rolled his eyes to the ceiling. Once an application had been approved and landed-immigrant status granted, there was very nearly nothing to compel most of these wealthy businessmen to do what they said they would do once they landed on Canadian soil. According to the objectives and procedures of the program as outlined in a manual prepared by Employment and Immigration Canada, there is provision for conditional landing, but it is to be used only "in those cases where the visa officer has serious doubts about the intentions of the entrepreneur and wishes to monitor the entrepreneur's steps towards establishing a business."

What immigration officers in Hong Kong hadn't anticipated when the program was conceived was that they would have to go head to head with a growing number of lawyers and consultants who have jumped onto the lucrative bandwagon of developing entrepreneurial schemes for wealthy

Chinese businessmen. Dozens of Canadian immigration lawyers and consultants have hung out their shingles in downtown Hong Kong. Almost daily, local newspaper ads trumpet the impending arrival of immigration lawyers and consultants from Vancouver, Calgary, Edmonton, Winnipeg, Toronto and Montreal offering local businessmen advice, for a healthy fee, on how they and their families can escape the threat of 1997. The services offered by many are straightforward and on the up and up, but there is an unsavoury cadre who specialize in dispensing bogus information while reaping thousands of dollars in the process. They hold seminars and colourful slide-shows in ritzy hotels, and private consultations in swank suites. Some charge upwards of $15,000 to fill out a simple application form, guaranteeing, as part of the service, that all who deal with them will be accepted as landed immigrants. Canadian immigration officers in the Hong Kong office will fill out the same form for free in 20 minutes; however, they offer no guarantee that the applicant will be successful. Other operators are experts in preparing fictitious yet extremely convincing business proposals to get their clients into Canada. Their fees often reach $60,000 and higher.

The antics of these Canadian shysters are renowned in Hong Kong. One local newspaper, after an investigation of Canada's entrepreneur promoters, headlined its front-page exposé "When Legal Eagles Become Vultures." William Sinclair recalled that when he first arrived in Hong Kong in 1981, he could count the number of Canadian lawyers doing business in the city on the fingers of one hand. He estimated that by 1985 no fewer than 140 were operating. And while he maintained that most were giving a respectable service, he was especially concerned about a sizeable contingent of opportunists who were giving Canada's immigration process a sordid reputation among influential Hong Kong businessmen. "I've seen some pretty severe situations. Some of these lawyers are absolutely horrendous in terms of all they're getting away with. They're generating a lot of negative publicity which affects Canada's image." The worst example of a rip-off that he had come across involved a businessman who paid $90,000 for "the processing of a very average, ordinary case, which was not worth more than a few hundred dollars of work."

These questionable activities have drawn the ire of many legitimate Canadian lawyers and consultants. Lawyer Mendel Green, who often travels to the Far East to advise entrepreneurs, said he was embarrassed by so many of his colleagues who used the 1997 jitters "to rip off clients and fill them with false hopes and false promises about things in Canada." Mr. Green said he was aware that lawyers and consultants have prepared fictitious business proposals for clients who have absolutely no intention of following through with their proposed venture once they get to Canada. "These Chinese businessmen are merely seeking a cure for the 1997 jitters, and that cure is ensuring that they and their families have landed-immigrant status in Canada." He noted that with a well-written proposal, an unscrupulous consultant or lawyer could "take a chimpanzee, dress him up in a business suit and just have him grunt and technically get him through [the immigration process]."

Particularly aggravating to the legitimate lawyers and consultants was the Canadian government's inability to stop the sleazy operators. Canada has no legal jurisdiction in Hong Kong and the local authorities were hamstrung by the difficulty of getting Chinese businessmen to come forward and admit they had been fleeced. Chinese culture dictates that it is important to save face and not to compromise family honour, so victims of the entrepreneurial scam have swallowed their pride and kept their mouths shut. Moreover, those who have reported haven't had much sympathy from Hong Kong authorities, who harbour a deep disdain for those who are able to buy their way off the island. "Our attitude is *caveat emptor*," said one high-ranking Hong Kong justice official. "You get what you pay for. But if we should ever happen to get a complaint of a suspected case of fraud, of course we'll investigate it." Even though they can do very little to keep the Canadian shysters off the island, the Canadian High Commission does keep its collective eye open for blatantly misleading ads in local newspapers, and when one appears a telephone call is made to the newspaper to set the record straight. An ad placed by a Vancouver lawyer simply stated that anyone with $500,000 can get into Canada as an entrepreneur.

In the busy lobby of a posh hotel on the Kowloon side of Hong Kong, a Vancouver immigration lawyer shook hands with a Chinese businessman and invited him up to his suite. In fact, Paul Poon wasn't really a businessman. He was a plant sent by a news reporter to find out what the lawyer meant by an advertisement he had placed in a local newspaper. The ad noted that the lawyer would be in the city on a particular week and would be seeing potential clients interested in immigrating to Canada. Mr. Poon told the lawyer that he was an intermediary for a very wealthy and extremely busy Chinese clothing manufacturer. The lawyer began to deliver his well-rehearsed spiel but quickly noticed that Mr. Poon wasn't paying close attention. "My honourable friend wants to be assured that his family can immigrate to your country," Mr. Poon interjected in a calm, detached tone. "He has too much business here right now and cannot leave Hong Kong. Do you understand?" The lawyer nodded and smiled. "I can prepare him a fantastic business proposal that will guarantee he will be accepted as a landed immigrant. But it will take a little time and it will take a certain sum of money."

"That is understood. How much money?" Mr. Poon asked.

"To start with I will need $15,000 to begin the paperwork and set up the procedure. After the interview is completed with our Canadian immigration people, I will require another $15,000, and when your friend and his family get their papers, I will require a final payment of $15,000," the lawyer explained.

"The money will be no problem for my honourable friend but he will need some assurances," Mr. Poon said.

"I'll guarantee he'll get into Canada. There will be no problem. I have the connections and I know the game," the lawyer
promised.

Back in Canada, government politicians and bureaucrats
grudgingly admit that there has been "some" abuse of the
program but they prefer to dwell on its positive aspects: the
money that has been invested in Canada and the jobs that
have been created. In separate interviews in late 1985, junior
Immigration Minister Walter McLean and Tory MP Jim
Hawkes, chairman of the Parliamentary Standing Committee on Labour, Employment and Immigration, boasted that
the program had a 77 per cent success rate, noting that the
numbers were confirmed in a very recent analysis of the
program. Immigration officials, however, refused to release
the study. "It is not for public consumption," Kirk Bell, director general of policy and program development for the Immigration Department, said flatly.

Nonetheless, a copy was obtained by the *Globe and Mail*.
The preamble noted that in May, 1985, Gaétan Lussier, deputy minister and chairman of the Canada Employment and
Immmigration Commission, initiated an "enquiry" into the
validity of claims about the amount of capital being invested
in Canada by entrepreneurs and the number of jobs being
created by the program. "It became clear from the enquiry
that there exists no systematic tracking capability and that,
on the whole, there is inadequate information on what happens to all entrepreneurs admitted to Canada," the confidential government report said. Furthermore, a quick analysis of
the monitoring efforts made by federal and provincial
authorities throughout Canada found stark inconsistencies,
with the most notable gaps existing in the major receiving
provinces of Quebec and British Columbia. The report concluded that the economic benefits attributed to the Entrepreneur Program "are based solely on declared intentions of the
successful applicants."

As a result, the department launched an intensive survey

over the summer and autumn months in hopes of getting a more comprehensive portrait of the program's effectiveness. The survey was set up to look at success, failure or abuse. Entrepreneurs were judged to be successful if they complied with the minimum requirements of the program and their business venture was a viable concern. Failures were those entrepreneurs who had established a business that was not at a break-even point after two years. Abusers were those who had established a business but not fulfilled prescribed employment and management standards. There was no category for those who did not even bother to establish a business.

The first hint that the program was in trouble came when a large block of entrepreneur immigrants could not even be located from the randomly selected sample of 1,056 case files. In the preliminary run-through, immigration officials could not find 395 of them. Of the 661 who were located, another 308 entrepreneurs did not take part in the survey because they were either away or simply refused to discuss their activities in Canada. In all only 353 entrepreneurs across Canada, or 18.8 per cent of the original number, were questioned, and from that group, the Immigration Department concluded that the program had a 77 per cent success rating. Several immigration officers in Toronto, Montreal and Vancouver later said the results confirmed their suspicions that many of the so-called entrepreneurs had no intention of ever starting a viable business concern in Canada and that their original business proposals were fictitious from the start. "The problem is that the people running the show in Ottawa don't want to hear about the problems because this is their pride and joy," a manager in Montreal said. "We don't know where most of these entrepreneurs are. They don't report to us and we don't do any serious follow-up work. It's a big joke." The survey also found that 40 per cent of those questioned, having previously stated their intention to establish themselves in the manufacturing sector, had switched to the retail or service sectors. This confirmed another suspicion held by immigration officers that many entrepreneurs who had stated in their applications that they would inject hundreds of thousands of dollars into the more job-intensive manufacturing industry later chose to invest the least amount of capital into "hole in the wall" retail and service outlets.

Not aware at first that the *Globe and Mail* had obtained a copy of the confidential study, Mr. McLean and senior officials in the Immigration Department sat down once again in late December to discuss the Entrepreneur Program with the author. They began by proudly citing the 77 per cent success rate. However, Mr. McLean appeared somewhat uneasy and admitted that he was surprised that the rate was so high. When asked how the success rate was reached, given that roughly 40 per cent of the entrepreneurs could not be found in the original random sample and that 308 people from the remaining 661 did not take part, Mr. McLean sheepishly replied: "Good question. I just got the first quasi-executive summary of the study and just had a preliminary briefing on the whole survey. . . ." Obviously annoyed, he tossed the question to Kirk Bell, who vehemently defended the results and conclusions of the survey. "They are statistically valid. Statistically, you can give a 77 per cent success rate across the board." Mr. Bell maintained that there was no reason to believe those who could not be found or who did not respond were more or less successful than those who had participated in the study. "They are to be considered the same. There is no reason, statistically, to believe otherwise." Yet the study itself concluded that "one must always be concerned with the potential bias that could be introduced as a result of systematic differences between those who respond and those who do not." It also pointed out that an extensive follow-up to locate all entrepreneurial immigrants would be "too costly, complex and time-consuming to pursue." It is not surprising that the survey had so few respondents when it was revealed that entrepreneurial application forms filed at the department's regional offices did not bother, in all cases, to record the intended address of the person at the time of landing or admission, nor were they updated to reflect changes of address as the person moved.

The study also pointed to "notable monitoring gaps" in Quebec. In several interviews with provincial and federal officials involved with the program, many mentioned that Quebec, which selects its own entrepreneurs but still has to get final approval from Ottawa, employed far less stringent criteria in assessing applicants. Several officials said that dozens of entrepreneurs who are selected each year by the Quebec government would never be accepted by the federal government on the basis of their application. They also noted that many of the Quebec-bound entrepreneurs simply hopped another airplane when they arrived at Montreal's Mirabel International Airport and went on to Ontario, Alberta or British Columbia. Renald Joubarne, a counsellor for the Entrepreneur Program in Quebec, has hotly defended Quebec's handling of entrepreneur applications and raved about a 75 per cent success rate. He also admitted that only 30 per cent of the entrepreneurs selected by the province ever show up in his office. Asked where the other 70 per cent are, Mr. Joubarne replied: "We don't know exactly where they are or how they are doing."

Somewhat red-faced over the public revelations of the program's poor monitoring, Mr. McLean announced that beginning in January, 1986, the Immigration Department would implement stricter controls. All entrepreneur newcomers would be granted conditional admission with a two-year period during which immigrant businessmen would have to realize their business ventures. He conceded that the new admission standard came about in part from the *Globe and Mail* investigation, and in part from the confidential study, which found that 90 per cent of the entrepreneurs who had had conditions attached to their entry went on to successfully establish businesses in Canada. In making the announcement, the minister said that virtually every entrepreneur would be placed on a conditional visa. Only a few exceptions would be made, for those with serious proposals that were already in place and ready to go.

A full year later, immigration statistics revealed that conditional visas were imposed on only about 30 per cent of the approximately 2,500 entrepreneurs approved in 1986. The rest continued to come in as landed immigrants. Admitted one Toronto lawyer in an interview in February, 1987, "I recently had two Hong Kong businessmen clients in my office asking me if they were required to do what they had indicated on their entrepreneur applications. They showed me a letter from the Immigration Department which outlined the terms of their conditions. However, the visas in their possession granted them landed-immigrant status and mentioned nothing about conditions. I told them that they were now landed immigrants and that legally there was nothing to compel them to live up to their end of the bargain. They thanked me and informed me that they weren't going to bother with their original business plan."

Despite the glaring lack of control, monitoring and follow-up, immigration officials continued to swear by the program. In November, 1986, they set the business immigrant quota at 4,000 for 1987, the same level as for the previous year. Crowed Minister of State for Immigration Gerry Weiner in *Maclean's* magazine: "We need people with a vision to help stoke our economy. It makes your mouth water when you know how many jobs immigrants create."

In January, 1986, the Conservative government introduced a new twist to the business immigrant program, the Investor Program, aimed primarily at even wealthier foreigners than those eligible for the entrepreneur scheme. Investors are described as persons who have a proven track record in business and have "a personal net worth of $500,000 or more." In order to qualify for immigration purposes, investors are required to commit, for a minimum period of three years, at least $250,000 to an investment project or venture which will contribute to business development and job creation. Unlike the Entrepreneur Program, which requires hands-on management skills, this new category allows immigrants to leave the work of managing their money in the hands of investment syndicates and others. Critics argued that the Investor Program was tantamount to selling Canadian citizenship with the rich being the only eligible buyers. They said that both the Investor and Entrepreneur Programs lack humanitarian concern, especially when there are so many deserving people that Canada should help.

Within months, several investor syndicates, mostly in Alberta and British Columbia, sprang up. Promoters began winging their way to Hong Kong to woo rich Chinese businessmen eager to get their hands on a Canadian passport. What bothered many immigration lawyers in Canada was that the promoters were failing to point out that the investor scheme was a high-risk venture. The $250,000 investment would be earmarked for projects assessed by each province as being of significant benefit to its economy and contributing to job creation for Canadians. Return on investment was not the first criterion in determining where the funds were placed. Like the Entrepreneur Program, the Investor Program is not closely monitored by either the federal or provincial governments. The syndicates are approved by the provinces, which, critics said, have not bothered to examine in detail how the funds will be managed.

Ultimately, of course, the decision whether to put up the $250,000 lies with the investors, and it is up to them to decide whether a Canadian passport is worth the financial risk. Because the program is recent, none of the syndicates has had time to establish a track record of success or failure. It is likely that a number of the well-managed syndicates will do well, but there is concern that some may run into serious difficulties.

The Entrepreneur and Investor Programs represent only a small portion of the total immigration to Canada, and if handled responsibly, they could prove to be a tremendous benefit to Canadians and new immigrants alike. The major problem with both programs is that they lack any meaningful and effective control. It is senseless and certainly misleading for immigration ministers and officials to tout figures each year when no one knows for sure just what is happening. For example, the Parliamentary Standing Committee on Labour, Employment and Immigration was told on December 4, 1986, that 1,259 entrepreneurs were issued visas in the first nine months of 1986. They declared a net worth of almost a billion dollars and they intended to create or retain 8,331 jobs in Canada. The fact remains that the department's lackadaisical approach makes these figures meaningless. The only thing that Canadians will know with any degree of certainty is the number of immigrants who have been selected: just what they do when they get here is anyone's guess.

In an interview on February 25, 1987, Kirk Bell, director general of policy and program development, was asked whether an entrepreneur had ever been deported for not fulfilling the terms of his entry into Canada. Under the Immigration Act a person is not guaranteed the right to remain in the country simply because he has been granted landed-immigrant status. He can lose this status. For those "unconditionally landed," the most common reasons for revoking a landing are committing a criminal offence and obtaining landed status by misrepresentation. Mr. Bell said misrepresentation involves serious offences such as getting landed status through false or forged documents. "It doesn't apply in the case of an entrepreneur who said he would open a high-tech factory and instead set up a candy store when he got here. That's not what is meant by misrepresentation." He argued that whether an entrepreneur set up the business he said he would or not is a moot point. "The point is they set up something else. They did something, got into something. It's not like they went on welfare. It isn't like they ripped us off. They went to work."

Mr. Bell's confidence notwithstanding, this serious flaw in what otherwise could be a dynamic and stimulating program lends considerable weight to the critics who argue that Canada is selling passports to the carriage trade, while ordinary immigrants are forced to wait years to find out whether they've been selected in the Canadian immigration lottery sweepstakes.

14 POLITICAL PREROGATIVE

FRED DARVIN, A CANADIAN VETERAN OF THE Second World War, wanted to come back to Canada from his home in Florida to live out his last years. As a young and proud Canadian, Mr. Darvin had joined the Essex Scottish Regiment and gone overseas. On August 19, 1942, his regiment took part in one of the bloodiest and most disastrous battles of the war, the Dieppe raid. One of almost 2,000 soldiers captured by the Germans, he spent the next three and a half years in a prison camp. A native of Manitoba, Mr. Darvin first moved to Windsor, Ontario, as a youth. After he left the army in 1945, he returned to Windsor where he worked briefly for Chrysler Canada Ltd. He was laid off after six months but soon found a job in Detroit in a tool-and-die shop. Mr. Darvin became a U.S. citizen and raised a family. In 1960, he moved to Fort Lauderdale, Florida, for the benefit of his two sons, who had muscular dystrophy. "The doctor told us they would live a little longer if we moved to a warmer climate," he recounted. The older boy died at 21, the second at 17. His daughter, who is married, still lives in Florida.

In 1983, Mr. Darvin develped circulation problems in his left leg. He had four operations on his arteries, and when it appeared that the problem was not getting better, he and his wife, Madeleine, decided to return to Canada. As a veteran, Mr. Darvin's medical treatment in Canada is paid for by the Department of Veterans' Affairs. The couple moved to Windsor in June, 1984, and Mr. Darvin, then 69 years old, checked into Windsor Western Hospital for yet another bypass operation. His leg was amputated shortly afterwards, because gangrene had set in.

The Darvins applied for landed-immigrant status from within Canada, thinking that the procedure would be straightforward. "I'm self-supporting. I get $564 [U.S.] a month in social security and $286 a month from the Department of Veterans' Affairs because I was a prisoner of war. So I can pay my own way," Mr. Darvin said. But the Immigration Department turned down his application because of "medical inadmissibility," citing a section in the Immigration Act which states that people with medical conditions likely to cause "excessive demands" on health and social services are inadmissible.

Ed Slater, director of service for the Dominion Command of the Royal Canadian Legion in Ottawa, took on Mr. Darvin's case, arguing repeatedly with immigration officials that the veteran would not be a drain on health services because he is entitled to "certain rights because he served his country during the Second World War. He's a veteran!" Mr. Slater got no concrete response to his pleas.

On September 4, 1986, Veterans' Affairs Minister George Hees wrote Employment and Immigration Minister Flora MacDonald asking that Mr. Darvin be allowed to remain in Canada. A month later, an assistant to Ms MacDonald wrote that after having "carefully and sympathetically" reviewed the case, "we are unable to identify sufficient grounds which warrant" issuing a minister's permit allowing Mr. Darvin to stay in the country. Seething with anger, Mr. Slater recounted that he was absolutely convinced that Ms MacDonald would personally look favourably on the request. "After all, this man fought for his country and he was a POW, and if he was good enough to fight for Canada, then we should welcome him back."

The *Globe and Mail* looked into the Darvin case in late November, 1985. A call to Ms MacDonald's office was not answered but a spokesman for the Immigration Department, Len Westerberg, pointed out that Mr. Darvin had given up his Canadian citizenship and would be treated no differently than any other foreigner wanting to immigrate to Canada. "He has to meet the requirements of the Immigration Act. His case has been reviewed right up to the minister's office and he's medically inadmissible and there are no extenuating circumstances that will change that."

The following morning, a front-page story in the *Globe and Mail* about Mr. Darvin's plight triggered a tremendous public outcry. Right across Canada, irate veterans, tearful veterans' widows and ordinary Canadians jammed the phone lines to the minister's office and the *Globe* to vent their outrage. Telexes and telegrams began to pour into the offices of Ottawa MPs. Embarrassed and visibly shaken, Ms MacDonald ordered a hurried review of the case, saying she had only become aware of Mr. Darvin's situation through the *Globe* story. "I can tell you that it's a case that was never brought to my attention," she told reporters in Ottawa. Yet although Ms MacDonald said she was not officially aware of the case earlier, Veterans' Affairs Minister George Hees had written her twice, on June 7 and September 4, 1985, to plead on Mr. Darvin's behalf. An aide to Mr. Hees said he did not know if Ms MacDonald ever actually read the letters.

In mid-afternoon, Ms MacDonald's press aide issued a statement: "The minister has made a decision. She has asked her officials to issue a [minister's] permit. [Mr. Darvin] will not be forced to leave the country."

According to secret documents in the possession of senior immigration officials, a man named Abraham Finkel had an extensive criminal record involving more than 20 run-ins with the law in Belgium, West Germany and Israel. One alleged conviction for highway robbery with violence earned Mr. Finkel a five-year sentence in a Belgian jail in 1956. That alone would ordinarily have made him ineligible for permanent-resident status in Canada. Under the Immigration Act, an individual who has been convicted of a crime that carries a maximum life sentence is inadmissible to Canada. However, the Act also provides for the granting of relief by the Cabinet or by the minister if either is satisfied that the person concerned is rehabilitated.

In 1979 a man named Abraham Finkel, an independently wealthy Israeli, his wife and teenage son were permitted to come to Canada from the United States in 1979 while Mr. Finkel's application to enter Canada as an entrepreneur was being processed at the Canadian visa office in Boston. The application was subsequently refused when the department learned of the applicant's alleged criminal past during a routine security check. However, Mr. Finkel refused to leave Canada, fiercely denying he had ever been convicted of any crime. He hired Montreal lawyer Robert Eidinger and began a long and bitter battle to remain in the country.

In a memorandum dated September 26, 1984, Gaétan Lussier, deputy minister of employment and immigration, said the refusal of Mr. Finkel's application was based on Interpol information supplied by the Royal Canadian Mounted Police, citing a series of warrants, arrests and convictions in Belgium, West Germany and Israel from 1956 to 1974. "Many incidents in this lengthy series are relatively minor; however, the list includes assault and robbery in Belgium and cheque-related offences in Israel involving a large amount of money."

For seven years, three immigration ministers — first John Roberts and subsequently Flora MacDonald and Walter McLean — refused to countermand the advice of their senior officials who recommended that Mr. Finkel not be allowed to become a landed immigrant, and that he should be deported from the country. Meanwhile, Gerry Weiner, then a backbench Conservative MP from Montreal's West Island, began making representations in 1985 and early in 1986 to Ms MacDonald and later to Mr. McLean to issue Mr. Finkel a minister's permit to allow him to remain legally in Canada, and to initiate the procedures to grant him permanent-resident status. Mr. Weiner had the support of several prominent leaders of Montreal's Jewish community who firmly believed that Mr. Finkel, a survivor of the Nazi death camps, was the victim of mistaken identity. Yet both Tory immigration ministers held fast. Ms MacDonald went so far as to show Mr. Weiner immigration files classified as secret to convince him that the department had the goods on Mr. Finkel, including fingerprints provided by the applicant to the RCMP which were said to match those of an individual named Abraham Finkel who had served time in a Belgian prison for robbery and assault in the mid-1950s.

On June 30, 1986, Mr. Weiner was appointed minister of state for immigration. One of his first official acts was to call Mr. Finkel to his Ottawa office and issue him a minister's permit as the initial step toward landed-immigrant status — despite a memo stamped secret and dated July 14, 1986, from Mr. Lussier, who dutifully informed the new minister that Mr. Finkel "has been convicted of offences which make him inadmissible under the Immigration Act." Mr. Lussier also recommended against favourable disposition of the case, pointing out to Mr. Weiner that the man "still refuses to admit to these convictions," and therefore "we cannot seek the necessary approval from your [Cabinet] colleagues because, in criminal cases, there must be evidence of rehabilitation."

During a meeting at Mr. Weiner's Ottawa office in August, 1986, Mr. Finkel provided the minister's political staff with the prerequisite letter of rehabilitation to start the landing process. In an interview in early April, 1987, Mr. Finkel admitted that Mr. Weiner's advisors did not like the wording, changed it and had it retyped, and he signed it. "But I never signed anything that said I am a criminal. I am not a criminal." The letter, he said, simply acknowledged that he is the man "referred to in the Belgian documents." He was immediately issued a minister's permit and the landing process was put in the works.

When the *Globe and Mail* learned of Mr. Weiner's decision in early November, 1986, the subsequent front-page story raised questions about the handling of the case, in particular the involvement of the minister of state for immigration. In a terse interview, Mr. Weiner huffed that while he valued the advice and guidance of his senior officials, he had acted in accordance with the terms of the Immigration Act in this case. He admitted that when he was a backbench MP for two years he had made representations on Mr. Finkel's behalf to Ms MacDonald and Mr. McLean. Asked whether there might not be a conflict of interest in his handling of the case now that he was minister of state for immigration, Mr. Weiner shot back: "I am the minister now. I make the decisions. I have that mandate. I based the decision on my own review of the case. And let me tell you, I did a complete and exhaustive review of this case."

The minister was reminded that for the first seven years while Mr. Finkel was in Canada, he had refused to admit that he was the man referred to in Interpol files in the possession of the department. He had hotly denied any criminal record and maintained that it was a case of mistaken identity. Did the department have the wrong man all along? Mr. Weiner countered that Mr. Finkel had made certain revelations "of a confidential and personal nature to the department. As a result of those revelations, I was pleased to recommend to Cabinet that the appropriate order-in-council be issued all in accordance with the terms of the Immigration Act." Mr. Weiner noted that the revelations, which he would not divulge, had not been made to the other immigration ministers.

Under heated questioning by Liberal Immigration critic Sergio Marchi, Mr. Weiner defended his decision in the House of Commons, arguing that his predecessors were faced with "a technical obstacle," in that Mr. Finkel had refused to admit his criminal past. The minister said the obstacle was removed when Mr. Finkel admitted that "he was the man in the convictions." In an aside, he noted that Mr. Finkel "has no criminal convictions" in Canada. Astounded by the response, Mr. Marchi called Mr. Weiner's decision "outrageous," especially when it "goes against his own departmental advice and the position taken by three former immigration ministers." Mr. Marchi also described the minister's explanation as nothing short of "a slap in the face to the thousands of legitimate immigrants who can't get into this country and it makes a mockery of the process. Why does an individual with over 20 criminal convictions get awarded special admission into this country when thousands of Canadians cannot even be reunited with their family members abroad?"

The case was immediately transferred to Employment and Immigration Minister Benoît Bouchard, the senior immigration minister, who said that he would make the final decision about the rehabilitation of Abraham Finkel. Then in a bizarre move, Gaétan Lussier, who had for years steadfastly recommended against accepting Mr. Finkel, abruptly reversed his decision in a secret memo to Mr. Bouchard in late November, 1986. Pointing out that although Mr. Finkel has "always steadfastly denied that he was, in fact, tried or convicted in Belgium, he has admitted that he is the person referred to in the Belgian document [describing the convictions in Belgium] and we have his fingerprints identifying him as the person so described." Mr. Lussier suggested that Mr. Finkel should be considered rehabilitated. At the start of May, 1987, Mr. Bouchard had yet to make a decision on the case.

In reaction to seeing his name published for the first time in a subsequent front-page story in the *Globe* on March 27, 1987, Mr. Finkel surfaced to argue his side of the story in public. In several conversations with the author in early April, Mr. Finkel reiterated that he had never been convicted of any crime and has never been in jail. "I have never been convicted of a crime in my life. The Immigration Department does not have one shred of proof that I have been convicted of any crimes. I have asked them to show me proof, to show me the documents of conviction. They have not been able to do so because these documents do not exist," he charged. "No official document or judgement exists that I have ever been convicted of any crime in any country. And I tell you now that if they can show me a *valid* document that [proves] I have been convicted of a crime, then I will leave Canada immediately." Asked why he signed the letter of rehabilitation, he shot back, "For my wife, for my son. I saw what this seven years had done to them. I wanted it to end for their sake, not mine. I was prepared to fight this through the courts."

Mr. Finkel said his problems started soon after he arrived in Montreal in 1979 when certain immigration officials tried to blackmail him. "They said it would cost me $50,000 to buy the papers for me and my family. I refused and this is when my troubles began." He refused to go into any detail about the blackmail attempt except to say that he can prove it. He also produced documents from the governments of Israel and West Germany that he said support his story. A document from the consulate general of Israel dated June 1, 1983, says that Mr. Finkel entered Israel in 1948 and became a citizen according to the Law of Return. "Since 1948, Mr. Finkel was never detained in Israel, nor sent to prison for any reason whatsoever," Vice-Consul Tamar Samash wrote. "I wish to emphasize that a person having a criminal record cannot obtain a police certificate from the Israeli police." The consulate general of the Federal Republic of Germany wrote on January 14, 1984, that the West German government had issued Mr. Finkel, at his request, a certificate of good conduct on February 12, 1982. "According and referring to this certificate . . . there were, on the date of issue, no police records kept on Mr. Finkel." Mr. Lussier had pointed out in his memorandum of September 26, 1984, that although Mr. Finkel has produced certificates of good conduct from Israel and West Germany, "it should be noted . . . that restrictions imposed by laws governing the release of criminal information in these two countries diminish the value of such documents."

During conversations in April, 1987, Mr. Finkel recounted an incident in Belgium that he felt might be at the root of his difficulties with the Immigration Department. He said that when he applied at the Canadian consulate in Boston in 1979, he informed officials there that he had been involved in a fracas in Belgium in the early 1950s but was never charged. He said that after the Second World War, he collaborated with a group of Israelis who hunted *capos* — Jews who had collaborated with the Nazis. In 1952, he said, his group attacked a former capo on a highway in Belgium late one night. The capo, whom Mr. Finkel identified as Albert Marian, was a prominent politician. "The police found him on the road with his car damaged. He said robbers beat him up and he identified me because he knows me from the concentration camps. He pressed charges, but we called him up and told him we would tell the real story so he withdrew the charges. I'm proud of this. I'm proud of what I did to this man," Mr. Finkel said.

He then asked angrily why immigration authorities allowed him to remain in Canada for eight years if he were "such a super criminal." He wondered why information about his case was leaked to the *Globe* shortly after Mr. Weiner had rendered his decision. "It was because Mr. Weiner is a Jew who was helping a Jew. Why for seven years was my case never exposed and then it suddenly appears in the *Globe?* Mr. Weiner took a decision because three other ministers did not have the courage or the decency to make a decision on my case. Mr. Weiner saw a man, his wife and son suffering, being tortured because no one had the guts to make a decision. He took the step and now he has been attacked for being a good human being."

When confronted with Mr. Finkel's story, Joe Bissett, executive director of the Immigration Department, said flatly, "We have the proof. I've got the official Belgian certificate of conviction. Fingerprints and all . . . Finkel [was] convicted of armed robbery at night on the highway." Mr. Bissett also noted that Mr. Finkel admitted that he was convicted in the letter of rehabilitation. "He may have told you that he did it under duress. It wasn't under duress at all. He had the choice of whether to sign it or not."

In an interview on May 5, 1987, Mr. Bouchard conceded that he was troubled by the case. Although he would not reveal then what his decision would be, his comments indicated he would grant the man landed-immigrant status. The minister cited several reasons. Mr. Finkel had been in the country eight years and had never been in trouble with the law. More importantly, he stressed, three immigration ministers had been involved in the case. Mr. Bouchard admitted they should never have allowed it to drag on for so long. They could have, and should have, made a decision. "How can I tell the man now to leave after eight years?" But the key factor in his decision, Mr. Bouchard said, was that the alleged crime was committed more than 30 years ago.

Every working day of every week, the immigration minister is bombarded with pleas to intervene in cases that have received a negative decision from immigration officers, supervisors, managers and senior departmental officials. The immigration minister is buttonholed by Members of Parliament in the House of Commons during question period and in caucus. MPs of every political stripe phone him urging his personal intervention to see that a particular individual or family is not deported by seemingly heartless bureaucrats. The minister also receives registered letters and urgent Telexes from lawyers, immigration consultants, church leaders, aldermen, employers, friends and family on behalf of people who want to remain in the country or who are having trouble immigrating from abroad.

With the stroke of a pen, the immigration minister has the power to change the entire direction of a case by issuing a minister's permit — even if he has received strong recommendations from his top officials not to waive normal procedure in a particular case. Section 37-1 of the Immigration Act provides that "the Minister may issue a written permit authorizing any person to come into or remain in Canada. . . ." This provision grants the minister legal authority to exercise a discretion that overrides the ordinary application of the law and regulations that would otherwise operate to exclude an individual from Canada. This discretionary power can be viewed as a useful tool to temper the rigid nature of written rules, which can never take into account all the circumstances that can arise in a given case. On the other hand, the minister's permit may also be viewed as the very antithesis of the principle of the rule of law, with the potential for unbridled arbitrariness and sheer exploitation for political gain. In other words, anyone with the right political connections and, even more, anyone who runs to the press and manages to get his heart-wrenching story published, gets a minister's permit. It can also be used as an influential weapon in a politician's arsenal when currying the favour of a particular bloc of ethnic voters.

In September, 1986, Tory backbench MP Andrew Witer, who represents the strongly ethnic Toronto riding of High Park-Swansea, reflected on the political power and force of minister's permits. In a confidential report to the Metropolitan Toronto Tory caucus, Mr. Witer unabashedly recommended that the immigration minister take full control of the issuing of minister's permits for what can only be interpreted as crass political gain. He noted that of the more than 6,500 minister's permits issued in the Ontario region in 1985, "only ten per cent were issued by the minister's office, the balance being issued by visa officers, Canada Immigration Centres and departmental staff. The political ramification of ministerial permits is obviously being allowed to fall by the wayside," Mr. Witer noted.

He went on to argue that the Progressive Conservative Party's immigration policy, although "positive and substantive," was not being fully communicated to the public. It is "political common sense that the minister's office gain control over the issuing of all minister's permits, rather than allowing politically non-aligned bureaucrats free rein with 90 per cent of them," he stressed. Mr. Witer recommended to his Metro Tory colleagues that the minister's office be the sole source of minister's permits. That way, ethnic voters would know where to go when they need a favour and would remember on election day who had helped them.

In a detailed report in June, 1983, entitled *Illegal Migrants in Canada*, W. Gerry Robinson, special advisor to Immigration Minister Lloyd Axworthy, wrote: "A regime which recognizes no rights in law but only permits privileges to be granted through the generosity of its officials does not conform to the principles of law. But a regime whose legal rules are so detailed and inflexible that they produce frequent anomalies and inequities will soon lose the respect of its citizens, which is the very foundation of the continued existence of the rule of law." It was obvious, Mr. Robinson pointed out, that a balance must be struck. The Immigration Act recognizes that there may be a need for the immigration minister to temper the strict application of the law and its regulations with individual judgement in specific cases.

Section 123 of the Act, with certain exceptions, provides that the minister may authorize such persons in the public service of Canada as he deems proper to exercise and perform any of the powers, duties and functions that may be or are required to be exercised by him under the Act. But any discussion of ministerial discretion must be considered in two distinct parts. The first concerns the issuing of minister's permits by senior immigration officials as delegated by the minister. The second involves cases where the minister responds to a request for personal intervention.

Each year thousands of minister's permits, which are valid for a period not exceeding 12 months and are renewable, are issued. The vast majority of decisions on the issuing of minister's permits are made by senior immigration officials under guidelines established by the department. Most of the cases are straightforward, involving, for example, a foreign university student who doesn't show up for a scheduled appointment with an immigration officer to renew his student visa allowing him to remain legally in Canada. The student may have forgotten about the appointment, or had a crucial exam that day, or fallen ill. The law states that once his visa has expired, he is illegally in Canada and he cannot renew the visa from inside the country. A minister's permit is the one piece of paper that will allow him to remain here legally and continue his studies. Otherwise, the student would be required to return home and reapply for a visa, a costly, time-consuming and absurd venture. Decisions such as this should not waste the valuable time of a minister of the

Crown. A public servant can simply issue the permit in the minister's name. Another major group that benefits from the issuance of minister's permits is people arriving in Canada claiming to be refugees. It can take several years before a refugee case is completed. In the interim, claimants are issued minister's permits allowing them to remain in the country and to work.

There are, however, decisions that are not always so easy to make and they are the ones most likely to come to the minister's office for review. Moreover, if the case has any hint of a political backlash, then it is certain to end up on the minister's desk. Sometimes a particular case demands the minister's intervention because of the arbitrariness and rigidity of some immigration officers and their managers. From the local immigration offices up through regional and national headquarters, there appears to be a strong management aversion to overrule the decisions of front-line officers, no matter how unfair or seemingly senseless. When family members, community groups and leaders, lawyers or politicians start questioning the rationale behind an immigration officer's decision, there is a tendency for the department to circle the wagons. Often immigration officials will hide under the cloak of anonymity, stating they are not permitted to discuss individual cases even though the person in question has gone to the press to plead his case in public.

In early January, 1987, a woman who had worked in Canada as a domestic for four years, saved $10,000, and had taken night courses, was ordered to leave the country because she was informed by immigration officials that she did "not have the initiative or resourcefulness" to be a permanent resident. Thirty-four-year-old Cecilia Changoo could not understand how immigration officials had arrived at their decision. Ms Changoo, whose common-law husband died in April, 1985, supported two daughters in St. Lucia. She entered Canada legally as a live-in domestic worker on November 27, 1982, and worked two years for one family and then two years for another. During this time, she saved her earnings and upgraded her education, successfully completing courses in accounting, word processing, hairdressing and nurse's aide training. Under the Immigration Department's Foreign Domestic Program, she was entitled to apply for permanent residence after demonstrating an ability to establish herself in Canada. Ms Changoo applied and was flatly rejected by immigration officials in Toronto in March, 1985, because, they ruled, she "had not demonstrated evidence for successful establishment in Canada."

Ms Changoo told the author that she had "no indication during the assessment that anything was wrong. I was told nothing. I was very much surprised when I got the letter. I did my best and everything I was supposed to" to qualify under the landing provisions of the Foreign Domestic Program. She then hired Sukhram Ramkissoon, a paralegal who specializes in immigration matters. Mr. Ramkissoon decided to wait a full year before asking the immigration minister to reconsider her case because he wanted to give his client an opportunity to establish herself more firmly. During that time, Ms Changoo saved more money and continued upgrading her qualifications at night school. In May, 1986, Mr. Ramkissoon received a letter from the office of Walter McLean, minister of state for immigration, saying a review had been carried out and it was found that Ms Changoo "did not demonstrate the adaptability, motivation, initiative or resourcefulness for establishment in Canada." She was advised to begin preparing to leave the country by mid-January, 1987.

Frustrated, Mr. Ramkissoon approached the *Globe and Mail* with his client to publicize the case. He noted that when Ms Changoo was selected abroad as a domestic, "she was assessed for her potential as an immigrant and she passed that assessment." He noted that people who enter Canada illegally and live underground for a period of three years or more are granted permanent status under much more relaxed selection criteria than those applied to his client. "And these people broke the law, lied and cheated to get into the country. Ms Changoo came here legally and worked very, very hard for four years only to be told that she didn't demon-

strate the adaptability, motivation, initiative or resourcefulness to establish herself here. I find that hard to accept. If my
client had exercised deceit by saying she was a refugee, she
would have been accepted now as a landed immigrant.
Where is the justice?" Mr. Ramkissoon asked.

Len Westerberg, a spokesman for junior Immigration Minister Gerry Weiner, said shortly after being called about the
case that the minister had directed the department to stay
any departure notice until Mr. Weiner had "an opportunity
to personally review the case." In early April, 1987, Mr.
Ramkissoon received a letter from Mr. Weiner's office stating
that the minister had "decided that favourable consideration
of her application is warranted." A minister's permit was
issued and processing for landed-immigrant status was
begun.

There are both positive and negative features to direct ministerial involvement in the exercise of discretionary power in
specific cases. On the one hand, it may have beneficial and
humane repercussions throughout the often bureaucratic
administration of our immigration law and policy. The minister's involvement can also provide informal guidance to officials in dealing with future cases and, more formally, in the
revision of immigration procedures and guidelines.

However, as special immigration advisor W. G. Robinson
pointed out in his report, a number of potential minefields
surround the minister's exercise of discretion in specific
cases. "By considering cases in isolation, the minister may
not be aware of a potential ripple effect on other similar cases.
Serious inroads may be made on general enforcement if individual cases are decided without regard for a great number of
identical cases which are being treated differently. Expectations which cannot realistically be met might be created
amongst other applicants." Mr. Robinson also argued that
there is a very real danger that the public will come to view
immigration decision-making as being significantly dependent on "who you know" rather than on individual merit. "If
public reaction is too influential upon decision-making,
applicants may come to view a successful public relations

campaign as the route to a successful determination of a case."

The overriding concern here is that if too many cases come to the minister's office, he or she will have to rely to a considerable degree upon political aides, who may not always be in the best position to weigh the effect a decision can have on immigration policy and regulations. For those especially tough and delicate cases, special care and attention must be taken to ensure that the fairest decision is reached. That requires the personal attention of the minister. Often ministers have been questioned by reporters on a particularly controversial case, such as the Darvin incident, only to plead ignorance of the facts. They have no recollection of the case because they never handled it. They let their personal staff deal with it and their signature on the minister's permit is nothing more than a rubber-stamp approval.

In all of this, the minister must not lose sight of the impact his decisions have on the officials who have been involved in the specific case at its earlier stages. In recent years, their morale has been sorely tested by the constant and often questionable reversal of decisions at the ministerial level. By and large, immigration officers take their job seriously and apply the rules and regulations diligently. They come to resent seeing their conscientious enforcement of the letter of immigration law overriden by their political masters. Similarly, the Canadian public loses confidence in the immigration system when they hear or read of some of the incredible gaffes committed by immigration ministers in their political attempt to be seen as compassionate and caring in a patently undeserving case, or resolute and unyielding in a seemingly deserving case.

In mid-May, 1986, newspaper headlines across Canada informed Canadians that Walter McLean, minister of state for immigration, had signed a minister's permit ordering his officials to begin landing procedures for a Chilean couple and their two children. The couple, Fernando Alfonso

Naredo Arduengo and his wife, Nieves del Carmen San Martín Salazar Arduengo, were once members of an intelligence unit of a militarized police force in Chile that kidnapped, tortured and murdered civilians in that country.

Transcripts of hearings before the Immigration Appeal Board (IAB) showed that Mr. Arduengo, who said he was an unpaid civilian member of the dreaded DICAR (Dirección de Intelligencia de Carabineros), had admitted to being present at as many as ten murders. According to the conclusions of an Immigration Appeal Board decision dated April 11, 1985, Mr. Arduengo took part in "at least two dozen incidents of torture which he says were always commenced by use of electric devices. Sometimes these interrogations were augmented by placing a suspect's head under water or butting lighted cigarettes on the subject's body." The report also stated that Mr. Arduengo had said that "his whole team of four persons, including himself, participated in each of the incidents of torture, although he himself at no time applied any force to any of the detainees but merely acted as a guard or as a witness to statements made by detainees."

Mrs. Arduengo told the IAB hearing that she had joined DICAR as a uniformed constable in 1975. Less than a year later, she was promoted to the intelligence unit, where she worked under the alias Sylvia Alvarez until she resigned in April, 1977. The IAB report said her duties "consisted of participation in detentions, surveillances and interrogations of detainees. She was issued a revolver and handcuffs and often brandished the revolver while effecting an arrest. Her most important and frequently performed duty was clandestine surveillance." The report noted that Mrs. Arduengo said that "she never actually participated in the physical infliction of pain."

The Arduengos claimed refugee status shortly after arriving in Toronto in February, 1978. The couple had two hearings before the IAB, one in 1978 and, after an appeal to the Federal Court of Canada for a new hearing and a number of delays, the other in 1985. On both occasions the board flatly rejected their refugee claim. In April, 1985, the IAB said in its report that the Arduengos' fear of persecution should they be returned to Chile was not well founded and concluded that their departure "was substantially motivated by economic considerations and not fear of any kind of persecution."

After their first rejection in 1978, Barbara Jackman, the couple's lawyer, wrote to Employment and Immigration Minister John Roberts asking that he issue a minister's permit giving them landed-immigrant status. Mr. Roberts refused. On March 12, 1985, after the second IAB rejection, Ms Jackman wrote to Mr. McLean, asking him to intervene in the case. Ms Jackman, who has represented many Chilean refugees, said she had interviewed the couple extensively and concluded: "I really believe that they felt sick about their government's actions and they reached a point where their fear of what would happen to them by leaving the DICAR was overcome by their disgust with it." The lawyer said that after interviewing the Arduengos, she had approached several people she knew to be active in the Chilean Left in Toronto and discussed the case without identifying her clients. "They all agreed that I should represent the Arduengos and had the same view that I had that the Arduengos were victims of the system in Chile."

When news of Mr. McLean's decision to issue a minister's permit became public in May, 1986, and instructions were given to department staff to prepare the necessary paperwork to grant the Arduengos landed-immigrant status, several prominent leaders in Toronto's Chilean community expressed outrage and anger. None could recall discussing the case with Ms Jackman. Patricio Mason, a spokesman for the Chilean exile community in Toronto, said: "We are enraged that the Canadian government would give people who have inflicted torture a reprieve on humanitarian and compassionate grounds when victims of torture, who have been trying for years to get their claims as refugees accepted, are being treated without any compassion." Juan Nunez, a spokesman for the Toronto Chilean Society, described DICAR as "the most repressive organ of the Chilean police." Its

crimes of murder, kidnappings and torture are well documented by Amnesty International, the Catholic Church in
Chile, and several international human rights groups, he
said.

The National Coordinating Committee of the Chilean Left
and Exiles in Canada added its voice to the public outcry.
"After carefully reviewing immigration files on the case, . . .
we have found no reason to extend either pardon or defence
to these former members of the clandestine operations
department of the dreaded DICAR. The Chilean exile community in Canada, which continues to fight for an end to the
repugnant Pinochet dictatorship, finds it offensive that Canada should become a refuge for those responsible for political
torture and murder elsewhere."

Mr. McLean steered clear of commenting on the case, refer-
ring all inquiries to his aide, Françoise Guenette. Ms
Guenette said the minister's intervention in the case centred
on the fact that the Arduengos "had admitted what they had
done. They have rehabilitated. They are now in Canada and
have Canadian-born children and if we send them back, we'd
be putting all those lives in jeopardy." She also confirmed
that Progressive Conservative MPs Michael Wilson and
David Smith and Liberal MP Donald Johnston made representations on behalf of the Arduengos to Mr. McLean. In late
May, in response to a growing public backlash, Mr. McLean
suspended his decision until he could review the case more
fully. However, the government was now in a difficult bind.
They could not force the Arduengos to return to Chile
because they would almost certainly be arrested and possibly tortured. A Royal Canadian Mounted Police report on the
couple states that because of the "vast knowledge" the couple have of intelligence operations in Chile, they "would be
severely dealt with should they return."

In May, 1987, almost a year later, the Arduengo case was
still in a state of limbo.

15 ALL IN THE FAMILY

FAMILY REUNIFICATION HAS REPEATEDLY BEEN described as the "cornerstone of Canada's immigration policy." In political speeches, that phrase ranks close behind the cliché "Canada is a nation built by immigrants." It is true that family reunification is one of the stated objectives of Canadian immigration policy. The 1976 Immigration Act declares that Canadian immigration policy and the rules and regulations under the Act shall be designed and administered in such a manner as to "facilitate the reunion in Canada of Canadian citizens and permanent residents with their close relatives abroad."

Canadian immigration officials maintain that family reunification, along with the selection of refugees, is accorded the "highest processing priority" and in the years 1981 to 1987 it has accounted for between 40 per cent and 55 per cent of the total annual arrival of immigrants to Canada. Yet in recent years, immigrant-aid organizations have been slamming Ottawa's immigration policy, charging that it is keeping families apart for years and sometimes forever. In November, 1986, a coalition of more than 50 ethno-cultural groups gathered in Ottawa and told reporters at a press conference that the government continues to present "discriminatory and insurmountable obstacles to family reunification" in favour of wealthy business immigrants. Pat Marshall, a counsellor with Ottawa-Carleton Immigrant Services, described the use of the "cornerstone" phrase in a recent speech by junior

249

Immigration Minister Gerry Weiner as "no more than empty rhetoric."

At the crux of the family reunification debate is the government's narrow definition of family that only covers limited nuclear-family relationships. Under immigration law, a Canadian citizen or landed immigrant is allowed to bring his immediate family to Canada. Family, under the government definition, basically consists of spouses, children under the age of 21, parents and grandparents who are at least 60 years of age and fiancé(e)s. Canadians and landed immigrants cannot, as a right, bring in members of the extended family such as siblings older than 21, parents under 60, cousins, nieces, nephews, aunts and uncles. Many immigrant-aid organizations have argued that the narrow family definition serves to prevent rather than foster family reunification because it fails to recognize strong de facto family relationships and to take into account the cultures of many immigrant groups in which extended family situations are commonplace and even necessary to economic survival.

Frederika Rotter, a lawyer who practises in the heavily ethnic Toronto community of Parkdale, stressed in a 1986 brief to junior Immigration Minister Walter McLean the numerous and important advantages which family reunification has for individual immigrants and the community at large. "A family member provides emotional support which is of great assistance in adjustment to a new life in Canada. Moreover, a family class or assisted relative immigrant has the advantage of being able to move into an existing network of social contacts. Family support has a significant impact on the speed with which newcomers settle into a new life, and their success at integrating into a Canadian community."

The ninth report of the Parliamentary Standing Committee on Labour, Employment and Immigration, dated June 17, 1986, dealt solely with the problems surrounding family reunification. The all-party Parliamentary committee noted yet again that while family reunification is "the cornerstone of Canada's immigration policy," it was clear to the members that applicants under the family-class category do not always receive the priority in processing that has been espoused by immigration officials. One of the key issues with which the committee attempted to grapple was the definition of family. It proposed that the present family and assisted-relative classes be reorganized into family class, assisted family class and assisted relatives. The first category would remain virtually the same as the current family definition. The assisted-family group would consist of the parents, non-dependent children and brothers and sisters of Canadian citizens and landed immigrants. This latter group would be assessed for immigration on a modified point system. In other words, they would get extra points during the selection process for having close family in Canada. The third category basically would apply to uncles, aunts, nieces, nephews and cousins, and they too would be awarded more points than are currently allotted under current selection criteria.

Immigrant-aid groups applauded the committee's attempt to broaden the family definition. But the government, which was required by statute to respond to the report within 120 days, replied on October 15 that while it had accepted most of the 59 recommendations made by the Standing Committee, it would defer on the recommendations dealing with membership and priorities in the family class. In a prepared statement, Gerry Weiner said: "The government is sympathetic to the rationale which in part has led the Standing Committee to its conclusions. These relate to the need to provide opportunities for adult siblings to join their relatives in Canada. . . . The concept and implications of the Assisted Family Class and the expansion of the definition . . . need to be more fully assessed by the government as part of a comprehensive policy review. They will also be discussed with the provinces before further action is taken."

Pat Marshall called "totally misleading" the minister's claim that the government, in accepting most of the Standing Committee's recommendations, is "reaffirming the government's commitment to the family class as the cornerstone of its immigration policy. . . . It is true that the government has accepted most of the recommendations but they all deal with administrative changes meant to streamline the process and have no impact on policy whatsoever," she said. "It is untrue that the government is committed to the family class as the cornerstone of the Immigration Act. The heart of the matter, recommendations 5 to 10 which form the critical policy changes hoped for not only by the Standing Committee but by all Canadians hoping to be reunited with their families, has been relegated to the obscurity of needing to be more fully assessed as part of a comprehensive policy review."

At a forum on immigration in the predominantly ethnic riding of Broadview-Greenwood in Toronto in early February, 1987, Mr. Weiner predictably stressed that the aim of the Tory government was to reunite families "faster than it has ever happened before because I understand the critical need for families to be together." The minister also indicated the government's thinking on expanding the definition of family. He began by noting that when he responded to the Standing Committee report in October, "it was clear that I was able to respond to almost all the recommendations, except to those that affect the opening of new categories" in family-class immigration. Mr. Weiner went on to say that if the categories were opened up as suggested by the committee, and, for example, children over 21 would be included in the new definition, "then instead of the moderate and controlled increase in immigration which we are now allowing for, it would have a meteoric increase." He added that the issue requires "a lot more thoughtful discussion in the community before we can even go in that direction." Mr. Weiner pointed out that the older children of Canadian landed immigrants can apply as independent immigrants under the selected worker category "but they must stand on their own merit."

But the problems with family reunification go much deeper than the question of definition. The Standing Committee found that the most common complaint with the existing program concerned excruciatingly long delays in processing applications. Committee members wondered why some cases drag on for years if, as immigration officials insisted, family-class processing was primarily a clerical exercise. It is true that time must be allotted for mail to arrive, for people to travel, for medical examinations and background checks to be completed. And even if all the documents are readily available and all the requirements are completed quickly, obtaining landed-immigrant status can still take several months. Some delays are the fault of foreign countries where the processing takes place. Postal services in certain countries may be extremely slow and unreliable. Travelling from one end of a country to the Canadian embassy to attend interviews may be difficult, and even more problematic when there is no embassy in that country. Medical facilities may be inadequate, leading to requests for repeat examinations. Further delays will occur in countries which have poor record-keeping practices, making official birth or marriage certificates extremely difficult to obtain. What is truly astonishing, however, is that the average waiting time for a family-class applicant to be accepted as a landed immigrant is about nine months, and cases taking two, three and four years to process are not unheard of.

Ironically, Canadian immigration officers processed two and a half times as many immigrants in 1967, with fewer resources, than they did in 1985. There are some valid explanations for the faster processing time two decades ago. First, Canada's traditional source countries of family-class immigrants were in the so-called developed countries of Europe, where communications hummed along without too much interruption and excellent record-keeping was a way of life. As the European demand to immigrate to Canada dropped, many Third World countries came to fill the void, bringing with them tremendous communications and documentation problems. However, that explanation, a favourite of bureaucrats at External Affairs, is seriously weakened when contrasted to the uneven distribution of Canadian immigration offices and personnel.

While Canada has turned toward Third World countries as the major source of family reunification immigration in recent years, it hasn't buttressed that move with resources and personnel. India, an extremely busy centre for potential immigration, has one Canadian visa office in New Delhi. There is one office for the entire Philippines in Manila. The distances applicants in these countries have to travel are vast and transportation is expensive and unreliable. By comparison, Western Europe is well served. West Germany has five Canadian visa posts and Spain has four. France has three and Italy, Switzerland and Britain have two each. Tiny Luxembourg and Monte Carlo have one each. The United States has no fewer than 12 Canadian immigration offices. Yet it is worth noting that the number of applications in a given year from prospective immigrants in India is virtually the same as for the United States.

The disproportionate distribution of posts and personnel is further reflected in processing time. The mean processing time from July to September, 1986, for family-class applications in Milan was 86 days. In London it was 101 days; in Paris, 154 days; The Hague, 106 days; and New York, 150 days. However, in Islamabad, it was 230 days; New Delhi, 286 days; Manila, 263 days; Hong Kong, 290 days.

To compound the problem, most of Canada's immigration offices abroad are still in the era of the manual typewriter, archaic filing systems and outdated procedures. At most of the busiest posts abroad very high volumes of files are still being handled manually. The age of the computer only just crept into Canada's Hong Kong offices in 1986, and only on a pilot basis. Until the computer age "arrives in earnest, files will continue to be lost and routine tasks will continue to consume a disproportionate amount of time," the Standing Committee noted in its report. It stressed that computer systems were a necessity to increase the efficiency of immigration posts abroad, especially the busiest ones, adding that the expenditure was urgent and would definitely save money in the long run. The committee also pointed out that Canada's ability to process the higher levels of immigration "projected for this [1986] and the coming years could well be in jeopardy if action is delayed."

Canada's immigration levels target for 1986 was set at 105,000 to 115,000. Its total intake was about 92,550 from overseas, and it was the fifth time in six years that Canada failed to reach its targeted levels. Government figures will, however, indicate that immigration for 1986 was about 99,100. The overseas shortfall was topped up by more than 6,545 former refugee claimants already in Canada who were selected as landed immigrants through the government's administrative review program announced on May 21, 1986.

A particularly unsavoury problem, several immigration critics have noted, has developed in high-traffic immigration posts in recent years, as limited resources and manpower are shifted to process wealthy immigrants wanting to establish business ventures in Canada. This problem is especially acute in Hong Kong, which already suffers major delays in processing family-class immigrants. It takes ten times more work to process an entrepreneur business proposal and application, yet there has been no allocation of additional resources to deal with the surge in this workload. Moreover, the mean processing time for an entrepreneur application was about 30 days less than for a family-class application during the three-month period from July to September, 1986. Many immigrant groups in Canada have charged that the government has shifted its "priority in processing family-class immigrants" to the entrepreneur class.

The Standing Committee was emphatic that an increase in resources for processing entrepreneurs should not be at the expense of other immigrant classes. It also recommended that full cost recovery for processing entrepreneurial applications should be implemented so that the program could become as self-sufficient as possible. However, this was one recommendation that the government did not support, arguing that all immigrants should be treated equally. In his reply to the Standing Committee, Mr. Weiner said the government intends "to maintain its egalitarian approach to the matter of cost recovery, so that all immigrants are essentially treated equally." This means one fee scale for all immigrant categories, regardless of such factors as the complexity of processing or the ability of applicants to pay in individual cases.

Delays also take place in Canada at Canada Immigration

Centres, where it can take weeks to get an interview with an immigration counsellor to discuss a family sponsorship. Once the interview is completed, it takes time to process and verify the necessary documentation — the application, financial forms and proof of relationship. Then it can take several weeks to send the documentation to Ottawa where it is put in a diplomatic bag or mailed to the appropriate post abroad. Adding to the difficulties of processing family-class applications is Canada's immigration law, which has become extremely technical and cumbersome. It is replete with exceptions and general and special regulations, and it is constantly subject to bureaucratic and political interventions. The delays are further exacerbated by the individual applicants themselves who often can't understand what is expected from them or are intimidated by the sheer volume of forms to fill out.

Tory MP Jim Hawkes, chairman of the Standing Committee, said many of the 59 recommendations made by the committee would help speed up reunification of families and decrease the delays in processing. The committee also submitted a detailed proposal for a new processing system, which, it said, would reduce the amount of processing time, both in Canada and abroad. It proposed that every sponsor be given a "family-class package" containing all the information and forms necessary for processing. This package would include general instructions, information on how to validate relationships, an application form, a medical form, and a list of local doctors who conduct medical examinations. It would be up to the sponsors to mail or otherwise deliver the package to their relatives, and the Canada Immigration Centre would send the application form and financial information to the appropriate post abroad. Once the applicants receive the package, they could collect the necessary documents and arrange for a medical exam. They would go to the immigration office only when a complete file has been assembled. Officers at the post would then arrange an interview, if necessary, and proceed with the verification and security checks before issuing a visa.

In tabling the government's response to the Standing Committee report in October, 1986, Mr. Weiner said his department had already taken initiatives to improve procedures and "reunite families more quickly." In the February issue of *Panorama*, a department newsletter, the minister boasted somewhat prematurely that "delays have now gone from years and months to weeks and days. . . ." In reality, it was far too early to tell what the effects of various department initiatives were. The department had only just launched a number of pilot projects aimed at somehow reducing the horrendous delays. Those projects were to be assessed around the end of the year and fully implemented some time in 1988, if they worked.

On May 1, 1982, the federal government imposed a restriction on the immigration of independent immigrants. The ruling has had a devastating effect on this once vibrant and important source of new immigrants. In 1981, about 21,000 independent immigrants came to Canada. By 1985, the number had dropped to 6,550. The government imposed the restriction in response to employment difficulties associated with the economic recession which began in late 1981. Total immigration to Canada dropped from 143,117 in 1980 to 84,300 in 1985 — the lowest recorded intake in the past 23 years. In 1985, the federal government recognized that immediate action was needed to address the imbalance among the three main streams of immigrants — family class, independent class and humanitarian — and after extensive consultations, it introduced a revised immigrant selection system to provide for a measured intake of independent immigrants beginning January 1, 1986. In that year, the selected worker or independent class jumped to 12,000 with an additional allotment of 14,000 for spouses and other dependents. For 1987, that figure increased to 17,000 to a maximum of 20,000, with corresponding numbers for spouses and dependents.

In addition, the government released a list of 119 designated occupational groups, most of which require higher skills and education, for which applicants can earn up to ten points. There was also a major revision to the selection criteria known as the points system, which has come under sharp criticism from immigrant-aid groups who have described it as discriminatory. The point system was questioned in the Parliamentary Standing Committee's ninth report, which identified it as an area of future investigation. "The committee has concerns that the point system may not be the most efficient or effective method of assessing immigrants. Further, we are unsure that it is providing sufficient landings to meet our current and projected immigration levels."

Of particular concern to immigrant-aid organizations was the ability of assisted relatives to meet the selection criteria as independent immigrants. Under the modified point system, an applicant would have to score 70 out of 100 to be accepted. A bonus of ten points was awarded to applicants who have relatives in Canada who are willing and have the ability to become guarantors by submitting undertakings of assistance. Under the old system, the passing mark was 50 and the bonus for assisted relatives was 15 to 30 points. Five points were also awarded for having any relative in Canada, a provision eliminated under the new criteria. Many advocates of family-class immigration argued that it would be virtually impossible to sponsor a brother or sister or any other relative when 45 of the possible points are linked directly to education and work experience. They charged that the new criteria were deliberately designed to favour the educated, professional immigrant, and weighted against the 23-year-old manual labourer in Greece, India, Hong Kong or Argentina who has a brother in Canada.

The following are some of the occupations opened up to prospective immigrants: personnel managers, draughtspersons, social workers, librarians, chiropractors, photographers, radio and television announcers, advertising artists, executive secretaries, group insurance representatives, advertising salespersons, railway workers, audio-video equipment operators, upholsterers, business machine repairers and motor vehicle fabrication and assembly workers.

To its credit, the Conservative government has opened the immigration gates to more independent immigrants in 1987. Its program to revive the independent category is an important step in the right direction. Aside from the entrepreneurial spirit and economic boost independent immigrants bring, they will also provide a much needed source for younger, skilled people to meet Canada's need for balance in the population's age profile and family make-up. The independent category must be allowed to grow proportionately as total immigration increases. Unfortunately, by its very nature, this group does not have much political clout in Canada. The pressure for higher immigration targets comes from recent immigrants who want to see their family members get in and they want to accomplish that by expanding the definition of family to include brothers and sisters, nieces, nephews, cousins and grandchildren. And the government, according to Mr. Weiner, is prepared to agree with them if it gets the support of the provinces and other key players in the consultation process.

There is a strong argument to be made for the expansion of the family class, but there also comes a time when grown adults make a decision for themselves and their immediate family to move, for whatever reason, and that decision doesn't give them the right to bring every one of their relatives along with them. Nor should it give an automatic right to people with relatives in Canada to come here. It can be argued that Canada's immigration policy should be much more flexible in its approach to potential immigrants with close family in Canada and the recommendations of the Parliamentary Standing Committee respond to those concerns. Those recommendations are sound, fair and just. However, if we are to believe the constant reminders by our political leaders that independent immigrants built Canada, then we should strongly support this important category of immigration. It is these very people who in past years brought with them the skills, the talent and the drive to make it in Canada, and it is these very people who should have an equal priority, along with refugees and family-class immigrants, to come to our country. Who you are, and not just who you know, should count in coming to Canada.

SELECTED
BIBLIOGRAPHY

Abella, Irving, and Troper, Harold. *None Is Too Many: Canada and the Jews of Europe, 1933-1948.* Toronto: Lester & Orpen Dennys, 1982.

Adelman, Howard. *Canada and the Indochinese Refugees.* Regina: L.A. Weigl Educational Associates Ltd., 1982.

Annual Report to Parliament on Future Immigration Levels. Ottawa: Canada Employment and Immigration Commission, 1982, 1983, 1984, 1985 and 1986.

Avery, Donald. *Dangerous Foreigners.* Toronto: McClelland & Stewart, 1979.

Billingsley, Brenda, and Muszynski, Leon. *No Discrimination Here?* Toronto: The Urban Alliance on Race Relations and the Social Planning Council of Metropolitan Toronto, May, 1985.

Canadian Immigration and Policy Study [Green Paper on Immigration and Population]. Ottawa: Department of Manpower and Immigration, 1975.

Canadian Immigration Policy, 1966 [White Paper on Immigration]. Ottawa: Department of Manpower and Immigration, 1966.

Equality Now! Report of the Special Committee on Visible Minorities in Canadian Society. Ottawa: March, 1984.

Henry, Frances, and Ginzberg, Effie. *Who Gets the Work.* Toronto: The Urban Alliance on Race Relations and the Social Planning Council of Metropolitan Toronto, 1985.

261

Hill, Daniel, and Schiff, Marvin. *Human Rights in Canada: A Focus on Racism*. Ottawa: Canadian Labour Congress and the Human Rights Research and Education Centre, University of Ottawa, 1986.

Immigration Levels, 1987: Public Consultation Issues. Ottawa: Canada Employment and Immigration Commission, May, 1986.

Lysenko, Vera. *Men in Sheepskin Coats*. Toronto: 1947.

Plaut, W. Gunther. *Refugee Determination in Canada*. Ottawa: Canada Employment and Immigration Commission, 1985.

Ramcharan, Subhas. *Racism: Nonwhites in Canada*. Toronto: Butterworths, 1982.

Ratushny, Ed. *A New Refugee Status Determination Process for Canada*. Ottawa: Canada Employment and Immigration Commission, 1984.

Refugee Perspectives 1986-1987. Ottawa: Refugee Affairs Division, Canada Employment and Immigration Commission, June, 1986.

Refugees: The Dynamics of Displacement. A Report for the Independent Commission on International Humanitarian Issues. London: the Commission, 1986.

Robinson, W.G. *Illegal Migrants in Canada*. Ottawa: Canada Employment and Immigration Commission, 1983.

Royal Commission on the Economic Union and Development Prospects for Canada, *Report*. Volume 2. Ottawa: the Commission, August, 1985.

Special Joint Committee of the Senate and the House of Commons, *Report to Parliament on Immigration Policy*. Ottawa: the Committee, 1975.

World Refugee Survey: 1986 in Review. Washington: U.S. Committee for Refugees, 1987.

1)

imperial forces - 196

Pg 96,97